PACEMAKER®

General Science

Third Edition

ANSWER KEY

to accompany Student Edition, Workbook,
and Classroom Resource Binder

GLOBE FEARON

Pearson Learning Group

REVIEWERS

We thank the following educators, who provided valuable comments and suggestions during the development of this book:

Philip Altshuler, River Ridge Middle/High School, New Port Richey, Florida
Anthony Arbino, Woodward High School, Cincinnati Public Schools, Cincinnati, Ohio
Shirley Johnson-Young, Memorial Middle School, Houston, Texas
Martha Kelly, Belleville Middle School, Belleville, New Jersey
Dorie Knaub, Downey Unified School District, Downey, California

Subject Area Consultants:
Gregory L. Vogt, Ed.D., Aerospace Education Specialist, Oklahoma State University.
Dr. Vogt has degrees in General Science, Earth Science, and Aerospace Education. He taught science in the Milwaukee Public Schools, helped design and run the Discovery World Museum of Science, Economics, and Technology also in Milwaukee, and is now part of the Teaching from Space Program at NASA's Johnson Space Center in Houston, Texas.
Dr. Lisa K. Wagner, Director of Education/Associate Professor South Carolina Botanical Garden, Clemson University, Clemson, South Carolina.

Pacemaker Curriculum Advisor: **Stephen C. Larsen**, formerly of the University of Texas at Austin

Executive Editor: Eleanor Ripp
Supervising Editor: Stephanie Petron Cahill
Lead Editor: Maury Solomon
Editor: Theresa McCarthy
Production Editor: Laura Benford-Sullivan
Assistant Editor: Kathy Bentzen
Designers: Susan Brorein, Jennifer Visco
Market Manager: Katie Kehoe-Erezuma
Research Director: Angela Darchi
Cover Design: Susan Brorein, Jennifer Visco
Editorial, Design and Production Services: Navta Associates
Electronic Composition: Linda Bierniak, Phyllis Rosinsky, Jeff Wickersty

ISBN 0-130-23436-2
Printed in the United States of America
9 10 V036 15 14 13 12 11 10

1-800-321-3106
www.pearsonlearning.com

Contents

Overview

PROVEN SOLUTIONS FOR TODAY'S CLASSROOMS

Today, students and educators alike face increased challenges. Students need preparation for the rigors of higher academic standards and challenging proficiency tests, as well as skills to successfully apply learning to daily life. Educators must meet the needs of diverse classrooms, create supportive learning environments for a range of learning styles, and keep content up-to-date. Both students and teachers need tools to meet the challenges of the twenty-first-century classroom.

THE SIX COMPONENTS OF THE PACEMAKER® CURRICULUM

Globe Fearon's *Pacemaker Curriculum* has consistently supplied students and educators with materials and techniques that are accessible, predictable, age-appropriate, and relevant. The six components of the new Third Edition of *General Science* provide a solid, well-balanced approach to teaching science content and building science skills.

The *Student Edition* presents content in concise, manageable lessons. All learning is reinforced through consistent practice, review, and application. Point-of-use strategies and answers are found in the *Teacher's Answer Edition*. More review, practice, and enrichment are provided in the *Workbook* and in the *Classroom Resource Binder*. Support for diverse classroom settings is provided in the *Teacher's Planning Guide*. Answers to <u>all</u> student materials are found in a separate *Answer Key*. Together, these six components form a complete and comprehensive program.

THIS SEPARATE ANSWER KEY

This *Answer Key* provides answers to all student materials in the *General Science* program. The booklet has been three-hole punched for easy insertion into the binder behind the tab marked "Answer Key." This booklet has three sections:

- The **Student Edition Answer Key** section is a duplicate of the answers found in the *Teacher's Answer Edition* and includes in Chapter Quizzes and Unit Reviews references to lessons and page numbers.

- The **Workbook Answer Key** section is the only source for answers to all exercises in the *Workbook*.

- The **Classroom Resource Binder Answer Key** section is the only source for answers to all the exercises and tests in the *Classroom Resource Binder*. This section also provides a correlation between all test items in the Test Preparation tab and lessons in the *Student Edition*.

Student Edition Answer Key

UNIT 1 THE WONDERS OF SCIENCE (p. 1)

1. 1. Describe a problem.   2. Gather information. 3. Suggest an answer.   4. Perform experiments. 5. Draw conclusions and report results.   **2.** 4. Perform experiments.   **3.** 5. Draw conclusions and report results.

Chapter 1 What Is Science? (p. 2)

Caption Examples include plants, animals, weather, and rocks, among many others.

1.1 From Atoms to Galaxies (p. 4)

Checkpoint 1   The study of nature and the universe
Checkpoint 2   Large objects such as galaxies and small objects such as atoms
Checkpoint 3   The facts that scientists have discovered and the process of discovering new facts
Checkpoint 4   Research leads to the discovery of new ideas.
Lesson Review   1. All that exists   **2.** Scientists study all the things in the universe.   **3.** An experiment is a kind of test that scientists use to discover or prove something. Scientists do research by studying things and performing experiments.   **4.** Do research
Great Moments in Science: The First Liquid-Fueled Rocket   Critical Thinking   The liquid-fueled rocket provided a way to launch objects into space.

1.2 Science at Work (p. 8)

Checkpoint 1   By helping solve people's problems or making life better for people
Checkpoint 2   Life, earth, and physical science
Checkpoint 3   Zoos, factories, laboratories, hospitals, parks, etc.
Modern Leaders in Science: Rita Rossi Colwell   Critical Thinking   There is a limited amount of money available, and some projects may not be worth supporting.
Checkpoint 4   By citizens supporting certain projects. Students might also say citizens can support certain projects by voting for the government officials who share their views.
Lesson Review   1. Examples include CDs, the Kurzweil Personal Reader, and wasps that feed on mealybugs in Africa.   **2.** Life science: living things; physical science: matter and energy; earth science: Earth and space   **3.** So they can make the right science-related choices   **4.** Facts will vary but should relate to life, earth, and physical science.

Lab Activity: Making Observations (p. 12)

1. You could tell a lot about the object such as its size, shape, color, etc.   **2.** Students might suggest adding more details to the observations.

Science in Your Life: Using Technology (p. 13)

Critical Thinking   People in the past may have used a simpler technology or a nontechnological means to achieve the same end, although with more effort or time.

Chapter 1 Review (pp. 14–15)

Vocabulary Review   1. research   **2.** galaxy
3. science   **4.** earth science   **5.** universe
6. experiment   **7.** observation   **8.** technology
Chapter Quiz   1. All that exists, including the planets, sun, stars, and space (p. 4)   **2.** Atoms are too small to be seen with the eyes alone. (p. 5)   **3.** The way people learn new facts (p. 5)   **4.** By making observations, doing experiments, and drawing conclusions (p. 5)   **5.** Possible responses: refrigerators, doorbells, phones (pp. 8–9)   **6.** It helps to solve problems or make life better for people. (p. 8)   **7.** Living things and how they behave (p. 9)   **8.** Matter and energy (p. 9)   **9.** Examples include medicine, farming, computers, forestry, and building. (p. 10)
10. Knowledge of science is used in many careers, and it can help a person make wise choices. (pp. 10–11)
Research Project   See the *Teacher's Planning Guide* or *Classroom Resource Binder* for a scoring rubric for the Research Project.

Chapter 2 The Process of Discovery (p. 16)

Caption Almost any process, object, or the materials of which an object is made involves scientific study.

2.1 The Scientific Method (p. 18)

Checkpoint 1   Describe the problem, gather information, suggest an answer, perform experiments, draw conclusions, and report the results
Checkpoint 2   The results raise new questions that the scientist wants to answer.
Lesson Review   1. To perform experiments and make new discoveries   **2.** Performing experiments that test the hypothesis   **3.** To be able to make better guesses
On the Cutting Edge: Artificial Skin   Critical Thinking   It causes healthy skin to grow over a wound, resulting in less scarring.

2.2 Measuring in Science (p. 21)

Checkpoint 1   The number ten and multiples of ten
Checkpoint 2   The meter
Checkpoint 3   Square meters and liters
Checkpoint 4   The gram
Checkpoint 5   Degrees Celsius and the second
Checkpoint 6   Use them to describe objects you are familiar with.
Lesson Review   1. The sizes or amounts of things
2. Metric units of length, volume, and mass
3. $\frac{1}{100}$; $\frac{1}{1,000}$; 1,000   **4.** A kilometer is too long to be useful in measuring such a small length.   **A Closer Look: The Atomic Clock   Critical Thinking**   They need to make very precise measurements.

2.3 Laboratory Science (p. 25)

Checkpoint 1   For doing experiments, making observations, and taking measurements
Checkpoint 2   Working with fire, chemicals, and other things can be dangerous.
Lesson Review   1. Metric rulers, graduated cylinders, petri dishes, Bunsen burners, microscopes, and balances   **2.** Know how to put them out and where to

find clean, running water   **3.** To avoid swallowing harmful chemicals or other dangerous substances
Great Moments in Science: A Lucky Mistake
Critical Thinking   So that you can tell if you've solved a problem

Lab Activity: Metric Measuring (p. 28)
1. Carelessness; not using the correct unit, for example, measuring in centimeters instead of millimeters   **2.** To check the measurement for accuracy

On-the-Job Science: Medical Lab Technician (p. 29)
1. Type A   **2.** The blood clumps with anti-A serum and does not clump with anti-B serum.   **Critical Thinking**   Answers include being organized and precise and having an interest in medicine or science.

Chapter 2 Review (pp. 30–31)
Vocabulary Review   1. meter   **2.** scientific method   **3.** liter   **4.** area   **5.** gram   **6.** volume   **7.** procedure   **8.** microscope
Chapter Quiz   1. The scientific method (pp. 18–19)   **2.** Talk to other scientists and read (p. 19)   **3.** To test the suggested answer (p. 19)   **4.** So they can share information easily (p. 22)   **5.** Ten (p. 22)   **6.** 1,000 (p. 22)   **7.** $\frac{1}{1,000}$ (p. 23)   **8.** Examples include chemicals, test tubes, and instruments (p. 25)   **9.** Read them over carefully (p. 26)   **10.** Tell the teacher immediately (p. 26)   **Research Project**   See the *Teacher's Planning Guide* or *Classroom Resource Binder* for a scoring rubric for the Research Project.

Unit 1 Review (p. 32)
1. B (p. 22)   **2.** B (p. 22)   **3.** A (p. 22)   **4.** D (p. 5)   **5.** D (p. 9)   **6.** C (pp. 18–19)   **7.** C (pp. 8–9)   **Critical Thinking**   To avoid accidents and mistakes during the experiment

UNIT 2 LIFE SCIENCE: PART I   (p. 33)
1. Trees and other plants   **2.** Bear and fish   **3.** The bear catching the fish

Chapter 3 The Study of Life (p. 34)
Caption Possible answers: They need to find food and shelter and learn to defend themselves.

3.1 A Home For Life (p. 36)
Checkpoint 1   Biology, or life science
Checkpoint 2   Botany, zoology, genetics, microbiology, ecology
Lesson Review   1. If the Earth were closer, it would be too hot for things to live. If the Earth were farther away, it would be too cold for things to live.   **2.** In size and shape   **3.** Organisms too small to be seen with the eye alone   **4.** About 15 times   **On the Cutting Edge: Is there Life on Other Planets?**
Critical Thinking   There are intelligent beings on other planets.

3.2 What Is Life? (p. 39)
Checkpoint 1   All organisms share these characteristics: They get and use food, move, grow,
reproduce, and respond to the environment.
Checkpoint 2   Plants make their own food. Animals eat plants, other animals, or both plants and animals. Both must break down food to use it.
Checkpoint 3   Animals move to find food, to get away from danger, and to find a mate. Plants move to get more sunlight.
Checkpoint 4   All
Checkpoint 5   Sexually and asexually
Checkpoint 6   To react to things in the environment
A Closer Look: Hatching Temperatures   Critical Thinking   The number of green turtles would decline, and eventually green turtles might die out.
Checkpoint 7   They range from one day to 5,000 years.
Lesson Review   1. Characteristics mentioned might describe appearance, getting and using food, moving, growing, reproducing, and responding to the environment.   **2.** Everything that surrounds you   **3.** Progress in medical science and nutrition   **4.** It does not have all of the characteristics of life.

Lab Activity: Observing Learning (p. 44)
1. Answers will vary, but the times should decrease.   **2.** Times should decrease.   **3.** The person learned how to get through the maze.

Science in Your Life: Plan a Flower Garden (p. 45)
1. Poppy, iris, carnation   **2.** In spring   **3.** Maps should include at least one of each kind of flower that blooms in spring, summer, and fall.

Chapter 3 Review (pp. 46–47)
Vocabulary Review   1. reproduce   **2.** genetics   **3.** life span   **4.** environment   **5.** biology   **6.** microbiology   **7.** waste   **8.** ecology
Chapter Quiz   1. Dog and dead fly because they are alive or once were alive (p. 36)   **2.** Animals (p. 37)   **3.** Botany (p. 37)   **4.** Getting and using food, moving, growing, reproducing, and responding to the environment (p. 39)   **5.** The sun's energy, water, and carbon dioxide (p. 40)   **6.** To find food, to move away from danger, and to find mates (p. 40)   **7.** To get sunlight (p. 40)   **8.** For many plants, seeds are needed to reproduce. (p. 41)   **9.** Answers will vary but might include a variety of objects and organisms as well as air and sunlight. (p. 42)   **10.** No; for example, life span of small dog: 14 years; life span of human: 76 years (p. 43)   **Research Project**   See the *Teacher's Planning Guide* or *Classroom Resource Binder* for a scoring rubric for the Research Project.

Chapter 4 Cells and Life (p. 48)
Caption The photo shows elodea leaf cells as they appear under a microscope. The cells have been magnified 100 times. The dark green spots are the chloroplasts.

4.1 The Basic Units of Life (p. 50)
Checkpoint 1   By looking at tree bark under a microscope
Checkpoint 2   One
Checkpoint 3   Cells
Lesson Review   1. Plant cells   **2.** Atoms that are

chemically bonded to one another   **3.** 112   **4.** Water is not an element because it is made of more than one kind of atom.   **On the Cutting Edge: Cloth That Can "Breathe"   Critical Thinking**   They do not allow hot air and perspiration vapor to pass out of the boots.

4.2 Understanding Cells (p. 53)
Checkpoint 1   Cytoplasm, cell membrane, nucleus, vacuoles, mitochondria
Checkpoint 2   From food molecules that are broken down in the cells
Checkpoint 3   A plant cell has a cell wall, bigger vacuoles, and chloroplasts.
Checkpoint 4   DNA molecules contain a code that controls the characteristics.
Lesson Review   1. Cytoplasm, cell membrane, nucleus, vacuole, mitochondria   **2.** Water and carbon dioxide   **3.** Make its own food   **4.** Compare the DNA in the strand of hair to the DNA in the hair of the suspect.
A Closer Look: DNA in Sponges   Critical Thinking Sponge DNA has a code for growing new parts.

Lab Activity: Making Models of Cells (p. 58)
1. Cell membrane, cytoplasm, nucleus, vacuoles, mitochondria   **2.** Cell wall and chloroplasts   **3.** That they share some characteristics but are different in some important ways

On-the-Job Science: Histologic Technician (p. 59)
1. Both are rounded and have similar parts.   **2.** The cancer cells are larger.   **Critical Thinking**   The dye makes the cells and their parts easier to see.

Chapter 4 Review (pp. 60–61)
Vocabulary Review   1. True   **2.** False, cell membrane   **3.** False, cell wall   **4.** True   **5.** False, chlorophyll   **6.** True   **7.** False, cytoplasm   **8.** True
Chapter Quiz   1. Cells (p. 50)   **2.** It is a list of all the elements. (p. 51)   **3.** Molecules are formed when atoms are joined by chemical bonds. (p. 51)   **4.** It controls all the other parts of the cell. (p. 53)   **5.** Food, water, wastes (p. 54)   **6.** Answers include to get and use food, move, grow, reproduce, and respond. (p. 54)   **7.** Food and oxygen (p. 54)   **8.** Plant cells have chlorophyll, animal cells do not. (p. 55)   **9.** A twisted ladder (p. 56)   **10.** It contains a code that controls eye color. (p. 56)   **Research Project** See the *Teacher's Planning Guide* or *Classroom Resource Binder* for a scoring rubric for the Research Project.

Chapter 5   The Kingdoms of Life (p. 62)
Caption Animal, plant, fungus

5.1 Classifying Organisms (p. 64)
Checkpoint 1   Kingdoms
Checkpoint 2   Phylum, class, order, family, genus, species
Lesson Review   1. They are all many-celled. They have cell walls. They use sunlight and chlorophyll to make food.   **2.** A species   **3.** They cannot reproduce together.

Great Moments in Science: Aristotle's Classification System   Critical Thinking   Aristotle would have put bats and pigeons in one group (in the air) and elephants in another (on land). Biologists today put bats and elephants in one group (mammals) and pigeons in another (birds).

5.2 Earth's Simplest Organisms (p. 67)
Checkpoint 1   Algae are plantlike and protozoa are animal-like.
Checkpoint 2   Bacteria have no nuclei to hold their DNA.
Checkpoint 3   Fungi do not have chloroplasts and cannot make their own food.
Lesson Review   1. A protozoan   **2.** One kind of true bacteria; used to make foods, such as cheese and yogurt   **3.** They grow in one place.   **4.** The Ancient Bacteria or True Bacteria Kingdoms
On the Cutting Edge: Fighting Dangerous Protozoa   Critical Thinking   If all of the mosquitoes were killed, there would be no way for the malaria protozoa to move from one person to another.

Lab Activity: Observing Protists (p. 70)
1. A green color, lack of movement   **2.** Movement, possibly consuming food   **3.** They come in a variety of forms.

Science in Your Life: Fighting Bacteria at Home (p. 71)
2a. Antibiotics, acne medicines, soaps, deodorants, ointments, and some adhesive bandages
2b. Cleansers, aerosol disinfectants, etc.   **Critical Thinking**   Students might suggest reading packaging labels, researching through consumer magazines, or doing an experiment.

Chapter 5 Review (pp. 72–73)
Vocabulary Review   1. classification   **2.** protozoan   **3.** Kingdom   **4.** biologist   **5.** alga   **6.** bacterium   **7.** fungus   **8.** species
Chapter Quiz   1. True bacteria, ancient bacteria, protist, fungus, plant, animal (p. 65)   **2.** Fungus, plant, animal (p. 65)   **3.** Phylum (p. 65)   **4.** Species (p. 65)   **5.** Protist (p. 67)   **6.** Ancient bacteria and true bacteria (p. 68)   **7.** Ancient bacteria (p. 68)   **8.** Fungi do not have chloroplasts, so they cannot make their own food. (p. 68)   **9.** By breaking down dead matter (p. 68)   **10.** Molds, yeasts, mushrooms (p. 69)   **Research Project** See the *Teacher's Planning Guide* or *Classroom Resource Binder* for a scoring rubric for the Research Project.

Chapter 6   The Animal Kingdom (p. 74)
Caption Moving around helps animals find food and mates, escape from predators, and leave an area when the food supply dwindles.

6.1 From Simple to Complex (p. 76)
Checkpoint 1   Animals can move around, they need to get food, and they have cells that do special jobs.
Checkpoint 2   Animal cells are specialized. The cells in a simpler organism are almost all alike.
Lesson Review   1. Animals must move around to get food. Plants make their own food.   **2.** Each cell's shape and size depend on its job.   **3.** Animals would

not be able to find food, escape enemies, or find a mate.

A Closer Look: Specialized Cells in Action   Critical Thinking   The heron would be unable to capture food or do the other things it must to survive.

6.2 Invertebrates (p. 79)
Checkpoint 1   They move around when they are young and must trap their food.
Checkpoint 2   A roundworm has more parts than a tapeworm. It can digest its own food.
Checkpoint 3   It protects the mollusk's body.
Checkpoint 4   In salt water
Checkpoint 5   An outer skeleton, jointed appendages, a body that is divided into segments
Lesson Review   1. False. Sponges are animals.
2. False. An earthworm uses its crop to store food.
3. True   4. It makes the skeleton flexible, which allows the arthropod to move.

6.3 Vertebrates (p. 84)
Checkpoint 1   Cold-blooded; have fins, scales, and gills
Checkpoint 2   Frogs, toads, salamanders
On the Cutting Edge: Researching Frog Slime   Critical Thinking   Other native peoples may use plants and animals that, like the phyllomedusa frog, produce medically important chemicals.
Checkpoint 3   Their bodies are covered with hard scales that keep in moisture.
Checkpoint 4   Possible answers: warm-blooded, vertebrates, feathers, wings, hollow bones
Checkpoint 5   Possible answers: warm-blooded, vertebrate, hair on its body, most give birth to live young, mother's body makes milk to feed young
Lesson Review   1. A backbone   2. Fish, amphibians, reptiles, birds, mammals   3. Fish and reptiles
4. They cannot feed while they are over water. The food they eat before they migrate gives them the energy they need to keep flying.

Lab Activity: Using a Two-Choice Key (p. 90)
No. This key is for spiders, and they do not have antennae.

On-the-Job Science: Pet Store Worker (p. 91)
1. Invertebrates—crayfish; fish—guppies, goldfish; amphibians—salamanders, frogs; reptiles—lizards, snakes, turtles; birds—parakeets, canaries; mammals—hamsters, gerbils   2. Guppies, crayfish, salamanders, goldfish, frogs, and possibly turtles   3. Parakeets, canaries, hamsters, gerbils

Chapter 6 Review (pp. 92–93)
Vocabulary Review   1. vertebrate   2. arthropod
3. migrate   4. parasite   5. cold-blooded
6. appendage   7. reptile   8. mollusk
Chapter Quiz   1. An animal can move around, must get its own food, and has specialized cells. (p. 76)
2. Invertebrates do not have a backbone. Vertebrates do. (pp. 79, 84)   3. Parasites live inside hosts. The hosts support the parasites. (p. 80)   4. Answers include snails, slugs, clams, oysters, squid, and octopuses. (p. 81)   5. Head, thorax, abdomen (p. 82)

6. Spiders have two body segments, four pairs of legs, and no antennae. Insects have three body segments, three pairs of legs, and antennae. (pp. 82–83)   7. Fish have gills, scales, and no legs. Mature amphibians have lungs, legs, and no scales. (pp. 85–86)
8. Answers include lizards, turtles, snakes, alligators, and crocodiles. (p. 87)   9. Hollow bones (p. 88)
10. Mammals have hair on their bodies. Mothers make milk in their bodies to feed their young. (p. 89)
Research Project   See the *Teacher's Planning Guide* or *Classroom Resource Binder* for a scoring rubric for the Research Project.

Chapter 7   The Plant Kingdom (p. 94)
Caption   Students may know that roots, leaves, seeds, and flowers are other plant parts.

7.1 Plants as Food Makers (p. 96)
Checkpoint 1   Plants make their own food, their cells have cell walls, and plants cannot move from place to place.
Checkpoint 2   Seeds produce new plants; roots hold plants in place and take in water and minerals from soil; stems hold a plant upright and carry water and food through a plant; leaves make food during photosynthesis.
Checkpoint 3   The soil does not have everything the plants need to grow.
Lesson Review   1. Seeds, roots, stems, leaves
2. The leaves   3. Sunlight, water, chlorophyll, carbon dioxide   4. Store extra food the plant has made
Modern Leaders in Science: Patricia Shanely   Critical Thinking   Write letters to lumber companies and politicians, voicing your opinions; refuse to buy products that require the cutting of rain forests; learn more about the rain forests.

7.2 Plant Reproduction (p. 101)
Checkpoint 1   The pistil is the female part of the flower that contains the ovary. Inside the ovary are egg cells. The stamen is the male part of a flower that holds pollen containing sperm cells. The petals are the colorful outer parts of a flower that attract insects and protect the inner parts of the flower.
Checkpoint 2   By the fleshy fruit that surrounds it
Lesson Review   1. Pollen is transferred from the stamen of a flower to the pistil of another flower.
2. A sperm cell and an egg cell join.   3. The environment might not be warm and wet enough.

Lab Activity: Germinating Seeds (p. 104)
1. Probably the warm, moist dish   2. Probably the warm, moist dish   3. Warm, moist conditions allow seeds to grow the best.

Science in Your Life: Products From Trees (p. 105)
1, 2. Answers might include items of furniture, cutting boards, musical instruments, or fireplace logs made from the wood in tree trunks; newspapers, paper towels, napkins, books, and magazines made from wood pulp; bulletin boards or bottle stoppers made from tree bark; maple syrup or turpentine made from tree sap.   **Critical Thinking**   Wood might be

hard to get for use as fuel or building material and might be expensive.

Chapter 7 Review (pp. 106–107)
Vocabulary Review 1. leaf **2.** stem **3.** stamen **4.** fruit **5.** photosynthesis **6.** pistil **7.** root **8.** egg cell
Chapter Quiz 1. Plants make their own food, plant cells have cell walls, plants cannot move from place to place (p. 96) **2.** Root, stem, leaf, seed (p. 97) **3.** Hold the plant in place, store extra food, take in water and minerals from the soil (p. 97) **4.** Water (p. 97) **5.** Food (p. 97) **6.** Photosynthesis (p. 98) **7.** Plants make food and oxygen. (pp. 98–99) **8.** They give off oxygen to the air that we need to breathe. (p. 99) **9.** Pollen moves from the stamen of a flower to the pistil of the same or a different flower. (p. 102) **10.** Fruit (p. 103) **Research Project** See the *Teacher's Planning Guide* or *Classroom Resource Binder* for a scoring rubric for the Research Project.

Chapter 8 Genetics: The Code of Life (p. 108)
Caption Answers may vary but could include the idea that parents pass on their traits to their offspring.

8.1 The Same But Different (p. 110)
Checkpoint 1 The traits are passed from parents to offspring when parents reproduce.
Checkpoint 2 Dominant and recessive traits
Lesson Review 1. Possible answers: color of skin, hair, and eyes; height; shape; personality traits such as being careful or reckless **2.** See the traits listed in the chart in Figure 8-1. **3.** From the crossbreeding of parents that have different traits **4.** All the offspring would be short.

8.2 The Building Blocks of Heredity (p. 113)
Checkpoint 1 A chromosome contains genes.
On the Cutting Edge: A Powerful Weapon Against Diabetes Critical Thinking The people pay less money for the insulin they need.
Checkpoint 2 They combine to form a complete set.
Checkpoint 3 A mutation
Lesson Review 1. Chromosomes **2.** Body cells divide once. Sex cells divide twice. Sex cells receive only half the number of chromosomes found in body cells. **3.** A mutation

8.3 Controlling Heredity (p. 116)
Checkpoint 1 The careful choosing of plants and animals for breeding
Checkpoint 2 Its environment
Checkpoint 3 By transferring new genes into organisms.
Lesson Review 1. By carefully choosing the plants they breed to produce offspring with better traits **2.** It allows scientists to change the genetic codes of organisms. **3.** Possible response: poor nutrition may stunt a person's growth.
A Closer Look: Cloning Animals Critical Thinking Farmers can use cloning to make many copies of an animal that has desirable traits.

Lab Activity: Observing Dominant and Recessive Traits (p. 118)
1. Answers will vary. **2.** Answers will vary. **3.** More students probably have dominant traits because to show a dominant trait they need to inherit the trait from just one parent. To show a recessive trait, they need to inherit the trait from both parents.

On-the-Job Science: Cattle Breeder (p. 119)
The breeds that students select for reproduction should have the traits that are desired in the new breed. **Critical Thinking** The cattle were produced by having dairy cattle reproduce with cattle that produced good-tasting meat.

Chapter 8 Review (pp. 120–121)
Vocabulary Review 1. False, recessive **2.** True **3.** True **4.** False, An offspring **5.** True **6.** False, hybrid **7.** True **8.** True
Chapter Quiz 1. Its traits (p. 111) **2.** No; it may reappear in later generations. (p. 112) **3.** Round seed is a dominant trait; wrinkled seed is a recessive trait. (p. 112) **4.** On the chromosomes in the nucleus (p. 113) **5.** 23; 46 (pp. 113–114) **6.** Its chromosomes (p. 114) **7.** The organism with the harmful mutation usually dies before it can reproduce. (p. 115) **8.** They carefully choose the animals that they breed. (p. 116) **9.** Answers may include the effect of nutrition on a person's body and the effect of soil quality and water on fruit production. (p. 116) **10.** They transferred the gene for human insulin to the DNA of the bacteria. (pp. 114, 117) **Research Project** See the *Teacher's Planning Guide* or *Classroom Resource Binder* for a scoring rubric for the Research Project.

Chapter 9 Evolution (p. 122)
Caption Obvious similarities are that it walked on four legs and had a tail and sharp teeth. The most obvious difference is that its upper canine teeth were very long.

9.1 Time and Change (p. 124)
Checkpoint 1 They change through the process of evolution.
Checkpoint 2 Bones, teeth, and footprints preserved in rock
Checkpoint 3 To get clues as to its evolution and ancestors
Lesson Review 1. Evolution **2.** To learn about species that have evolved or have become extinct **3.** They can learn how closely the DNA of the extinct organism resembles the DNA of living organisms.

9.2 Theories of Evolution (p. 127)
Checkpoint 1 That traits an organism developed during its lifetime could be inherited
Checkpoint 2 Organisms with helpful traits live longer and are more likely to have offspring.
Checkpoint 3 They may introduce traits that help organisms to survive better.
Lesson Review 1. Traits an organism develops during its lifetime **2.** The ones with traits that are best suited to their environments **3.** It would be

helpful because it would make the rabbit harder to see against the snow.

Great Moments in Science: Jumping Genes
Critical Thinking The result of a single experiment could be a mistake. If repeating the experiment produces the same result, the result is more believable.

Lab Activity: Studying Natural Selection (p. 132)
1. The number of brown dots should decrease and white dots increase for each succeeding generation.
2. Animals that blended into the environment (white dots) survived and reproduced, passing along their helpful trait of color.

Science in Your Life: Changing the Course of Natural Selection (p. 133)
1. $\frac{1}{1,000}$ **2.** 10   **3.** 100 resistant; 1,000 normal
4. More resistant   **Critical Thinking** The new pesticide would be effective at first, but mosquitoes might eventually become resistant.

Chapter 9 Review (pp. 134–135)
Vocabulary Review   **1.** theory   **2.** natural selection
3. extinct   **4.** evolution   **5.** fossil   **6.** naturalist
7. paleontology
Chapter Quiz   **1.** Changes with time (p. 124)
2. How organisms from the past are different from organisms of today (p. 125)   **3.** They compare the genetic code of different organisms to find out if they evolved from the same ancestor. (p. 126)   **4.** The limbs have bones that are very similar. (p. 126)
5. They are passed on to its offspring. (p. 127)
6. Most organisms have more offspring than can survive; offspring must compete for food and space; organisms that survive have traits that are best suited to the environment; natural selection passes along helpful traits to offspring. (pp. 129–130)   **7.** Offspring must compete for food and space. (p. 130)
8. Organisms that survive have traits that are best suited to their environment. (p. 130)   **9.** The first involves new combinations of existing genes; the second occurs when a whole new gene is formed. (p. 130)   **10.** Mutations that introduce a helpful trait (p. 130)   **Research Project** See the *Teacher's Planning Guide* or *Classroom Resource Binder* for a scoring rubric for the Research Project.

Unit 2 Review (p. 136)
1. C (p. 39)   **2.** D (p. 55)   **3.** B (p. 65)   **4.** A (p. 76)
5. B (p. 101)   **6.** D (p. 113)   **7.** C (p. 125)   **Critical Thinking** Algae are plantlike protists, and protozoa are animal-like protists.

UNIT 3 LIFE SCIENCE: PART II (p. 137)
1. Respiratory   **2.** Muscular   **3.** Skin

Chapter 10 The Human Body (p. 138)
Caption His brain for thinking and his thumbs for grasping

10.1 From Cells to Systems (p. 140)
Checkpoint 1   Cells form into tissues, tissues form organs, and organs form systems.
Checkpoint 2   Messages are passed along to the brain by way of nerve cells all around the body. The brain interprets those messages and sends information to the body on how to react.
Checkpoint 3   Eyes, ears, tongue, nose, and skin. They allow us to see, hear, taste, smell, and pick up sensory messages. The skin also keeps the body from drying out, keeps out bacteria, and regulates body temperature.
Checkpoint 4   The brain
Lesson Review   **1.** The brain   **2.** Sweet, sour, salty, bitter   **3.** The human brain is bigger and more complex.   **4.** Nails protect the sensitive skin on the fingers and toes from heat and cold and from blows.

10.2 Your Body at Work (p. 145)
Checkpoint 1   For support and protection of internal organs and for movement
Checkpoint 2   Attach muscle to bone
Lesson Review   **1.** 206 (in adults). They support the body and protect internal organs. They also allow movement.   **2.** Voluntary and involuntary   **3.** Most actions carried out by involuntary muscles help keep the body alive and functioning properly.

10.3 Reproduction (p. 147)
Checkpoint 1   The body develops sexually and becomes capable of reproduction.
Checkpoint 2   The ovaries and the uterus
Checkpoint 3   A fetus will begin to grow in the woman's uterus.
Lesson Review   **1.** When the reproductive organs begin to mature, around age 10–13 for girls, 13–16 for boys   **2.** The unfertilized egg cell and blood cells lining the uterus are shed.   **3.** The baby's shape changes, organs develop, and so on.
A Closer Look: Premature Babies   **Critical Thinking** Fetal problems could be detected and treated to help prevent premature birth.

Lab Activity: Tasting What You Smell (p. 150)
1. Probably the apple only   **2.** Most or all   **3.** They work together to help you recognize and enjoy foods.

On-the-Job Science: Fitness Instructor (p. 151)
1. 10 minutes, heart rate 125   **2.** 20 minutes, heart rate 145   **3.** 5 minutes, heart rate 125   **Critical Thinking** Almost every body system is affected, but especially the respiratory, circulatory, and muscular systems. Exercise of these systems increases stamina, strength, metabolic rate, and energy.

Chapter 10 Review (pp. 152–153)
Vocabulary Review   **1.** organ   **2.** tissue   **3.** system
4. fetus   **5.** hormone   **6.** puberty   **7.** skeleton
8. joint
Chapter Quiz   **1.** Blood and muscle (p. 140)
2. Examples are the heart (pumps blood) and the eyes (sight). (pp. 140, 142)   **3.** Digestive—breaks down food; Circulatory—moves blood (p. 140)   **4.** Sight—eyes; Hearing—ears; Taste—tongue; Smell—nose;

Touch—skin (pp. 142–143) **5.** Skin, by sweating (p. 143) **6.** In the brain (p. 141) **7.** Support and protection of organs (p. 145) **8.** Possible answer: muscles in the arm; heart (p. 146) **9.** Hormones (p. 147) **10.** Sperm—testes (male); egg—ovaries (female) (pp. 147–148) **Research Project** See the *Teacher's Planning Guide* or *Classroom Resource Binder* for a scoring rubric for the Research Project.

Chapter 11 Getting Energy Into and Around the Body (p. 154)

Caption The people moving the most are using the most energy. Those moving least are using the least energy.

11.1 Digestion (p. 156)

Checkpoint 1 The energy to carry out daily activities

Checkpoint 2 It breaks down food into molecules your cells can use.

Lesson Review **1.** Food **2.** By chewing, the use of enzymes, and involuntary muscles **3.** Food would not be broken down into small enough pieces to pass through the intestines.

11.2 Respiration (p. 158)

Checkpoint 1 It gets oxygen to their cells.

Checkpoint 2 It gets oxygen to the body's cells and removes waste gases.

Lesson Review **1.** Air goes down the throat to the larynx, trachea, bronchi, then lungs. **2.** Through the walls of the air sacs **3.** We depend on plants for the oxygen we breathe and for our food.

11.3 Circulation (p. 160)

Checkpoint 1 to pump blood to every part of the body

Checkpoint 2 A liquid (plasma) and three solids (red blood cells, white blood cells, and platelets)

Checkpoint 3 Blood vessels to the heart become clogged.

Lesson Review **1.** The circulatory system moves blood around the body. **2.** An artery carries blood away from the heart; a vein returns blood to the heart. **3.** When the blood vessels become clogged, the heart muscle cannot get the oxygen it needs to pump.

Modern Leaders in Science: Antonia Coello Novello **Critical Thinking** By educating people to the dangers of smoking, she helped them decide to quit or not to start smoking.

Lab Activity: How Much Air Is There? (p. 164)

1. It went down to make room for the air.
2. Whoever displaced the most water with their breath

Science in Your Life: The Activity Pyramid (p. 165)

Critical Thinking It encourages them to set up a good routine and become more active.

Chapter 11 Review (pp. 166–167)

Vocabulary Review **1.** True **2.** True **3.** False, trachea **4.** True **5.** False, plasma **6.** False, platelet **7.** True **8.** False, vein

Chapter Quiz **1.** Down the esophagus (p. 156) **2.** Into the large intestine (p. 157) **3.** The respiratory and circulatory systems (pp. 158–161) **4.** To the lungs (p. 156) **5.** Carbon dioxide and water vapor (p. 159) **6.** Open and close to control the flow of blood (p. 160) **7.** Arteries, veins, capillaries (p. 161) **8.** Red blood cells carry oxygen and carbon dioxide throughout the body; white blood cells fight off bacteria and sickness in the body; platelets help stop bleeding. (p. 162) **9.** Bad; it can lead to heart disease. (p. 162) **10.** Do not smoke, eat fewer fatty foods, and get plenty of exercise. (p. 162) **Research Project** See the *Teacher's Planning Guide* or *Classroom Resource Binder* for a scoring rubric for the Research Project.

Chapter 12 Staying Healthy (p. 168)

Caption Possible answer: We get different benefits from different foods.

12.1 Fighting Disease (p. 170)

Checkpoint 1 From animals or from other humans

Checkpoint 2 Helps protect against and fight off disease

Checkpoint 3 They invade and eventually destroy living cells. While inside the cell, viruses use parts of the living cell to make more viruses.

Lesson Review **1.** Viruses are smaller; bacteria are living things, while viruses do not appear to be alive. **2.** AIDS, influenza, colds, polio, chicken pox, measles, mumps **3.** Once bacteria enter the body, white blood cells start to destroy them. If the bacteria reproduce faster than the white blood cells can handle, the body will produce more white blood cells. This is when a person begins to feel sick.

A Closer Look: The Fight Against AIDS **Critical Thinking** Answers include abstaining from sexual contact and making sure donated blood was tested for HIV.

12.2 Nutrition (p. 174)

Checkpoint 1 Eating the right combination and amounts of nutrients

Checkpoint 2 Carbohydrates, fats, proteins, vitamins, minerals, water

Checkpoint 3 The bread, cereal, rice, and pasta group; the vegetable group; the fruit group

Lesson Review **1.** All six kinds of nutrients: carbohydrates, fats, proteins, vitamins, minerals, and water **2.** Too much cholesterol can build up in the arteries and block the flow of blood. **3.** It helps people choose foods for a healthy diet. **4.** Include more foods from breads, cereals, and grains; fruits; and vegetables. Choose fewer foods that are high in fat.

12.3 Guarding Your Health (p. 178)

Checkpoint Good nutrition, not smoking, and getting exercise

Lesson Review **1.** It causes blood vessels to become narrow. **2.** Exercise keeps muscles, including the heart, strong. It also keeps blood vessels open and helps prevent heart disease. **3.** Good nutrition, not smoking, and exercise

On the Cutting Edge: Using Electricity to Kill Bacteria **Critical Thinking** Many people become sick from eating foods with harmful bacteria in them.

Lab Activity: Making a Healthy Meal (p. 180)
1. Students should indicate whether they chose a variety of foods—five or more kinds. **2.** Katrina's meal; six foods likely provide more kinds of vitamins and minerals than two foods do.

On-the-Job Science: Cafeteria Attendant (p. 181)
1. B, E; **2.** A, C; **3.** H; **4.** D; **5.** F; **6.** G
Critical Thinking It would have too many sweets and no fruit.

Chapter 12 Review (p. 182)
Vocabulary Review 1. disease **2.** defense **3.** virus **4.** nutrition **5.** carbohydrate **6.** vitamin **7.** cholesterol **8.** protein
Chapter Quiz 1. Mosquitoes, fleas, pigs (p. 170)
2. The hairs filter the air you breathe. (p. 171)
3. White blood cells surround the bacteria and try to break them down. (p. 171) **4.** Answers will vary but may include colds, influenza, polio, chicken pox, measles, mumps, and AIDS. (p. 172)
5. Carbohydrates, fats, proteins, vitamins, minerals, water (p. 174) **6.** Carbohydrates give the body energy. (p. 175) **7.** Meat, fish, nuts, beans, dairy products (p. 175) **8.** Fats, oils, and sweets; because fat can build up on blood vessel walls and lead to heart disease (p. 175) **9.** Answers will vary but could include lung cancer, emphysema, and heart disease. (p. 178) **10.** Exercise keeps your muscles in good working order and keeps your blood vessels open wide. (p. 178) **Research Project** See the *Teacher's Planning Guide* or *Classroom Resource Binder* for a scoring rubric for the Research Project.

Chapter 13 Depending on Each Other (p. 184)
Caption Possible answers include that zebras need plants for food. They also need air for breathing, water for drinking, and sunlight for keeping warm.

13.1 Living Together (p. 186)
Checkpoint 1 They are recycled.
Checkpoint 2 A community is made of many populations that live in a habitat.
Checkpoint 3 Organisms find it easier to survive.
Checkpoint 4 A community may change into a different type of community.
Lesson Review 1. Air, water, food **2.** All the populations living in the same place **3.** Examples include water, air, and soil. **4.** The types of organisms change.
A Closer Look: Changing Communities Critical Thinking There was no food for the deer mice to eat.

13.2 Using Nature's Resources (p. 190)
Checkpoint 1 A producer can make its own food. A consumer must eat other organisms for food.
Checkpoint 2 Fossil fuels, which include coal, oil, and natural gas
Checkpoint 3 Evaporation and condensation

Checkpoint 4 Oxygen and carbon dioxide
Checkpoint 5 Examples include fossil fuels, water, air, soil, minerals, forests, and wildlife.
Lesson Review 1. Algae→little fish→big fish
2. Water evaporates from the land into the air. Water vapor in the air condenses and falls back to the land in the form of rain or snow. **3.** Photosynthesis gives off oxygen used for respiration in plants and animals. This produces carbon dioxide. The carbon dioxide is then used by producers for photosynthesis. **4.** If used wisely, Earth's supply of fossil fuels may last longer.
On the Cutting Edge: Less Gasoline for Cars of the Future Critical Thinking The materials should also be strong and durable.

Lab Activity: Making Models of Food Chains (p. 196)
1. The organisms depend on each other for food; each one is part of several food chains. **2.** A food web

Science in Your Life: Recycling Garbage (p. 197)
Critical Thinking Answers include using cloth napkins instead of paper ones, writing on both sides of sheets of paper, reusing containers, and using refillable pens.

Chapter 13 Review (pp. 198–199)
Vocabulary Review 1. ecosystem **2.** recycling **3.** habitat **4.** natural resource **5.** solar energy **6.** condensation **7.** food web **8.** conservation
Chapter Quiz 1. A population consists of one kind of species. A community consists of different species. (p. 187) **2.** Plants take in water through their roots. (p. 187) **3.** They change into different types of communities. (p. 188) **4.** Yes; plants→rabbits→foxes (pp. 190–191) **5.** Humans are consumers because they must eat food. (p. 190) **6.** Decomposers break down dead organisms into molecules that plants can use. (p. 191) **7.** Oil, coal, natural gas (p. 191) **8.** Evaporation (p. 192) **9.** Photosynthesis and respiration (p. 193) **10.** Answers can include to ensure that they will be available in the future and to preserve ecosystems. (pp. 194–195) **Research Project** See the *Teacher's Planning Guide* or *Classroom Resource Binder* for a scoring rubric for the Research Project.

Unit 3 Review (p. 200)
1. A (pp. 190–191) **2.** C (pp. 190–191) **3.** B (pp. 190–191) **4.** D (p. 141) **5.** A (pp. 158–159) **6.** C (p. 171) **7.** B (p. 175) **Critical Thinking** All members of a community must work together for the community to survive.

UNIT 4 PHYSICAL SCIENCE: PART I (p. 201)
1. 65 feet per second **2.** 1.3 seconds

Chapter 14 The Properties of Matter (p. 201)
Caption Answers might include that the Hope diamond is much larger and that it is blue instead of colorless.

14.1 From Molecules to Matter (p. 204)
Checkpoint 1   Physical science
Checkpoint 2   They are both branches of physical science.
Checkpoint 3   Because they cannot be broken down further
Checkpoint 4   A nucleus, electrons, neutrons, protons
Lesson Review   1. Possible responses; color, shape, odor, hardness   **2.** Chemistry and physics   **3.** Metals and nonmetals; families   **4.** 12
On the Cutting Edge: Looking at Atoms   Critical Thinking   We could learn more about matter and how things work, which could lead to better products and improved health.

14.2 More About Matter (p. 208)
Checkpoint 1   Density is determined by how much mass is in a given space.
Checkpoint 2   Solid, liquid, gas
Checkpoint 3   In a compound, a mixture, or a solution
Lesson Review   1. Solids and liquids   **2.** The parts of a mixture do not combine chemically.   **3.** A jar filled with water; The jar of water has more mass than the same volume of air.

Lab Activity: Part of the Solution (p. 212)
1. Salt, yes; chalk, no   **2.** Chalk   **3.** Salt

On-the-Job Science: Concrete Worker (p. 213)
1. A   **2.** C. The particles are many different sizes. Small particles fill the spaces.   **3.** C; because it is dense   **Critical Thinking**   The holes will make the concrete less dense, weakening it.

Chapter 14 Review (pp. 214–215)
Vocabulary Review   1. True   **2.** False, gas   **3.** False, compound   **4.** False, neutron   **5.** True   **6.** True   **7.** False, solid   **8.** True
Chapter Quiz   1. Chemistry; it involves the study of matter. (p. 205)   **2.** Possible answers: orange, round, smooth (pp. 204, 208)   **3.** Nucleus: center of atom; electrons: outside the nucleus; neutrons and protons: inside the nucleus (p. 206)   **4.** An electrical charge opposite that of protons (p. 207)   **5.** How much mass something has for its size (p. 208)   **6.** It spreads out to fill the big container (p. 210)   **7.** Steam; molecules in gas are less tightly packed than in liquids or solids. (p. 210)   **8.** A compound; the atoms bond and are not just mixed together. (p. 211)   **9.** Soil and water do not join chemically. (p. 211)   **10.** It spreads evenly throughout the water. (p. 211)   **Research Project**
See the *Teacher's Planning Guide* or *Classroom Resource Binder* for a scoring rubric for the Research Project.

Chapter 15   Energy and Matter (p. 216)
Caption   When a tree is chopped down, no change takes place in the substances that make up the tree. In a fire, the substances that make up the tree change to other substances.

15.1 Energy in All Things (p. 218)
Checkpoint 1   To make something move

Checkpoint 2   When it is in motion
Lesson Review   1. Energy   **2.** Potential and kinetic   **3.** From digested food   **4.** Kinetic energy changed to potential energy.

15.2 The Different Forms of Energy (p. 220)
Checkpoint 1   The sun
Checkpoint 2   Hot; because the molecules in a hot object move faster
Checkpoint 3   The electron
Checkpoint 4   Chemical
Checkpoint 5   Mechanical
Checkpoint 6   Nuclear fission
Checkpoint 7   It can change forms.
Lesson Review   1. Heat, light, electrical, chemical, mechanical, nuclear   **2.** Electrical   **3.** Be sure students provide reasons in their answers.

15.3 Changing Matter Using Energy (p. 223)
Checkpoint 1   Adding or taking away heat energy
Checkpoint 2   Physical and chemical
Lesson Review   1. It freezes and becomes a solid.   **2.** A change in odor and color   **3.** Chemical; the fried egg has different properties than the raw egg.   **4.** As the balloon cooled, water vapor in the balloon condensed.
Modern Leaders in Science: Roy Plunkett   Critical Thinking   Chemical change

Lab Activity: Changing Forms of Energy (p. 226)
1. It increased.   **2.** The mechanical energy of the moving sand grains changed to heat energy.

Science in Your Life: Cooking and Energy (p. 227)
Critical Thinking   The body uses them for life processes and to move, or they are stored for later use.

Chapter 15 Review (pp. 228–229)
Vocabulary Review   1. kinetic energy   **2.** electrical energy   **3.** nuclear fusion   **4.** heat energy   **5.** chemical energy   **6.** potential energy   **7.** nuclear fission   **8.** light energy
Chapter Quiz   1. None (p. 218)   **2.** Potential energy, a book sitting on a table; kinetic energy, a falling book (p. 218)   **3.** Heat energy, burning match; light energy, the sun; electrical energy, electric current; chemical energy, food; mechanical energy, a bicycle; nuclear energy, nuclear fission (pp. 220–221)   **4.** Nuclear fission (p. 221)   **5.** No. Energy cannot be created or destroyed. It just changes form. (p. 222)   **6.** It changes into a gas. (p. 223)   **7.** Energy (p. 224)   **8.** Answers might include breaking it. (p. 224)   **9.** Answers might include burning it. (p. 224)   **10.** Answers might include that energy is given off, gases are released, and the substances that make up the wood change identity. (p. 224)   **Research Project**
See the *Teacher's Planning Guide* or *Classroom Resource Binder* for a scoring rubric for the Research Project.

Chapter 16   Force and Motion (p. 230)
Caption   The bobsled might travel up and over the wall of the track.

16.1 What Is Force? (p. 232)

Checkpoint 1 The object is pushed or pulled.

Checkpoint 2 The mass of the objects and the distance between them

Checkpoint 3 Weight changes with the pull of gravity, while mass stays the same.

Checkpoint 4 Rolling friction, sliding friction, fluid friction

Checkpoint 5 Centripetal force causes the object to move in a curved path.

Lesson Review   1. Less. The moon is less massive than Earth and has less gravitational pull.
2. Rolling friction between the wheels and sidewalk
3. Centripetal force   **4.** A change in the distance between them would cause a change in the gravitational pull; Closer objects exert a stronger gravitational pull.

16.2 Inertia and Motion (p. 238)

Checkpoint An object will stay at rest or in motion unless it is acted upon by a force.

Lesson Review   1. Sir Isaac Newton   **2.** A force
3. The bus has greater mass and therefore greater inertia.

On the Cutting Edge: Technology in Theme Parks Critical Thinking The force of gravity

Lab Activity: Weight and Friction (p. 240)

1. The sandpaper causes the most friction. The pencils cause the least.   **2.** The greater the surface friction, the more force is needed to move an object across the surface.

On-the-Job Science: Truck Driver (p. 241)

1. 185 feet   **2.** 305 feet   **3.** Its greater weight gives it more inertia.   **Critical Thinking** The last stop. At each stop, she adds mass to the truck, which gives it more inertia.

Chapter 16 Review (pp. 242–243)

Vocabulary Review   1. force   **2.** gravity   **3.** motion
4. weight   **5.** friction   **6.** centripetal force   **7.** inertia
8. lubricant
Chapter Quiz   1. Possible answer: Dragging a sled (p. 232)   **2.** Possible answers: Hitting a baseball, golfball, or tennis ball (p. 232)   **3.** Gravity (p. 233)
4. Weight can change depending on the gravitational pull on the object. Mass stays the same wherever an object is. (p. 234)   **5.** Friction (p. 235)   **6.** Sliding friction (p. 235)   **7.** Centripetal force (pp. 236–237)
8. Inertia (p. 238)   **9.** A large car. It has greater mass. (p. 239)   **10.** Gravity, inertia, friction (pp. 233, 235, 238)   **Research Project** See the *Teacher's Planning Guide* or *Classroom Resource Binder* for a scoring rubric for the Research Project.

Chapter 17 Machines at Work (p. 244)
Caption Lifts heavy loads

17.1 All Kinds of Work (p. 246)

Checkpoint 1 They change the speed, direction, or amount of a force.

Checkpoint 2 Effort force and resistance force
Lesson Review   1. To make it easier to do work

2. Your lifting; gravity   **3.** Higher, because a higher mechanical advantage increases the effort force
Great Moments in Science: A Perpetual Motion Machine   Critical Thinking Answers include electricity, moving water or steam, gasoline burning, and a push or pull from a person.

17.2 Simple and Compound Machines (p. 249)

Checkpoint 1 Lever, pulley, inclined plane, wedge, screw, wheel and axle

Checkpoint 2 Their effort force, resistance force, and fulcrum are in different positions.

Checkpoint 3 By changing the direction of the effort force

Checkpoint 4 They spread the work out over a greater distance.

Checkpoint 5 The wheel

A Closer Look: The Great Pyramid at Giza   Critical Thinking Wedges, because wedges can be used to cut things

Checkpoint 6 A compound machine is made up of two or more simple machines, so it can do more complicated jobs. A compound machine often runs on fuels.

Lesson Review   1. Answers could include scissors, broom, and fly swatter.   **2.** Inclined plane   **3.** Pencil sharpener (wheel and axle, wedges); scissors (lever, wedges)   **4.** The wheels help reduce friction, the resistance force.

On the Cutting Edge: Robots at Work   Critical Thinking Robots cannot reason. They take some jobs that people could do.

Lab Activity: Working With Levers (p. 256)

The closer the fulcrum is to the load, the less force is needed to move the load.

Science in Your Life: Machines as Tools (p. 257)

1. Pastry brush, tongs, slotted spoon   **2.** Pizza cutter
3. Apple corer, pizza cutter, pastry scraper   **4.** The pizza cutter is made of a wheel and axle and a wedge (the edge of the wheel).   **Critical Thinking** Answers could include variations of the following tools: forks, graters, mashers, bottle openers, peelers, spatulas, knives, and whisks.

Chapter 17 Review (pp. 258–259)

Vocabulary Review   1. inclined plane   **2.** wedge
3. lever   **4.** mechanical advantage   **5.** load   **6.** work
7. fulcrum   **8.** pulley
Chapter Quiz   1. By changing the amount, direction, or speed of a force (p. 246)   **2.** Resistance force (p. 247)   **3.** Effort force (p. 247)   **4.** Between the effort force and the resistance force (p. 250)   **5.** Close to the load (p. 251)   **6.** Pulley (p. 251)   **7.** Wedge and screw (p. 252)   **8.** Wheel and axle (p. 253)
9. Compound machines (p. 254)   **10.** The handle is a wheel and axle. The blades are wedges. (p. 254)
Research Project See the *Teacher's Planning Guide* or *Classroom Resource Binder* for a scoring rubric for the Research Project.

Unit 4 Review (p. 260)

1. D (p. 206) **2.** A (p. 206) **3.** C (p. 211) **4.** C
(pp. 218–219) **5.** A (pp. 223–224) **6.** B (p. 247)
7. D (p. 250) **Critical Thinking** Gravity pulls it on
the downhill part of the track, making it go faster. As
the car glides onto the uphill part of the track, rolling
friction between the wheels and the track slows its
speed.

UNIT 5 PHYSICAL SCIENCE: PART II (p. 261)

1. In waves **2.** As a flow of electrons **3.** Sound
energy

Chapter 18 Heat, Light, and Sound (p. 262)

Caption They are all forms of energy.

18.1 Heat and Matter (p. 264)

Checkpoint 1 Heat is the total kinetic energy of the
particles in a substance. Temperature is the measure of
the average kinetic energy of the particles in a
substance.
Checkpoint 2 Heat moves quickly through a good
conductor but very slowly through a poor conductor.
Checkpoint 3 Warm air rises and pushes cooler air
down, which gets heated and rises.
Checkpoint 4 Radiation
Lesson Review **1.** The particles move faster, and
the substance becomes hotter. **2.** Temperature
3. Because there is no matter in a vacuum. **4.** The
bathtub of water; it has more molecules of water.
**Great Moments in Science: The Mercury
Thermometer** **Critical Thinking** It allowed
scientists and researchers to make more accurate
temperature measurements.

18.2 Light (p. 269)

Checkpoint 1 Wavelength, amplitude, and
frequency
Checkpoint 2 Visible light, ultraviolet light, infrared
light; their wavelengths
Checkpoint 3 Pass through the object, get absorbed
into the object, bounce off the object, or be bent by
the object
Checkpoint 4 Red, orange, yellow, green, blue,
indigo, and violet lights
Lesson Review **1.** Light, sound, water, TV and radio
signals **2.** It either passes through the object, is
absorbed by it, bounces off of it, or is bent by it.
3. The different wavelengths of white light bend
different amounts and separate into a spectrum.
4. Red, orange, green, blue, indigo, violet

18.3 Sound (p. 274)

Checkpoint 1 Solid
Checkpoint 2 By matter that vibrates
Lesson Review **1.** A vacuum **2.** The sound becomes
louder. **3.** The vibrations of the string
On the Cutting Edge: Sonar **Critical Thinking**
Scientists can get a picture of the ocean floor by
sending sound waves down into the ocean and
measuring how long it takes them to return to the
surface.

Lab Activity: Combining Colors of Light (p. 276)

1. Three **2.** That they are primary colors because
they form the others

On-the-Job Science: Store Manager (p. 277)

1. Yes. They both start with 978. **2.** No. The
company codes are different: 03273 and 05275.
Critical Thinking Change the bar code number to
the correct price.

Chapter 18 Review (pp. 278–279)

Vocabulary Review **1.** insulator **2.** spectrum
3. vacuum **4.** conduction **5.** prism **6.** radiation
7. refraction **8.** frequency
Chapter Quiz **1.** Heat is the total kinetic energy
of the particles in a substance. Temperature is the
average kinetic energy of the particles. (p. 264)
2. By molecules bumping into each other (p. 266)
3. It is less dense than the surrounding cool air.
(p. 267) **4.** Wavelength, amplitude, frequency
(p. 269) **5.** Makes the light brighter (p. 269)
6. Reflection is the bouncing of light off an object.
Refraction is the bending of light. (p. 271) **7.** It has
a different wavelength. (p. 272) **8.** The color of light
that the object reflects (p. 273) **9.** Sound (p. 274)
10. The amplitude of the sound waves (p. 275)
Research Project See the *Teacher's Planning Guide* or
Classroom Resource Binder for a scoring rubric for the
Research Project.

Chapter 19 Electricity and Magnetism (p. 280)

Caption Both produce light. Students may also say
that both involve electricity.

19.1 All Charged Up (p. 282)

Checkpoint 1 The movement of electrons
Checkpoint 2 By two objects with opposite charges
attracting each other
Checkpoint 3 The movement of electrons between
a cloud and an object with a positive charge
Lesson Review **1.** The electrons **2.** They have
opposite charges and attract each other. **3.** The heat
of lightning warms the air, making it expand quickly.
4. Repel. Each balloon would have a negative charge.
**Great Moments in Science: Benjamin Franklin and
Lightning** **Critical Thinking** Both attract lightning
and carry its charge toward the ground.

19.2 Electrical Currents (p. 286)

Checkpoint Start the flow of electrons through a
conductor
Lesson Review **1.** Electricity travels through it easily.
2. Both are batteries that produce electrical current.
Wet cells use an acid solution. Dry cells use a paste.
3. If the electricity goes out, you can use the generator
to produce some electricity.

19.3 Electrical Circuits (p. 288)

Checkpoint Electricity can flow through a closed
circuit but not through an open one.
Lesson Review **1.** Circular **2.** Opens or closes a
circuit **3.** The wire will not stop the circuit from
becoming overloaded.

19.4 Magnetism (p. 290)

Checkpoint 1 Iron, nickel, cobalt
Checkpoint 2 In the area called the magnetic field
Lesson Review 1. Stones that are attracted to each other, iron, and anything else that is strongly magnetic **2.** One end points toward the north, and the other points toward the south. **3.** They line up so their magnetic pull is all in one direction. **4.** The needle will be attracted to the magnet and no longer point north and south.

Lab Activity: Identifying Conductors and Insulators (p. 292)

1. Anything made of metal is a conductor. Anything made of plastic, rubber, wood, paper, cork, glass, or chalk is an insulator. **2.** By determining if electricity will easily travel through it

Science in Your Life: Using Electricity (p. 293)

1. Washing machine, 25; Stove, 120; Dishwasher, 30; TV, 54 **2.** Refrigerator, stove, TV, dishwasher, washing machine **Critical Thinking** Suggestions include watching less TV and washing clothes only when there are full loads.

Chapter 19 Review (pp. 294–295)

Vocabulary Review 1. electrical conductor
2. battery **3.** magnetic field **4.** discharge **5.** static electricity **6.** electrical insulator **7.** generator
8. fuse
Chapter Quiz 1. Electricity is caused by the movement of electrons (p. 282) **2.** Negative (p. 282) **3.** Neutral (p. 283) **4.** The electrons (p. 284) **5.** Metals are excellent electrical conductors. Rubber is not (p. 286) **6.** A chemical reaction in the dry cell causes parts of the cell to become negative and positive. Current flows when these parts are connected. (p. 287) **7.** Electrical energy (p. 287) **8.** It provides a circular, unbroken path for electrons to flow through. (p. 288) **9.** Strong magnetism (p. 290) **10.** At the poles (p. 290) **Research Project** See the *Teacher's Planning Guide* or *Classroom Resource Binder* for a scoring rubric for the Research Project.

Chapter 20 Energy Resources (p. 296)

Caption Windmills are most practical to use in areas that get strong winds much of the time. These include mountain passes and Great Plains states such as North Dakota, South Dakota, and Texas.

20.1 Fossil Fuels (p. 298)

Checkpoint 1 Fossil fuels
Checkpoint 2 The supply of fossil fuels will eventually run out, and burning fossil fuels causes air pollution.
Lesson Review 1. 84% **2.** Answers include to run cars, heat homes, and provide power for factories.
3. Answers include taking a bus instead of a car, riding a bike, walking, and insulating homes.
4. Plastic is made from fossil fuels. If plastic is recycled, less plastic needs to be made, and this means using less of fossil fuels.
On the Cutting Edge: Electric Cars Critical Thinking Advantages: An electric car does not pollute the air and is less noisy. Disadvantages: An electric car isn't convenient to use for long trips, and it takes a long time to recharge the battery compared to filling a tank with gasoline.

20.2 Other Energy Resources (p. 300)

Checkpoint 1 Nuclear fission produces radioactive wastes. Scientists are unable to control the nuclear fusion process.
Checkpoint 2 Absorbs sunlight and changes it into heat energy
Checkpoint 3 Moving water turns the blades of a turbine, which runs the generator.
Checkpoint 4 The heating of rock inside the Earth
Checkpoint 5 Windmills use wind to power electric generators. Power plants near the oceans capture the energy in waves and tides.
Lesson Review 1. e **2.** a **3.** b **4.** f **5.** d
6. c **7.** g **Critical Thinking** The wind is free, and it does not pollute.
A Closer Look: Energy From Garbage Critical Thinking Garbage is constantly being produced. Fossil fuels are not.

Lab Activity: Absorbing Solar Energy (p. 306)

1. The black paper. The temperature reading of the thermometer under the black paper was higher than that of the thermometer under the other color papers.
2. So they can absorb more solar energy and produce more heat for the house

On-the-Job Science: Nuclear Reactor Operator (p. 307)

1. C, A, B **2.** A **3.** B **Critical Thinking** Drawings should show the temperature at 530°F at 0% power and 570°F at 100% power.

Chapter 20 Review (pp. 308–309)

Vocabulary Review 1. True **2.** True **3.** False, geothermal energy **4.** True **5.** False, solar collector **6.** False, geyser **7.** True
Chapter Quiz 1. Coal, oil, natural gas (p. 298) **2.** By burning them (p. 298) **3.** It pollutes the air. (p. 298) **4.** Nuclear fission and nuclear fusion (pp. 300–301) **5.** Nuclear fission (p. 300) **6.** It is clean, plentiful, and free. (p. 303) **7.** By moving water striking and turning the blades of a turbine (p. 303) **8.** The heat from hot rocks is used to run electric generators (p. 304) **9.** To pump water, grind grain, and produce electricity (p. 304) **10.** Power plants must be built near oceans, where the conditions are just right. (p. 304) **Research Project** See the *Teacher's Planning Guide* or *Classroom Resource Binder* for a scoring rubric for the Research Project.

Unit 5 Review (p. 310)

1. B (pp. 269–270) **2.** B (pp. 269–270) **3.** A (pp. 269–270) **4.** C (p. 283) **5.** D (pp. 288–289)
6. C (pp. 298, 300) **7.** B (p. 303)

UNIT 6 EARTH SCIENCE: PART I (p. 311)

1. Green **2.** Pink and purple **3.** Lakes

Chapter 21 Planet Earth (p. 312)

Caption Landmasses, clouds, oceans

21.1 Spaceship Earth (p. 314)

Checkpoint 1 In a closed, curved path called an orbit

Checkpoint 2 Gravity drew a huge cloud of gases and dust together to form the planets and the sun.

Lesson Review **1.** The sun and all the planets and other objects that circle around it **2.** About 4.5 billion years ago **3.** The Earth **4.** The planets each move in their own orbits. This keeps them separated from one another.

21.2 Features of the Earth (p. 316)

Checkpoint 1 Water

Checkpoint 2 Core, mantle, crust

Checkpoint 3 It revolves around the sun and spins on its axis.

Checkpoint 4 The tilt of the Earth on its axis

Lesson Review **1.** Africa, Antarctica, Asia, Australia, Europe, North America, South America **2.** Core: center of the Earth; mantle: middle layer; crust: outer layer. They also differ in thickness and what they are made of. **3.** The spinning of the Earth on its axis **4.** The number of daylight hours would never change, and there would be no change of seasons.

21.3 Dividing Up the Earth (p. 321)

Checkpoint 1 To help people find different places and features on Earth

Checkpoint 2 Because the Earth rotates 15° of longitude in 1 hour (15 × 24 = 360)

Lesson Review **1.** The equator is the 0-degree line of latitude, while the prime meridian is the 0-degree line of longitude. **2.** About 15 degrees **3.** 1:00 P.M.

Great Moments in Science: Setting Up the Time Zones **Critical Thinking** It would be difficult to keep track of appointments that were in different places several miles apart.

Lab Activity: Making a Model of the Seasons (p. 324)

1. No. The amount of sunlight remains about the same all year. **2.** The seasons would be more intense. Nights would be longer in winter, shorter in summer.

Science in Your Life: Topographic Maps (p. 325)

1. 2 **2.** From the west because it is less steep **3.** East **Critical Thinking** It would show where steep areas are located and where it would be easier to hike.

Chapter 21 Review (pp. 326–327)

Vocabulary Review **1.** solar system **2.** orbit **3.** continents **4.** mantle **5.** crust **6.** axis **7.** line of latitude **8.** prime meridian

Chapter Quiz **1.** Clouds of gas and dust were drawn together; 4.5 billion years (p. 315) **2.** Water covers so much of the planet. (p. 316) **3.** The crust, the mantle, and the core; the crust (p. 318) **4.** $365\frac{1}{4}$ days, or one year (p. 319) **5.** The Earth rotates on its axis every 24 hours and revolves around the sun every $365\frac{1}{4}$ days. (p. 319) **6.** Halfway between the North and South poles (p. 321) **7.** East to west (p. 321)

8. North to south (p. 321) **9.** An area in which the same time is used; Pacific, Mountain, Central, Eastern (p. 322) **10.** You gain one hour for each new time zone. (p. 323) **Research Project** See the *Teacher's Planning Guide* or *Classroom Resource Binder* for a scoring rubric for the Research Project.

Chapter 22 The Earth's Crust (p. 328)

Caption Students should reason that the cloud of dirt and ash they see bursting from the volcano filled the sky, blocking the sun.

22.1 Plate Tectonics (p. 330)

Checkpoint 1 They sit on the plates, which float and drift on the softer rock of the mantle.

Checkpoint 2 Trenches and mountains. One plate can be forced under the other, forming a trench, or two plates can pile up against each other, forming a mountain.

Checkpoint 3 When plates slide past each other, parts of the plates may lock in place. When the pressure becomes great enough, the plates slip with a jolt, causing an earthquake.

Great Moments in Science: Putting the Puzzle Together **Critical Thinking** The continents are carried along on the plates, which move on the hot, softer rock of the mantle.

Checkpoint 4 Melted rock squeezes up from within the Earth.

Lesson Review **1.** True **2.** True **3.** False, mantle **4.** The upward movement of magma can cause movement in the ground under the volcano.

A Closer Look: Pompeii **Critical Thinking** The volcano erupted suddenly, allowing gas and ash to trap people before they could escape.

22.2 Rocks and Minerals (p. 336)

Checkpoint 1 Igneous: hardened magma; sedimentary: rock particles or the remains of living things that stick together and harden; metamorphic: rocks that change chemically under high temperatures or pressure

Checkpoint 2 One or more minerals

Checkpoint 3 Natural processes, such as running water and freezing and thawing, break rock into tiny pieces that become part of soil.

Checkpoint 4 By rivers and glaciers

Lesson Review **1.** Color, shape, hardness, texture **2.** Rain, running water, ice, plants, animals, chemicals **3.** They clear soil and rock in their paths as they move. **4.** The surface would be mostly solid rock because there would be no processes to break it down.

Lab Activity: Recognizing Types of Soil (p. 340)

1. The soil with the most organic matter because plants need nutrients to grow **2.** The soil with the smallest particles

On-the-Job Science: Geologist (p. 341)

1. Sample 2; Sample 1 **2.** They are both yellow and shiny, but Sample 3 is much harder than Sample 1. **3.** Use a magnet to identify Sample 4. **Critical Thinking** Properties tell geologists how a mineral can be used. For example, a mineral that is very hard would have different uses than a mineral that is soft or can be crumbled into powder.

Chapter 22 Review (pp. 342–343)

Vocabulary Review 1. True **2.** True **3.** True
4. False, sedimentary rock **5.** True **6.** False, weathering **7.** False, erosion **8.** False, volcano
Chapter Quiz 1. The Earth's crust is made up of plates that slowly shift position while floating on the mantle. (p. 331) **2.** A trench (p. 332) **3.** Mountains (p. 332) **4.** Movements of the Earth's plates (p. 333) **5.** Both are caused by the movement of the Earth's plates. (pp. 333–334) **6.** Igneous, sedimentary, metamorphic (pp. 336–337) **7.** Minerals (p. 338) **8.** Weathering breaks down rock into smaller pieces. (p. 338) **9.** Rivers slowly carve away rock and move soil to shape river valleys. (p. 339) **10.** Rock and soil get worn away by water, wind, or ice. (p. 339)
Research Project See the *Teacher's Planning Guide* or *Classroom Resource Binder* for a scoring rubric for the Research Project.

Chapter 23 The Earth's Atmosphere (p. 344)

Caption Descriptions might refer to dark storm clouds; high, wispy clouds; and clouds that cover the entire sky.

23.1 Air All Around Us (p. 346)

Checkpoint 1 Nitrogen and oxygen
Checkpoint 2 Five; troposphere, stratosphere, mesosphere, ionosphere, thermosphere
Lesson Review 1. Dust, water vapor, and other gases **2.** About 600 miles (960 km) **3.** Ionosphere; contains many electrically charged particles that reflect radio signals. **4.** The gases would escape into space. Earth would have little or no atmosphere.

23.2 Properties of Air (p. 349)

Checkpoint 1 Gravity near the Earth's surface is very strong and pulls air molecules close together.
Checkpoint 2 They block it during the day and trap the heat from it at night.
Checkpoint 3 The uneven heating of the atmosphere, which forms convection currents
Lesson Review 1. Weight, heat, movement
2. By changing to heat energy when it strikes the ground and radiating into the air **3.** A circular motion of air **4.** Sea breezes help keep the shore cooler.

A Closer Look: Jet Streams Critical Thinking
They would be flying against the jet stream and would need to use more fuel and take more time than if they avoided the jet stream.

23.3 Water and Air (p. 353)

Checkpoint 1 Sleet, snow, hail
Checkpoint 2 Cirrus: thin and feathery; stratus: cover whole sky; cumulus: puffy
Lesson Review 1. By evaporating off the ground, lakes, oceans, rivers, plants, and animals **2.** Cloud droplets become heavy and fall to the ground. **3.** From water droplets or ice particles that collect in the atmosphere **4.** They evaporate

On the Cutting Edge: Cloud Seeding Critical Thinking During a drought to save crops or during a forest fire

Lab Activity: Making a Cloud (p. 356)

1. Step 7 **2.** The presence of more particles in the air from the smoke **3.** Water vapor, a cooling of temperature, particles in the air

Science in Your Life: Wind Chill Temperature (p. 357)

1. −5°F **2.** 0°F **3.** Probably a heavy jacket or coat and gloves because the wind chill temperature is below freezing. **Critical Thinking** The wind chill will make it feel like 30°F.

Chapter 23 Review (pp. 358–359)

Vocabulary Review 1. dew point **2.** stratosphere
3. air pressure **4.** barometer **5.** precipitation
6. atmosphere **7.** humidity **8.** troposphere
Chapter Quiz 1. Troposphere, stratosphere, mesosphere, ionosphere, thermosphere (pp. 347–348)
2. The weight of gases pressing on Earth (p. 349)
3. They reflect the sunlight back into the outer atmosphere (p. 349) **4.** Warmer air rises; cool air takes its place. This movement of air is wind. (p. 350)
5. Mountains, valleys, big bodies of water (p. 351)
6. Sea breeze (p. 351) **7.** Some water vapor turns to liquid water. (p. 353) **8.** Sleet is rain that freezes as it falls. Snow falls from a cloud as crystals. Hail is made up of hard pieces of ice. (pp. 353–354) **9.** Cirrus, stratus, cumulus (pp. 354–355) **10.** A special kind of cumulus cloud (p. 355) **Research Project** See the *Teacher's Planning Guide* or *Classroom Resource Binder* for a scoring rubric for the Research Project.

Chapter 24 Weather and Climate (p. 360)

Caption Destroy power lines, cutting off electricity and communication; cause fires from ruptured gas lines; shoot deadly debris through the air

24.1 Air on the Move (p. 362)

Checkpoint 1 Weather is the atmosphere's condition at a certain time, while climate is the average weather in an area over many years.
Checkpoint 2 A warm front forms when a warm air mass meets and runs over a cold air mass. A cold front forms when a cold air mass meets and moves under a warm air mass.
Checkpoint 3 They have instruments that collect weather data that meteorologists use to make forecasts.
Lesson Review 1. There may be precipitation, then the temperature will drop. **2.** Weather stations, satellites, weather balloons, ocean buoys, airplanes, radar **3.** People would be unprepared for hazardous weather and would get caught in storms without warning.

24.2 Storms (p. 365)

Checkpoint 1 Warm, moist air rising quickly because of a cold front or mountains; sun heating the Earth's surface

Checkpoint 2 Air moving from high-pressure to low-pressure areas
Checkpoint 3 Cyclone, hurricane, typhoon, tornado. All are caused by low pressure, warm air rising, and circling winds.
Lesson Review **1.** Electric charges build up in thunderheads and are discharged as lightning. **2.** High pressure: clear weather; low pressure: stormy weather **3.** Their energy comes from warm ocean waters.
A Closer Look: More About Hurricanes Critical Thinking Because there are no winds in the eye, and the sun sometimes shines

24.3 The Earth's Climate Zones
Checkpoint 1 Latitude, mountains, large bodies of water, ocean currents
Checkpoint 2 Tropical, polar, temperate. Tropical is hot. Polar is cold. Temperate varies between both.
Lesson Review **1.** They block moisture, creating a dry climate on their leeward side. **2.** Polar: no true summer; tropical: no true winter **3.** In a temperate climate, people would need clothes for both cold winters and warm summers. In tropical climates, for example, people always wear warm-weather clothes.
Great Moments in Science: Benjamin Banneker and the *Farmer's Almanac* Critical Thinking Because farmers depend on weather to plant, grow, and harvest crops

Lab Activity: Observing Fronts (p. 372)
1. Answers will vary depending on weather conditions. **2.** If students find precipitation (especially short and heavy) and wind followed by a drop in temperature, a cold front has probably passed. If students find a longer period of light precipitation followed by a rise in temperature, a warm front has probably passed.

On-the-Job Science: Television Meteorologist (p. 373)
1. At 2:00 P.M. **2.** 2:00 P.M. and 3:00 P.M. **3.** It dropped. **Critical Thinking** They were recorded during summer because the temperatures are very high.

Chapter 24 Review (pp. 374–375)
Vocabulary Review **1.** climate **2.** meteorology **3.** air mass **4.** typhoon **5.** hurricane **6.** front **7.** weather **8.** tornado
Chapter Quiz **1.** Weather (p. 362) **2.** The weather of an area changes with the temperature and humidity of the air mass over it. (pp. 362–363) **3.** It brings short, heavy bursts of precipitation, followed by a drop in temperature. (p. 363) **4.** It produces calmer weather than cold or warm fronts (p. 364) **5.** Thunderstorms (p. 365) **6.** High pressure usually means clear weather, while low pressure usually means rainy or stormy weather. (p. 366) **7.** They are both stormy cyclones with high winds. (p. 367) **8.** They interrupt the flow of moist global winds, causing land on the side of a mountain facing the wind to get a lot of rainfall. (p. 369) **9.** Because the air is too cold to hold much water (p. 370)

10. Tropical climates are warm all the time, have heavy rainfall, and no true winter. Temperate climates have warm summers, cold winters, and precipitation varies. (p. 370) **Research Project** See the *Teacher's Planning Guide* or *Classroom Resource Binder* for a scoring rubric for the Research Project.

Unit 6 Review (p. 376)
1. C (p. 318) **2.** C (p. 321) **3.** B (pp. 322–323) **4.** B (p. 331) **5.** A (p. 337) **6.** D (p. 347) **7.** D (p. 363)
Critical Thinking Answers should refer to the conditions of temperature and precipitation in that climate.

UNIT 7 EARTH SCIENCE: PART II (p. 377)
1. Lightning, earthquake, thunderstorm, volcanic eruption **2.** Soil formation, glacier carving valley, mountain formation **3.** No, not compared to millions of years.

Chapter 25 The Earth's History (p. 378)
Caption Clues about the rocks, weather, and early life at different times in the Earth's past

25.1 The Story in the Rocks (p. 380)
Checkpoint 1 The oldest rocks are usually at the bottom. The youngest rocks are usually at the top.
Checkpoint 2 That it changes over time
Lesson Review **1.** It can bend the layers or turn them upside down. **2.** Geologists compare the decay rates of certain radioactive elements to tell when they formed. **3.** That the area was once under water because fish live in water
On the Cutting Edge: Greenland Ice Core Project Critical Thinking Ash and volcanic rock thrown from the volcano

25.2 Geological Time (p. 382)
Checkpoint 1 Nearly 4 billion years
Checkpoint 2 Plants and sea life flourished at this time.
Checkpoint 3 Dinosaurs
Checkpoint 4 Late in the Cenozoic era
Checkpoint 5 They don't know, but the sun will eventually die out, and there can be no life on Earth without sunlight.
Lesson Review **1.** Precambrian era **2.** Paleozoic era **3.** Dinosaurs and other reptiles **4.** Scientists would not know as much about past life and climates.

Lab Activity: Identifying Fossils From Rock Layers (p. 386)
1. No. The correct order from bottom to top, based on the fossils, is 3, 1, 2. **2.** Yes. Layers 1 and 2 must have been overturned because older fossils are on top of younger ones. **3.** That sometimes they are not in order because of uplifting and folding

Science in Your Life: Going on Dino Digs (p. 387)
1. B2 **2.** A2 because it is closer to the bones already found **3.** B1 **4.** Dinosaur eggs **Critical Thinking** Many leaf fossils and a tree trunk fossil were found nearby, indicating a forest.

Chapter 25 Review (pp. 388–389)

Vocabulary Review **1.** True **2.** False, Mesozoic **3.** True **4.** False, huge **5.** True **6.** True **7.** False, billion

Chapter Quiz **1.** Uplifting and folding can rearrange rock layers. (p. 380) **2.** They break down into other elements. (p. 380) **3.** The Earth's continents and climate have changed a lot over time. (p. 381) **4.** Precambrian, Paleozoic, Mesozoic, Cenozoic (pp. 382–384) **5.** The formation of the Earth (p. 382) **6.** The Mesozoic era (p. 383) **7.** Huge glaciers flowed south from the Arctic and covered the northern parts of the Earth (p. 384) **8.** Mammals such as humans (p. 384) **9.** 100,000 to 120,000 years (p. 385) **10.** It will change. (p. 385) **Research Project** See the *Teacher's Planning Guide* or *Classroom Resource Binder* for a scoring rubric for the Research Project.

Chapter 26 The Earth's Oceans (p. 390)

Caption Small rocks, the bases of large rocks, more of the vegetation

26.1 Features of the Ocean (p. 392)

Checkpoint 1 Weathered and eroded rocks on land
Checkpoint 2 Surface currents and undersea currents
Checkpoint 3 Continental shelf, continental slope, ocean basin
Lesson Review **1.** Salt **2.** A current of warm water that flows through the Atlantic from the Gulf of Mexico north toward Newfoundland **3.** The crust of the ocean floor moves away from the mid-ocean ridge as magma pushes up through openings at the ridge. **4.** Oceans are deep-water environments that cannot be easily explored without special equipment.

26.2 Waves and Tides (p. 397)

Checkpoint 1 Wind
Checkpoint 2 Earthquakes on the ocean floor
A Closer Look: Seismic Sea Waves Critical Thinking So people can move quickly inland away from the coast
Checkpoint 3 The combined gravity of the sun and the moon
Lesson Review **1.** As the shallow ocean floor near shore drags on a wave, its faster-moving top spills over as a breaker. **2.** They travel fast and pile up on shore. **3.** Spring tides are especially high or low tides. Neap tides are neither very high nor very low. **4.** Swimmers caught in it can be dragged out to sea.
On the Cutting Edge: Exploring the Ocean Floor Critical Thinking By eating the remains of living organisms that sink to the bottom

26.3 Ocean Resources (p. 401)

Checkpoint Answers might include resources listed in the chart on p. 401.
Lesson Review **1.** Algae are the first step in many food chains and produce most of the Earth's oxygen. **2.** Cobalt, copper, manganese, nickel **3.** Because freshwater supplies are scarce

Lab Activity: Making a Cold-Water Current (p. 402)

1. As it melts, blue streaks of the water drift toward the bottom of the jar. The cold water is denser, and sinks through the warmer, less dense water in the jar. **2.** Density currents operate in the same way. Cold ocean water sinks. But in the ocean, there are also warm currents that rise to complete the cycle.

On-the-Job Science: Underwater Photographer (p. 403)

1. Octopus **2.** All of them **Critical Thinking** The sea is their natural environment, so they are better adapted to deep dives.

Chapter 26 Review (pp. 404–405)

Vocabulary Review **1.** mid-ocean ridge **2.** tide **3.** ocean basin **4.** salinity **5.** density current **6.** ocean current **7.** seismic sea wave **8.** continental shelf

Chapter Quiz **1.** 70 percent (p. 392) **2.** Wind (p. 394) **3.** A difference in the densities of ocean waters (p. 394) **4.** Warmth makes currents rise, while coldness makes them sink. (p. 394) **5.** Along the mid-ocean ridge (p. 395) **6.** They are all parts of the ocean floor. The continental shelf is the gentle slope from the shore out to the continental slope. The continental slope is the steep cliff that extends from the shelf down to the ocean basin, which is the bottom of the ocean floor. (p. 396) **7.** Wind (p. 397) **8.** The pull of the gravity of the sun and moon on the Earth (p. 399) **9.** During high tide, water is as high as it can get on shore. During low tide, water is as low as it can get on shore. (p. 399) **10.** Possibilities include: fish for food; seaweed in cosmetics, foods, paints, dyes, paper; oil and natural gas fuel; ocean water used for drinking after removing salt. (p. 401) **Research Project** See the *Teacher's Planning Guide* or *Classroom Resource Binder* for a scoring rubric for the Research Project.

Chapter 27 Exploring Space (p. 406)

Caption The planet's distinctive set of rings

27.1 The Last Frontier (p. 408)

Checkpoint 1 Space and all of the objects in it
Checkpoint 2 The Milky Way
Lesson Review **1.** By shape **2.** Spiral galaxy **3.** Meteorologists study weather on Earth. Astronomers study objects that are far away in space.
A Closer Look: A Telescope in Space Critical Thinking Astronauts from the space shuttle can repair it in orbit.

27.2 The Solar System (p. 410)

Checkpoint 1 A star
Checkpoint 2 Inner planets are small and rocky. Outer planets (except Pluto) are large, gaseous, have rings, and many moons.
Checkpoint 3 An asteroid is a small, rocky object. A comet is a ball of ice and dust.
Lesson Review **1.** Hydrogen and helium gases **2.** Inner: Mercury, Venus, Earth, Mars; Outer: Jupiter,

Saturn, Uranus, Neptune, Pluto   **3.** They are all fairly small objects in space.

27.3 Space Exploration (p. 416)
Checkpoint 1   The United States and the Soviet Union
Checkpoint 2   It is reusable.
Lesson Review   1. *Gemini* tested equipment and techniques needed to get people to the moon. *Apollo* took people to the moon.   **2.** Building a space station and perhaps sending people to Mars   **3.** Answers will vary but should include reasons such as to find new worlds, mine minerals, or learn about the universe.
Modern Leaders In Science: Mae Jemison   Critical Thinking   The information can improve space travel for future astronauts.

Lab Activity: Observing the Phases of the Moon (p. 418)
1. Students should see two.   **2.** 3–4 days   **3.** The last phase observed will depend on when students begin observations. Students should use their observations and the chart above to choose the next phase in the sequence.

Science in Your Life: Artificial Satellites (p. 419)
1. *Tiros 1*   **2.** *SOHO*   **3.** *MAGSAT* and *LAGEOS 1*
Critical Thinking   Possible answer: They allow scientists to study the Earth in ways that would not be possible from the ground.

Chapter 27 Review (pp. 420–421)
Vocabulary Review   1. True   **2.** False, a meteoroid   **3.** False, meteorite   **4.** False, astronomy   **5.** True   **6.** False, comet   **7.** False, meteor
Chapter Quiz   1. The Milky Way (p. 408)   **2.** A star made mostly of hydrogen and helium (p. 410)   **3.** The sun, the nine planets, and other objects that orbit the sun (pp. 410–411)   **4.** Mercury, Venus, Earth, Mars, Jupiter, Saturn, Uranus, Neptune, Pluto (p. 411)   **5.** Mercury, Venus, Earth, Mars, Pluto (pp. 411–412, 414)   **6.** Jupiter, Saturn, Uranus, Neptune (pp. 413–414)   **7.** They might be remains of a planet that broke up or be material left over from when the solar system formed. (p. 415)   **8.** Gas from the comet (p. 415)   **9.** It begins to burn up and makes a streak of light. (p. 415)   **10.** Students might list any three events described in Lesson 27.3 such as the first spaceflight or mission to the moon. (pp. 416–417)
Research Project   See the *Teacher's Planning Guide* or *Classroom Resource Binder* for a scoring rubric for the Research Project.

Unit 7 Review (p. 422)
1. A (p. 383)   **2.** D (p. 382)   **3.** A (p. 385)   **4.** C (pp. 393–394)   **5.** C (p. 399)   **6.** A (p. 410)   **7.** C (p. 411)   **Critical Thinking**   Mars is closer. Mars is also a rocky planet with a solid surface that a spacecraft could land on. Jupiter has no solid surface. Astronauts could not land on it or explore it easily.

Workbook Answer Key

UNIT 1 THE WONDERS OF SCIENCE

Chapter 1 What Is Science?

1.1 From Atoms to Galaxies Ex. 1
A. 1. e **2.** f **3.** a **4.** b **5.** d **6.** c **B. 7.** No
8. Yes **9.** Yes **10.** Yes **11.** No **12.** No **13.** Yes
14. No

Critical Thinking
Answers should indicate whether each technology is used to make people's lives easier, safer, or more enjoyable.

1.2 Science at Work: Science as Solution Ex. 2
A. 1. b **2.** c **3.** a **4.** a **5.** c **6.** b **B.** Earth Science:
8, 9, 12 Physical Science: 7, 10 Life Science: 11, 13

Critical Thinking
Answers might refer to medical-related careers that combine life science and physical science or astronomy careers that combine earth science and physical science.

1.2 Science at Work: Making the Right Choices Ex. 3
A. Answers will vary, but the money that students allocate for the various projects should total $4,000,000,000. **B.** Answers will vary, but students should give reasons why they divided the money as they did and why certain projects affecting human health are the most important.

Critical Thinking
Answers will vary, but students should give a reason.

Chapter 2: The Process of Discovery

2.1 The Scientific Method: The Five Steps Ex. 4
A. 1. Describe the problem. **2.** Gather information.
3. Suggest an answer. **4.** Perform experiments.
5. Draw conclusions and report the results.
B. 6. Danny might choose two areas of lawn that are the same size and time himself cutting one area with the blue lawn mower and the other with the red lawn mower. **7.** Maria might time herself taking the bus to school one day and walking the next. **8.** Dawn might grow grass in a tray of soil, then tilt that tray and another tray of bare soil, sprinkle water over both, and see how much soil is washed away in both.

Critical Thinking
Possible answers include a chart, a graph, a speech, an outline, an illustration, a poster, and a written report.

2.1 The Scientific Method: Using the Five Steps Ex. 5
Answers will vary but should show an understanding of the five steps of the scientific method.

Critical Thinking
Answers should include problems that would reasonably stem from the original experiment, such as: Does the time of day affect your ability to learn? or Do you learn better indoors or outdoors?

2.2 Measuring in Science: Comparing Metric and Nonmetric Units Ex. 6
1. a **2.** a **3.** c **4.** b **5.** 16 **6.** 9.6 **7.** 41.6
8. 4,800

Critical Thinking
Students might suggest reading food labels to compare English measurements with their metric equivalents.

2.2 Measuring in Science: Changing Values Using Metrics Ex. 7
A. 1. 2,000 **2.** 1.5 **3.** 170 **4.** 2,500
B. 5. kilogram **6.** meter **7.** milliliter

Critical Thinking
Possible items include the length of a baseball bat or the height of the classroom door, the area of the classroom floor or a sheet of paper, the volume of a carton of juice or a can of soup, and the mass of a pineapple or a bowling ball. The actual measurements may be estimates but should be reasonable.

2.3 Laboratory Science Ex. 8
Answers will vary, but answers to questions 2–5 should be consistent with the answer to question 1.

Critical Thinking
Answers may include three of the following:
Rule 1: Being prepared before beginning an experiment can help prevent mistakes.
Rule 2: Keeping a clean work area can help prevent accidents. Having out only the equipment that you need could help prevent using the wrong equipment during the experiment.
Rule 3: Using equipment that is damaged can lead to accidents and inaccurate results.
Rule 4: Knowing how to put out fires can help prevent injuries and damage to property.
Rule 5: Tasting or eating in the lab can lead to poisoning or illness.
Rule 6: Wearing goggles can prevent eye injury.
Rule 7: Wearing a lab apron can prevent damage to clothing.
Rule 8: Being careful when working with sharp objects can help prevent injuries.
Rule 9: Following all instructions exactly can help prevent accidents and mistakes from occurring and can lead to better results.
Rule 10: Telling a teacher about an accident can help limit the amount of damage or injury that may result.

UNIT 2: LIFE SCIENCE: PART I

Chapter 3: The Study of Life

3.1 A Home for Life: Earth's Position Ex. 9
A. 1. They would melt. **2.** They would boil and evaporate. **3.** They would dry up or burn up. **4.** It would dry up. **B. 5.** They would freeze. **6.** They would grow. **7.** They would freeze and die. **8.** They would have no plants to eat and would also freeze and die.

Critical Thinking

Stories should reflect an understanding of how warming up or cooling down on Earth would affect life on the planet.

3.1 A Home for Life: Dividing Up Life Science Ex. 10

A. 1. microbiology **2.** zoology **3.** botany **4.** ecology **5.** genetics **B. 6.** c **7.** e **8.** a **9.** d **10.** b

Critical Thinking

Accept reasonable answers. What might be studied: possible answers include plants, animals, or the interaction of them; Where it would be studied: possible answers include in the field, in a laboratory, at a zoo, in a hospital; Different tools used: possible answers include lab equipment such as microscopes, binoculars for observing in the field, and computers.

3.2 What Is Life? Characteristics of Life Ex. 11

A. 1. insect, fish, mouse **2.** fox, eagle, frog **3.** trees, waterlilies **4.** fox, mouse, frog, insect, eagle, duck **5.** eagle, duck, insect **6.** frog, duck, fish

Critical Thinking

Descriptions should refer to questions 1, 2, 4, and 6.

3.2 What Is Life? Charting Life's Characteristics Ex. 12

1. All rows of boxes should be checked except those next to rock, computer, and glass. Students may say that some of these non-organisms do some of the life functions, such as glass can "grow" when blown. However, point out that all columns must be checked for it to be considered living. **2.** housefly, grass, pine tree, crab, shrub, squirrel **3.** Answers will vary but should focus on how the thing does not fulfill all the life functions.

Critical Thinking

Answers should explain how the organism gets and uses food, moves, grows, reproduces, and responds to its environment.

Chapter 4: Cells and Life

4.1 The Basic Units of Life Ex. 13

A. 1. c **2.** a **3.** d **4.** b **B. 5.** eyepiece **6.** coarse adjustment knob **7.** objectives **8.** stage **9.** fine adjustment knob **10.** mirror

Critical Thinking

Elements that are found in humans, such as oxygen, carbon, and hydrogen, might be signs of life on other planets.

4.2 Understanding Cells: Parts of Cells Ex. 14

1. cell membrane **2.** mitochondrion **3.** chloroplast **4.** cell wall **5.** vacuole **6.** nucleus **7.** cytoplasm **8.** cytoplasm **9.** mitochondrion **10.** cell membrane **11.** nucleus **12.** vacuole **13.** Produce their own food; chloroplast

Critical Thinking

Answers should indicate that an increase or decrease in cell size is caused by the movement of materials into or out of the cell, respectively.

4.2 Understanding Cells: Comparing Plant and Animal Cells Ex. 15

1. animal cell and plant cell; holds the cell together **2.** animal cell and plant cell; controls all parts of the cell **3.** plant cell; absorbs sunlight so the plant can make food **4.** animal cell and plant cell; other cell parts float in this **5.** animal cell and plant cell; help the cell store and use energy **6.** animal cell and plant cell; store food, water, and wastes **7.** plant cell; contain chlorophyll used to trap sunlight **8.** plant cell; covers a plant cell membrane

Critical Thinking

The equation describes respiration. During respiration, the cell uses oxygen to release energy from food. Wastes in the form of water and carbon dioxide also are produced during this process.

4.2 Understanding Cells: DNA Ex. 16

1. False. DNA molecules are larger than most other molecules found in cells **2.** True **3.** True **4.** False. The nucleus in a cell contains DNA. **5.** False. Thousands of smaller molecules make up a DNA molecule. **6.** False. A DNA molecule has the shape of a twisted ladder.

Critical Thinking

Characteristics completely or partly controlled by DNA might include eye color, skin color, face shape, hair color, baldness, height, weight, tendency toward certain diseases, artistic abilities, athletic abilities, and intelligence. Characteristics not controlled by DNA might include various personality traits.

Chapter 5: The Kingdoms of Life

5.1 Classifying Organisms: Species Ex. 17

1. The creature does not belong to any known kingdom because it has characteristics of bacteria, fungi, and plants. **2.** Drawings will vary, but they may show some characteristics of a bacterium, fungus, and plant. **3.** Accept reasonable names students can explain. The names may be descriptive of a feature or features of the creature.

Critical Thinking

Yes, since they can reproduce with each other, they must belong to the same species.

5.1 Classifying Organisms: The Kingdoms of Life Ex. 18

A. 1. Bacteria **2.** Protist **3.** Fungus **4.** Animal **5.** Plant **B. 6.** Plants can make their own food, but a mushroom cannot. **7.** Bacteria do not have nuclei, but protozoa do. **8.** Human bodies do not have chlorophyll.

Critical Thinking

Organisms that are very different except for their size, such as blue whales and redwood trees, would be in the same kingdom.

5.2 Earth's Simplest Organisms: Identifying Simple Organisms Ex. 19

A. 1. alga **2.** fungus **3.** bacterium **4.** protozoan
5. fungus **6.** alga **B. 7.** cytoplasm **8.** protists
9. Fungus Kingdom **10.** chloroplasts

Critical Thinking
Find out if it has a nucleus. If it does not, it is a bacterium. If it does, find out if it absorbs its food. If it does, it is a fungus. If it does not, it is a protist.

5.2 Earth's Simplest Organisms: Friends or Enemies? Ex. 20

A. 1. Bacteria are used to make foods, such as cheese and yogurt. **2.** Some protists have shells that are used to make chalk. **3.** Fungi help break down the bodies of dead animals and plants. Students may also answer that some fungi, such as mushrooms, are good to eat. **B. 4.** Some bacteria cause sickness and even death. **5.** Some protists cause diseases, such as malaria. **6.** Molds make food spoil. Some fungi cause diseases, such as athlete's foot.

Critical Thinking
Students should disagree. Destroying all bacteria would get rid of the ones that are useful for things such as making food. It would also eliminate bacteria that live inside and around people without doing any harm.

Chapter 6: The Animal Kingdom

6.1 From Simple to Complex Ex. 21

A. 1. (a, b, c) **2.** a, b **3.** c **4.** a, b, c **5.** b **6.** a, c
7. b, c **8.** a **9.** a, b, c

Critical Thinking
They are animals. They move around when they are young, so they cannot be plants. They are made of specialized cells, so they cannot be protists, monera, or fungi.

6.2 Invertebrates: Grouping by Type Ex. 22

A. 1. earthworm, roundworm, tapeworm **2.** clam, octopus, oyster, slug, snail, squid **3.** sand dollar, sea star **4.** ant, bee, butterfly, cockroach, crab, crayfish, flea, grasshopper, lobster, mite, mosquito, scorpion, spider, tick

Critical Thinking
If it has a soft body inside, it is a mollusk. If it has jointed appendages and a body that is divided into segments, then it is an arthropod.

6.2 Invertebrates: Sponges, Worms, Mollusks, and Spiny-Skinned Animals Ex. 23

A. 1. worm **2.** mollusk **3.** sponge **4.** spiny-skinned
5. mollusk **6.** worm **B. 7.** b **8.** a **9.** a, b **10.** a, b
11. a **12.** c

Critical Thinking
Crop—examples include a refrigerator, a pantry, a cupboard, and any kind of food container; like a crop, they're used for storing food. Gizzard—examples include a food processor, a blender, and a meat grinder; like a gizzard, they're used for grinding food.

6.2 Invertebrates: Arthropods Ex. 24

A. 1. An arthropod is an animal with an <u>outer</u> skeleton. **2.** Arthropods have jointed <u>appendages</u>.
3. <u>Insects</u> are the largest group of arthropods. **4.** An insect's body has <u>three</u> main parts. **5.** Insects have feelers, which are called <u>antennae</u>. **6.** A crustacean's front pair of legs are called <u>claws</u>. **B. 7.** (3) **8.** 3
9. 2 **10.** 4 **11.** 2 **12.** 5

Critical Thinking
Students might mention the number of pairs of legs, the number of body segments, the presence or absence of antennae, or the presence or absence of wings.

6.3 Vertebrates: Organizing Major Groups Ex. 25

A. First level: The Animal Kingdom. Second level: Invertebrates, Vertebrates. Third level (under Invertebrates): sponges, worms, mollusks, spiny-skinned invertebrates, arthropods. Third level (under Vertebrates): fish, amphibians, reptiles, birds, mammals. Students may do a fourth level, breaking arthropods into insects, spiders, and crustaceans.
B. First level: Vertebrates. Second level: Cold-blooded, Warm-blooded. Third level (under Cold-blooded): fish, amphibians, reptiles. Third level (under Warm-blooded): birds, mammals.

Critical Thinking
A warm-blooded animal would find it easier to live in extreme kinds of weather because its body temperature does not change much. Even if the weather was very hot or cold, the animal's temperature would stay about the same.

6.3 Vertebrates: Characteristics Ex. 26

A. 1. c **2.** e **3.** b **4.** a **5.** d **B. 6.** Answers will vary. **7.** Reptiles if a snake, amphibians if a frog, mammals if a lion, birds if an eagle **8.** Cold-blooded if a snake or frog; warm-blooded if a lion or an eagle
9. Scales if a snake, slippery skin if a frog, fur if a lion, feathers if an eagle

Critical Thinking
Answers will vary, but students should give reasons for their opinions. Students may think that endangered animals are particularly important to protect. Or they may think that the needs of people are more important.

Chapter 7: The Plant Kingdom

7.1 Plants as Food Makers: Food From Plants Ex. 27

A. 1. P **2.** N **3.** N **4.** N **5.** P **6.** A **7.** P **8.** P
9. P **10.** P **B. 11.** (wheat flour [seed])
12–14. vegetable oil, seed; sugar, stem or root; walnuts, seed; carrots, root; lemon rind, fruit

Critical Thinking
Animals either eat plants directly or they eat other animals that eat plants. Also, plants provide oxygen that animals need.

7.1 Plants as Food Makers: Plant Parts Ex. 28

A. 1. The <u>seed</u> is the part of a seed plant from which a new plant can grow. **2.** Most of a plant's chlorophyll is found in its <u>leaves</u>. **3.** Plants make sugar using sunlight, water, chlorophyll, and <u>carbon dioxide</u>.
B. 4. leaf **5.** stem **6.** root **7.** Roots hold the plant in place, store extra food, and soak up water and minerals from the soil. **8.** Leaves make food through photosynthesis. **9.** Stems hold up plants so the leaves can get sunlight. Stems also carry water and food up the plant and store extra food.

Critical Thinking
Without chlorophyll, plants could not make food, and people and animals would not have anything to eat. Also, there would be more carbon dioxide and less oxygen in the air, which would affect living things.

7.2 Plant Reproduction: Pollination Ex. 29

A. 1. petal **2.** pistil **3.** pollen **4.** stamen **5.** ovary
B. 6. a. Pollen would not stay on the pistil as easily.
7. b. Flowers are needed for seed plants to reproduce and produce fruit. **8.** c. Pollen must land on the pistil for pollination to occur.

Critical Thinking
Flower petals' bright colors, unique shapes and patterns, and strong smells make the plant easy for insects to identify and find.

7.2 Plant Reproduction: Producing Seeds and Fruit Ex. 30

A. 1. pollination. Pollen is transferred from the stamen of one flower to the pistil of another flower.
2. fertilization. A sperm cell joins with an egg cell in the ovary of the flower. **3.** germination. A young plant breaks out of its seed and begins to grow.
B. 4. Wind carries the seed as the "wings" of the seed twirl through the air. **5.** Animals carry the seeds as tiny hooks attach to the animals' fur.

Critical Thinking
Students' designs should account for a way to scatter the seeds from the parent plant.

Chapter 8: Genetics: The Code of Life

8.1 The Same But Different Ex. 31

A. 3, 1, 5, 2, 4 **B. 6.** Descriptions will vary but may include single-celled, very small, lacking in specialized cells, having DNA in its cytoplasm. **7.** Descriptions will vary but may include lacking in specialized cells, single-celled, green, red, or brown; may have a shell.
8. Descriptions will vary but may include having cells with cell walls, many-celled, growing in one place, lacking in chlorophyll. **9.** Descriptions will vary but may include many-celled, having chlorophyll, having cells with cell walls, growing in one place. **C. 10.** b
11. c **12.** a

Critical Thinking
The recessive trait—shortness—was hidden in the hybrids but not lost. That is why the trait reappeared in the offspring of the hybrids.

8.2 The Building Blocks of Heredity: Genes Ex. 32

A. 1. cell **2.** nucleus **3.** chromosome **4.** gene
B. 5., 6. Drawings will vary. Students should show the nucleus inside the cell and the chromosome inside the nucleus. The gene should be shown on the chromosome. **C. 7.** Mutation **8.** Examples of harmful mutations include those that cause diseases or deformations of body parts. **9.** Examples of helpful mutations include those that make the organism stronger or healthier or more likely to resist attacks by other organisms. **10.** Egg cells and sperm cells have only half the number of chromosomes found in body cells.

Critical Thinking
Mutations are passed down to offspring through the chromosomes in the parents' sex cells.

8.2 The Building Blocks of Heredity: Producing Offspring Ex. 33

A. 1. 32 **2.** 26 **3.** 12 **4.** 32 **5.** 39 **B. 6.** During fertilization, a <u>sperm cell</u> joins with an egg cell.
7. A <u>DNA</u> code is found in an organism's genes.
8. An animal cell gets <u>half</u> of its chromosomes from its mother. **9.** A sperm cell is a <u>sex</u> cell. **10.** Sex cells reproduce by dividing <u>twice</u>.

Critical Thinking
Having half the number of chromosomes in the sex cells ensures that the offspring have the same number of chromosomes as their parents have. If the sex cells had the same number of chromosomes as in body cells, each generation of offspring would have twice the number of chromosomes as the previous generation.

8.3 Controlling Heredity Ex. 34

1. Environment. Christina's plant didn't produce tomatoes because it didn't get enough water and sunlight. **2.** Genetics. Annie was a good runner and jumper even though she didn't exercise because her parents passed down those traits to her. **3.** Genetics. Hiroko's roses were more beautiful than Bob's because her plants had genes that caused the plants to produce beautiful flowers.

Critical Thinking
Possible traits include skin color, hair color, height, weight, body shape, intelligence, and personality.

Chapter 9: Evolution

9.1 Time and Change: Paths of Evolution Ex. 35

1. Path should be drawn from First Living Organisms to Bony fish. **2.** Path should be drawn from First Living Organisms to Arthropods. **3.** Circle should be drawn around the bottom of the tree, from First Living Organisms to the intersection of the Bony fish and the Arthropod branches.

Critical Thinking
Algae evolved from an ancestor that also evolved into plants.

9.1 Time and Change: Relationships Among Organisms Ex. 36

1. Bacteria and blue-green algae   **2.** Mosses   **3.** Bony fish, amphibians, reptiles, birds, and mammals (Students may respond to the pictures and answer fish, frog, turtle, bird, and dog.)   **4.** Just below the branch that leads to bony fish. Students should write vertebrates on the tree just below the branch that leads to bony fish.   **5.** Conifers and flowering plants   **6.** Just below the branch that leads to conifers. Students should write seed plants on the tree just below the branch that leads to conifers.   **7.** No organisms evolved from fungi.   **8.** Sponges
9. Mollusks   **10.** Mosses

Critical Thinking
The first living things most closely resembled today's bacteria and blue-green algae. This is indicated by their position at the bottom of the evolutionary tree of life.

9.2 Theories of Evolution: Darwin's Theory Ex. 37

A. 1. Most organisms have more offspring than can survive.   **2.** Offspring compete for food and space.   **3.** Organisms that survive have traits that are best suited to the environment.   **4.** Natural selection passes along helpful traits to offspring.   **B. 5.** 4   **6.** 1
7. 2   **8.** 3   **9.** 4   **10.** 2   **11.** 1 (If students' answers in Part A are correct but out of order, that will affect their responses to Part B. Check the numbers they write in Part B against their answers in Part A.)

Critical Thinking
The parents should take music lessons to develop musical skill, so that they can pass on this skill as a trait to their offspring.

9.2 Theories of Evolution: Mutations Ex. 38

A. 1. Harmful. The butterfly probably could not fly with wings that small.   **2.** Helpful. With a large mouth, the fish could capture larger animals to eat.
3. Harmful. With a short neck, the giraffe could not reach tender leaves at the tops of tall trees.
4. Harmful. With short legs, the zebra could not run from its enemies as quickly.   **5.** Helpful. Deep roots would help the pine tree get water that lies deep in the ground.

Critical Thinking
No. The animal cannot reproduce if it does not make sperm cells, so there is no way that it can pass on this trait to offspring.

UNIT 3: LIFE SCIENCE: PART II

Chapter 10: The Human Body

10.1 From Cells to Systems: The Basic Plan Ex. 39

A. 1. c   **2.** d   **3.** b   **4.** a   **B.** Answers will vary depending on which body parts students choose.
5. (Biceps/muscular system. The muscular system allows movement.)   **6–9.** Brain/nervous system. The nervous system receives and sends messages, controls body functions, and stores information.
Heart/circulatory system. The circulatory system pumps blood throughout the body.
Skin/immune system. The immune system protects the body from the environment.
Stomach/digestive system. The digestive system breaks down food into usable parts.
Ovaries/reproductive system. The reproductive system makes offspring.
Lungs/respiratory system. The respiratory system takes in oxygen from the air.
Backbone/skeletal system. The skeletal system supports the body and protects the organs.

Critical Thinking
Answers will vary but should demonstrate students' understanding that a system is a group of different parts that work together to perform a single task or function. Some examples are a school, a city, and a car.

10.1 From Cells to Systems: Nerves and Senses Ex. 40

A. 1. cerebrum   **2.** cerebellum   **3.** brain stem
B. Answers will vary.

Critical Thinking
Answers will vary.

10.2 Your Body at Work Ex. 41

A. 1. muscular   **2.** muscular   **3.** skeletal   **4.** skeletal
5. skeletal   **6.** skeletal   **7.** muscular   **8.** skeletal
B. 9. muscular   **10.** skeletal   **11.** muscular
12. muscular   **13.** muscular   **14.** skeletal

Critical Thinking
Answers will vary depending on which bone students choose. The skull is shaped somewhat like a bowl, which is the best shape to surround the oval-shaped brain. The backbone is like a long pole, to which the arms, legs, and head are attached. It is also hollow to surround the ropelike spinal cord. The hip bone is shaped like a saddle. It forms part of the area of the body where you sit.

10.3 Reproduction Ex. 42

A. 1. False. During <u>puberty</u>, the reproductive system develops.   **2.** True   **3.** False. Females release one egg each month from their <u>ovary</u>.   **4.** False. <u>A fetus</u> will begin to develop when an egg cell is fertilized by a sperm cell.   **5.** True   **6.** False. A fetus usually takes <u>38</u> weeks to develop.   **7.** False. The <u>reproductive</u> system controls the release of sperm cells and egg cells.   **8.** True.   **9.** False. Menstruation stops in women at about the age of <u>50</u>.

Critical Thinking
Answers will vary but may include the fact that most women over 50 will not want to bear children, the bodies of older women may be unable to safely carry and deliver a baby, or the bodies of older women may not produce the hormones needed to release eggs.

Chapter 11: Getting Energy Into and Around the Body

11.1 Digestion: The Digestive System Ex. 43
1. mouth **2.** esophagus **3.** stomach **4.** small intestine **5.** large intestine **6.** anus **7.** Mouth breaks food into pieces and releases enzymes.
8. Esophagus carries food to the stomach. **9.** Muscles and enzymes in stomach further break down food.
10. Food molecules pass through walls of small intestine into the blood. **11.** Large intestine collects food wastes. **12.** Feces leave the body through the anus.

Critical Thinking
Students would eat more often. Their meals would probably be smaller but more frequent.

11.1 Digestion: Breaking Down Food Ex. 44
1–5. Answers should reflect the functions of the digestive organs as stated in 7–12 of Exercise 43. Students should include details such as food being pushed down the esophagus by muscles and moving in a wavelike motion in the stomach.

Critical Thinking
An assembly line puts something together in stages. The digestive system takes something (food) apart in stages.

11.2 Respiration: The Respiratory System Ex. 45
A. 1. b **2.** a **3.** d **4.** c **B. 5.** False. Respiration gets oxygen to the cells. **6.** True **7.** False. Oxygen in the air passes through the air sacs into your blood.
8. False. The oxygen in the air comes from plants.

Critical Thinking

Respiration in Plants	Respiration in Animals
Plants take in air through small holes in leaves.	Animals take in air through nose and mouth.
Plants absorb oxygen from air.	Animals absorb oxygen from air.
Plants use oxygen to break down stored food to release energy.	Animals use oxygen to help break down food to use as fuel.
Plants give off carbon dioxide as a waste product.	Animals give off carbon dioxide as a waste product.

11.2 Respiration: Exchanging Oxygen and Carbon Dioxide Ex. 46
A. 1. carbon dioxide **2.** oxygen **3.** air sacs **4.** cells
B. 5. d **6.** c **7.** a **8.** b

Critical Thinking
A cold or allergies may cause the passages in your nose to become blocked. Then air has another way to get into your body.

11.3 Circulation: The Circulatory System Ex. 47
A. 1. vein **2.** heart **3.** capillaries **4.** artery
B. 5. heart **6.** vein **7.** artery **8.** connect arteries to veins

Critical Thinking
Plasma is the liquid part of blood. Red blood cells carry oxygen and carbon dioxide throughout the body. White blood cells fight off bacteria and sickness. Platelets help injuries stop bleeding.

11.3 Circulation: Heart Disease Ex. 48
A. 1. Heart B. The artery is partly clogged. This narrows the artery and increases the blood pressure.
2. Students should fill in the artery to show that it is completely blocked. This blockage prevents oxygen, which it needs to keep pumping, from getting to the heart. **B. 3.** Drawing should have an *X* because fatty foods can cause blood vessels to become blocked.
4. Drawing should have a circle because exercise makes the heart pump more blood and helps keep blood vessels unclogged. **5.** Drawing should have an *X* because smoking can cause heart disease.

Critical Thinking
Lists of heart-healthy foods will vary, but may include foods such as fish, lean meat, fruits, vegetables, and low-fat dairy products. Students should explain that these foods are heart healthy because they are low in fat, cholesterol, and/or sodium and will not clog arteries and/or raise blood pressure.

Chapter 12: Staying Healthy

12.1 Fighting Disease Ex. 49
A. 1. Covering your face while sneezing helps to prevent the spread of disease. **2.** Animals such as mosquitoes, fleas, and pigs can spread disease.
3. Washing your hands helps to prevent the spread of disease. **B. 4.** bacteria **5.** diseases **6.** white blood cells **7.** viruses **8.** DNA

Critical Thinking
It is easier to get the flu when you are already fighting off a cold because your immune system is already weak, and that's why you got the cold. Also, the immune system has to work to fight off the cold, and so it may not be able to fight off the flu.

12.2 Nutrition Ex. 50
A. 1. d **2.** a **3.** f **4.** e **5.** c **6.** b **B. 7.** hot turkey sandwich **8.** macaroni and cheese or rice **9.** collard greens **10.** milk **11.** carrot cake **12.** macaroni and cheese or rice (whichever is not given as answer to number 8)

Critical Thinking
Answers should reflect an understanding of the Food Guide Pyramid.

12.3 Guarding Your Health Ex. 51
A. Answers will vary but may include smoking, heart disease, drug use, AIDS, and teen pregnancy.
B. Answers will vary but may include education, fitness programs, better nutrition, and medical research.

Critical Thinking
Answers will vary but should reflect an understanding of the relationship of the health problem with the approach to fighting it.

Chapter 13: Depending on Each Other

13.1 Living Together Ex. 52
A. 1. 3 **2.** 2 **3.** 4 **4.** 1 **B. 5.** b **6.** e **7.** a **8.** f
9. c **10.** d

Critical Thinking
Answers may include populations of algae, plants, mollusks, fish, and whales, along with rocks, water, and trash.

13.2 Using Nature's Resources: Food Chains and Webs Ex. 53
A. Producers: trees, bushes, other plants; Consumers: Possible answers: girl, boy, mosquito, squirrel, bird, worm, fungi, mold, bacteria; Decomposers: fungi, mold, bacteria
B. Grass, mouse, snake, hawk; Students may not know the correct order of all organisms in the food chain but should know that it begins with grass—the producer.

Critical Thinking
Answers will vary somewhat but should generally state that the food web would be thrown out of balance. Students may cite any of the following as explanations: The insects would increase because there are no frogs to eat them. The insects would then eat more water plants. Without frogs to eat, the bass would eat more minnows. The turtles would have nothing to eat, so they would disappear.

13.2 Using Nature's Resources: Water and Air Ex. 54
1. Oxygen and Carbon Dioxide Cycle. Labels should show that the deer carries on respiration. The plant carries on photosynthesis. Arrows should show that the plant gives off oxygen and takes in carbon dioxide. The deer takes in oxygen and gives off carbon dioxide. **2.** Water Cycle. Labels should point to the river, ocean, rain, clouds, and water vapor in the air. Arrows and labels should show that condensation causes water to move from the air to the Earth in the form of rain. Water moves from the Earth to the air by the process of evaporation. **3.** cellular respiration
4. carbon dioxide **5.** photosynthesis **6.** oxygen
7. condensation **8.** evaporation **9.** river **10.** ocean

Critical Thinking
Photosynthesis uses the sun's energy to produce food. Evaporation uses the sun's energy to change liquid water into water vapor.

13.3 Using Nature's Resources: Natural Resources and Conservation Ex. 55
A. 1. b **2.** d **3.** c **4.** e **5.** a **B.** Possible answers:
6. Making paper, furniture, or floors **7.** Breaking up concrete to make gravel or blocks **8.** Melting the steel and reforming it into pipes or beams **9.** Letting the wastes decompose and using it as fertilizer

10. Using the tires as playground equipment or cutting up the rubber and using it as road-building material **11.** Melting the plastic to form new items
Critical Thinking
Answers may include not wasting water, keeping the air and bodies of water clean, using less of fossil fuels, and protecting plants and animals.

UNIT 4: PHYSICAL SCIENCE: PART I

Chapter 14: The Properties of Matter

14.1 From Molecules to Matter: Elements and Physical Science Ex. 56
A. 1. Al **2.** C **3.** chlorine **4.** Cu **5.** hydrogen
6. mercury **7.** S **8.** tin **B. 9.** physics
10. chemistry **11.** physics **12.** chemistry

Critical Thinking
Possible answers: The universe is made of matter and energy. The two branches of physical science deal with matter and energy. Matter can be living or nonliving. There are six kinds of energy.

14.1 From Molecules to Matter: The Atom Ex. 57
A. 1. nucleus **2.** electron **3.** proton **4.** neutron
B. 5. 6 **6.** carbon **C. 7.** c **8.** a **9.** b

Critical Thinking
Ideas might include associating electrons with electricity and motion to remember that electrons form a cloud around the nucleus. Students might associate the *p* of *proton* with the *p* of *positive*. Other ideas include the mnemonic device "pen" to remember proton, electron, and neutron.

14.2 More About Matter: Properties Ex. 58
A. Sample answers are provided. **1.** black **2.** solid
3. none **4.** cylindrical **5.** white **6.** liquid
7. slightly sweet, sour, or spoiled **8.** shape of container **9.** colorless **10.** gas **11.** none **12.** no definite shape **13.** white **14.** solid **15.** none
16. rectangular, flat **17.** light golden brown
18. liquid **19.** like flowers **20.** shape of container
21. yellow **22.** solid **23.** woody **24.** long, round, or hexagonal **B.** Sample answers are provided.
25. rub it with sandpaper **26.** same shape, shinier and lighter in color **27.** boil it **28.** becomes a gas
29. mix with something that smells **30.** now has an odor **31.** burn it **32.** odor and color change, becomes ash **33.** pour it into another container
34. now has the shape of its new container
35. break it in half **36.** each piece is half as long

Critical Thinking
Air is a gas solution (mixture of nitrogen, oxygen and other gases). Steel is another solid solution (iron with small amounts of other elements).

14.2 More About Matter: Vocabulary Practice Ex. 59

A. 1. compound **2.** correct **3.** solid **4.** correct **5.** density **B. 6.** compound **7.** mixture **8.** mixture, solution

Critical Thinking

The balloon itself is a solid, the water is a liquid, and the air in the balloon is a gas.

Chapter 15: Energy and Matter

15.1 Energy in All Things Ex. 60

A. 1. work **2.** matter **3.** energy **4.** mass **5.** potential **6.** kinetic **B. 7.** potential **8.** kinetic **9.** potential **10.** kinetic **11.** kinetic **12.** potential **13.** kinetic **14.** kinetic

Critical Thinking

The car has kinetic energy because it is moving. It has potential energy because it is able to move faster.

15.2 The Different Forms of Energy: Identifying Them Ex. 61

A. 1. electrical **2.** light **3.** nuclear **4.** chemical **5.** heat, light, or chemical **6.** mechanical **B.** Possible answers: **7.** heat cooking breakfast **8.** mechanical riding a bicycle **9.** light using electric lights at school **10.** chemical using energy stored in food **11.** electrical using electric hair dryer

Critical Thinking

The person gets energy from the chemical energy from food.

15.2 The Different Forms of Energy: How They Are Used Ex. 62

A. Students should list heat, light, electrical, chemical, and mechanical energy. **B.** Student descriptions will vary but should include examples of how energy is used, including as light and heat from the sun, heat from the grill, for motion from the bicycles and runner, and to power the radio.

Critical Thinking

Examples include light energy changing to heat energy in a greenhouse or in a car sitting in sunlight; chemical energy in food changing to mechanical energy as a person moves; and the chemical energy in a match changing to light and heat energy when the match burns.

15.3 Changing Matter Using Energy: Matter and Heat Energy Ex. 63

A. 1. (melting) **2.** freezing **3.** evaporation **4.** condensation **B.** 6, 5, 7 **C. 8.** The cool night air causes water vapor to condense into liquid water. **9.** The dew disappears because it evaporates.

Critical Thinking

Air next to the cold glass becomes cool enough for water vapor in the air to condense on the outside of the glass.

15.3 Changing Matter Using Energy Ex. 64

A. 1. physical change **2.** chemical change **3.** chemical change **4.** physical change **5.** physical

change **6.** chemical change **7.** chemical change **8.** physical change **9.** chemical change **10.** chemical change **B. 11.** chemical change **12.** Gasoline changes to exhaust gases. **13.** The car changes shape and probably volume.

Critical Thinking

Physical changes might include breaking something, pouring milk from a gallon container into a glass, or boiling water during cooking. Chemical changes might include the burning of fuel in a car or bus or the changes that occur when food cooks.

Chapter 16: Force and Motion

16.1 What Is Force? Mass and Weight Ex. 65

1. No **2.** The one at sea level will weigh more because it is closer to the center of the Earth, so more gravity will be pulling on it. **3.** Yes; mass is the amount of matter in something and never changes no matter where you are. **4.** If the quarter at the equator weighs less, it must be farther away from the center of the Earth. Therefore, you can infer that the Earth bulges slightly, and so there is a greater distance from the equator to the center of the Earth than from either of the poles to the center of the Earth.

Critical Thinking

The rock weighs much less on the moon because there is much less gravity on the moon than on Earth.

16.1 What Is Force? Friction and Centripetal Force Ex. 66

A. 1. Sliding friction **2.** Fluid friction **3.** Rolling friction **B. 4.** b **5.** c **6.** c **7.** a **8.** b **9.** c

Critical Thinking

Tires have treads to make the tire surface rougher so as to increase friction. This increases the ability of the vehicle to slow down and stop when necessary. Students should explain their tread design in terms of its ability to produce enough friction.

16.2 Inertia and Motion: Forces in Sports Ex. 67

1. Gravity makes the baseball fall to the ground. **2.** The baseball would never come down. **3.** Friction acts on it. **4.** Centripetal force **5.** Gravity **6.** To reduce friction **7.** Friction with the water **8.** Inertia

Critical Thinking

Answers should take into account that there is less gravity on the moon compared to the Earth and that thrown objects will take longer to return to the surface.

Chapter 17: Machines at Work

17.1 All Kinds of Work Ex. 68

A. 1. d **2.** c **3.** a **4.** e **5.** b **B. 6.** (pulling) **7.** friction **8.** (sack of cement) **9.** lifting of plant **10.** gravity **11.** plant **12.** pushing up barbells **13.** gravity **14.** barbell

Critical Thinking

Students' examples of work should involve a force moving something through a distance.

17.1 Simple and Compound Machines: Identifying Machines Ex. 69
1. pulley   **2.** inclined plane   **3.** wheel and axle
4. lever   **5.** wedge   **6.** screw

Critical Thinking
Picture 2 shows both a wheel and axle and an inclined plane being used. Using the wheel and axle helps reduce the resistance force, friction, between the box and the inclined plane.

17.2 Simple and Compound Machines: Designing Machines to Solve Problems Ex. 70
1–3. Answers will vary, but at least two simple machines should be mentioned in each answer.

Critical Thinking
Students may mention energy shortages, pollution, and hunger. Machines may help by producing energy more cheaply or using less energy, using nonpolluting types of fuel or cleaning up polluted areas, and producing food more efficiently.

UNIT 5: PHYSICAL SCIENCE: PART II

Chapter 18: Heat, Light, and Sound

18.1 Heat and Matter: Heat Energy Ex. 71
A. 1. total   **2.** average   **3.** particles   **4.** temperature
B. 5. The air near the heater is warmer and therefore less dense than the air above it.   **6.** In waves   **7.** Heat moved from the burner to the handle by conduction.

Critical Thinking
When sunlight strikes the Earth's surface, much of the radiation changes into heat energy.

18.1 Heat and Matter: Heat on the Move Ex. 72
A. 1. solid, conduction   **2.** liquid, convection   **3.** gas, radiation   **4.** solid, conduction   **5.** gas, convection
B. 6. cool water   **7.** warm water

Critical Thinking
The burner on the stove heats the bottom of the pan by conduction. Heat from the hot pan moves through the milk by convection.

18.2 Light: Understanding Waves Ex. 73
A. 1. trough   **2.** wavelength   **3.** amplitude   **4.** crest
B. 5. Wave A   **6.** Wave C   **7.** Wave B   **8.** Wave A
9. Wave B   **10.** Wave C

Critical Thinking
Dropping the marble into the water from increasing heights will increase the amplitude of the water waves produced because the waves will have more energy. You can also use a larger marble to create waves with more amplitude.

18.2 Light: What Are Its Properties? Ex. 74
A. 1. spectrum   **2.** refraction   **3.** amplitude
4. reflection   **5.** wavelength   **B. 6.** B   **7.** A   **8.** Mirror or a shiny surface   **9.** A change in the speed of light as the light passes from one material to another

Critical Thinking
The light waves would not reflect off the surface. They would be absorbed.

18.3 Sound: Comparing Sound and Light Ex. 75
A. 1. light or sound   **2.** light   **3.** light or sound
4. sound   **5.** sound   **6.** light   **7.** light or sound
8. light   **9.** light or sound   **10.** sound   **B. 11.** b
12. c   **13.** a

Critical Thinking
The particles in a liquid are closer together than the particles in a gas. Therefore, vibrations can pass from particle to particle faster in a liquid than in a gas.

18.3 Sound: How Sound Travels Ex. 76
A. 2, 6, 1, 4, 5, 3   **B. 1.** Arrow should point to the bar.   **2.** Arrow should point to the drumhead.
3. Arrow should point to the string.

Critical Thinking
The funnel helped a person hear better by directing more sound waves into the person's ear.

Chapter 19: Electricity and Magnetism

19.1 All Charged Up: Static Electricity Ex. 77
A. 1. e   **2.** c   **3.** g   **4.** d   **5.** f   **6.** b   **7.** a
B. Sketches will vary, but all should show a bolt of lightning extending from a cloud to some other object, such as a tree or the ground. Positive (+) signs should be drawn on the top of the cloud and the top of the other object, where the lightning is striking. Negative (–) signs should be drawn on the bottom of the cloud, in the lightning, and, if a tree is drawn, on the bottom of the tree.

Critical Thinking
Students may say it is a good idea because lightning contains a lot of energy. They may say it is a bad idea because lightning cannot be produced on demand and is too dangerous or too hard to control.

19.1 All Charged Up: Comparing Present and Past Ex. 78
A. 1–6. Accept any six electrically powered devices.
B. 7–9. Answers for pre-electricity days may include such things as using candles for light, sunlight to dry clothes, and fire to heat homes.

Critical Thinking
They would have seen lightning and static electricity.

19.2 Electrical Currents Ex. 79
A. 1. All <u>metals</u> are excellent electrical conductors.
2. Electricity does not travel easily through an electrical <u>insulator</u>.   **3.** A battery changes chemical energy into <u>electrical</u> energy.   **4.** A generator can be used to start the flow of <u>electrons</u>.   **B. 5–7.** Accept anything made of metal.   **C. 8–10.** Accept anything made of rubber, plastic, wood, or paper.

Critical Thinking
The wires that lead from the pacemaker to the heart are insulated.

19.3 Electrical Circuits Ex. 80

A. 1. light bulb **2.** switch **3.** battery **4.** The direction of electron flow **5.** The flow of electrons would stop because the circuit would not be complete. **6.** The flow of electrons would stop because the battery is their source. **7.** At the light bulb, as heat (Students may also say as light.)

Critical Thinking
Too many electrical devices may be plugged into the same electrical outlet.

19.4 Magnetism Ex. 81

A. 1. False. If you smash a magnet with a hammer, it will lose its magnetism. **2.** True **3.** False. A magnet is any solid substance that attracts iron or steel. **4.** True **5.** False. The like poles of magnets repel each other, and the opposite poles attract each other.

Critical Thinking
The needle on the compass would always point north. You could use this information to figure out the other directions and find your way.

Chapter 20: Energy Resources

20.1 Fossil Fuels: How Are They Used? Ex. 82

A. 1–10. Answers will vary. Students might identify fossil fuels, moving water, nuclear fission, sunlight, muscle power, and hot water from inside the Earth as energy sources they used. **B. 11.** Answers will vary. **12.** Drying clothes or hair, brewing tea, or heating a home are some activities that could be done using solar energy. **13.** Answers will vary. Muscle power could be used to walk or ride a bike instead of traveling by vehicle. Chopping food or kneading dough could be done by hand instead of using kitchen appliances. Clothes could be hand washed instead of machine washed.

Critical Thinking
Answers will vary. Students might predict that the lack of fossil fuels would have a great impact on people's activities. Or students might predict that people will have prepared themselves for the eventual unavailability of fossil fuels by using other sources of energy, and so their activities would not be affected.

20.1 Fossil Fuels: Saving or Wasting? Ex. 83

A. 1. save **2.** save **3.** save **4.** save **5.** save **6.** waste **7.** save **8.** waste **9.** save **10.** waste **B. 11.** Answers will vary **12.** Answers will vary.

Critical Thinking
Faster cooking time means less fuel use and less time preparing meals.

20.2 Other Energy Resources: Producing Energy Ex. 84

1. True **2.** False. A dam is used to trap moving water to produce hydroelectric energy. **3.** False. A machine with blades that can be turned is a turbine. **4.** True **5.** True **6.** False. The fuel used in nuclear fusion is seawater.

Critical Thinking
People get energy from the sources that are available to them. Available sources vary according to where people live and, in some cases, what they can afford.

20.2 Other Energy Sources: Advantages and Disadvantages Ex. 85

A. 1–14. Answers should take into account availability, wastes produced, expense, and pollution factors. **B. 15–18.** Answers should take into account availability.

Critical Thinking
Answers should show an understanding that a desirable energy source would be readily available, inexpensive, safe to use, and clean.

UNIT 6: EARTH SCIENCE: PART I

Chapter 21: Planet Earth

21.1 Spaceship Earth Ex. 86

A. 1. b **2.** d **3.** c **4.** a **B. 5.** 3 **6.** 2 **7.** 1

Critical Thinking
Gravity gets weaker as objects get farther away from each other.

21.2 Features of the Earth: The Earth's Surface Ex. 87

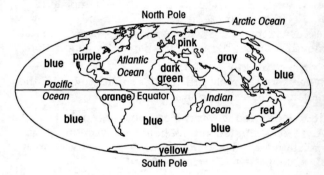

Critical Thinking
Answers will vary.

21.2 Features of the Earth: Land, Layers, and Seasons Ex. 88

A. 1. False. Each of the Earth's seven large landmasses is called a <u>continent</u>. **2.** False. An imaginary line called the <u>equator</u> circles the Earth halfway between the North and South poles. **3.** False. The center of the Earth is called the <u>core</u>. **4.** True **B. 5.** Winter **6.** Fall **7.** Summer **8.** Spring

Critical Thinking
The lengths of day and night would always remain the same. Also there would be no change of seasons.

21.3 Dividing Up the Earth: Lines of Latitude and Longitude Ex. 89

1. Lines of latitude **2.** Nairobi **3.** 90° N **4.** Manaus and San Jose **5.** Accra **6.** 30°W **7.** The North Pole and the South Pole

Critical Thinking

All the lines of longitude meet at two places, the North Pole and the South Pole. When you reach the North Pole, you begin to head toward the South Pole, so you are traveling southward.

21.3 Dividing Up the Earth: Time Zones Around the World Ex. 90

A. 1. From 9:00 A.M. to 10:00 A.M. **2.** 3:29 P.M.
B. 3. 3:00 P.M. **4.** noon

Critical Thinking

People did not need time zones in the past because travel and communication were much slower than they are today. For travelers, the change in time would have been so gradual that they would not have noticed it.

Chapter 22: The Earth's Crust

22.1 Plate Tectonics: Breaks in the Earth's Crust Ex. 91

A. 1. lava **2.** magma **3.** geologists **4.** volcanoes
5. earthquake **B. 6.** The Earth's crust is made of several <u>plates</u>. **7.** Plates drift because they float on the hot, soft rock of the <u>mantle</u>. **8.** Most geologists think that all of the Earth's <u>continents</u> were once part of Pangaea.

Critical Thinking

No. Because of the slow drifting of continents on the Earth's surface, the landmasses and seas around them will have different positions and shapes.

22.1 Plate Tectonics: Shifting Plates Ex. 92

A. 1. A mountain range will form. **2.** A trench will form. **3.** An earthquake will occur. **4.** A volcano may erupt. **B.** Volcano descriptions should include lava, ash, or rock pouring out of the volcano. Students might also include loud noise, people shouting, ground shaking, or destruction associated with the eruption. Earthquake descriptions should include shaking of the Earth and nearby buildings, possible destruction of built objects, and panicky people. Accept any other reasonable details.

Critical Thinking

They both often occur near plate boundaries.

22.1 Plate Tectonics: Earthquakes and Volcanoes Ex. 93

A. 1. earthquake **2.** earthquake **3.** volcano
4. earthquake **5.** volcano **B. 6.** gas and ash
7. magma **8.** vent **9.** lava

Critical Thinking

Accept any reasonable answers. Scientists might look at the history of earthquakes in a certain place to predict when another one might occur. They might use instruments to record movements along a fault. An increase in these movements might be a sign that an earthquake is about to happen. An increase in volcanic activity might also be a sign that an earthquake could be near.

22.2 Rocks and Minerals: Kinds of Rock Ex. 94

A. 1. d **2.** a **3.** c **4.** f **5.** g **6.** e **7.** b
B. 8. sedimentary **9.** metamorphic **10.** igneous.

Critical Thinking

Weathering and erosion can break down igneous rock on Earth's surface. The particles of rock can then be deposited in layers that are pressed together over a long period of time to become sedimentary rock.

22.2 Rocks and Minerals: Weathering and Erosion Ex. 95

A. 1. Check **2.** No check **3.** Check **4.** Check
5. No check **6.** No check **B. 7.** True **8.** False. When water freezes, it expands and acts like a wedge to break rock. **9.** True **10.** False. Glaciers create valleys as they flow downhill.

Critical Thinking

The rock with rounded edges. The flowing water and the rocks tumbling against each other in the water slowly chip away at sharp edges and round them.

22.2 Rocks and Minerals: Predicting the Effects of Erosion Ex. 96

1. The river should be flowing through a deeper channel, with higher banks at its edges. **2.** The gullies should be deeper and wider, and some parts of the hillside should be completely eroded, with bare areas of soil. **3.** Students should draw a thinner layer of soil.

Critical Thinking

Accept any reasonable answers, such as trees and other plants that grow; animals that grow; the moon, which appears to change shape with its phases; or clouds that form and reform, depending on atmospheric conditions.

Chapter 23: The Earth's Atmosphere

23.1 Air All Around Us Ex. 97

A. 1. thermosphere **2.** ionosphere **3.** mesosphere
4. ozone **5.** stratosphere **6.** troposphere **B. 7.** d
8. e **9.** c **10.** a **11.** b

Critical Thinking

Possible answers include carrying a tank of oxygen and wearing very warm clothing.

23.2 Properties of Air: Pressure and Temperature Ex. 98

1. Air pressure is the weight of <u>gases</u> pressing down on the Earth. **2.** A barometer is an instrument that measures air <u>pressure</u>. **3.** Energy from the sun reaches the Earth as <u>radiation</u>. **4.** The <u>uneven</u> heating of the atmosphere causes convection currents to form. **5.** Heat causes the molecules in matter to move <u>faster and spread out</u>. **6.** At night, clouds act as a blanket and make the land <u>warmer</u>. **7.** Heat energy radiating from the <u>Earth</u> warms the atmosphere.

Critical Thinking

Daytime and nighttime temperatures would differ more in the desert. Because there are fewer clouds to trap the Earth's heat at night, the temperature would be lower. Daytime temperatures would be higher because there are fewer clouds to block the sun.

23.2 Properties of Air: Wind Ex. 99
1. It will likely be quite windy since warm air is rising and cool air is moving in to take its place.
2. Trade winds **3.** Westerlies

Critical Thinking
Washington's west coast has milder weather because the ocean keeps the land cooler in summer and warmer in winter.

23.3 Water and Air: Precipitation Ex. 100
A. 1. fog **2.** water vapor **3.** sleet **4.** hail **5.** rain
6. snow **B. 7.** 4 **8.** 3 **9.** 1 **10.** 5 **11.** 6 **12.** 2

Critical Thinking
It probably would not be a good day for a picnic. Even though it is sunny in the morning, with the humidity high and the temperature dropping, clouds and rain are likely to develop.

23.3 Water and Air: Clouds Ex. 101
A. 1. c **2.** f **3.** e **4.** b **5.** d **6.** a **B.** Cirrus clouds: made of ice crystals, usually bright white, thin and feathery, seen in mountains. Stratus clouds: broad, flat layers; low in sky, often sign of stormy weather, gray colored, made of water droplets. Cumulus clouds: made of water droplets; sign of fair weather; big, puffy; low in sky

Critical Thinking
Moisture in your breath condenses into tiny water droplets when your breath meets the cold air. This forms a small cloud.

Chapter 24: Weather and Climate

24.1 Air on the Move Ex. 102
A. 1. air mass **2.** front **3.** climate **4.** weather
5. occluded front **B. 6.** Los Angeles **7.** A low pressure system and cold front will pass, bringing rain and cooler temperatures.

Critical Thinking
A cold front has passed. You know this because there was a brief but heavy shower, and the temperature dropped after the rain.

24.2 Storms Ex. 103
A. 1. thunderhead **2.** wind **3.** hurricane
4. tornado **B. 5.** cumulus clouds **6.** lightning
7. low air **8.** funnel-shaped

Critical Thinking
No. High pressure systems usually bring clear weather.

24.3 The Earth's Climate Zones Ex. 104
A. 1. Manila **2.** New York **3.** Light clothing
B. 4. Accept all reasonable answers including (good) never have to wear heavy clothing, (bad) it is always very hot. **5.** Accept all reasonable answers including (good) experience all seasons, (bad) have to cope with cold winters. **6.** Accept all reasonable answers

including (good) can ice skate and sleigh ride much of the time, (bad) summers are never hot enough for participation in sports such as swimming outdoors.

Critical Thinking
Answers will vary depending on where students live and the climate zone they choose. Accept answers that cover the impact on how students would get around, leisure time, outdoor activities, school, jobs, clothing, and available foods.

UNIT 7: EARTH SCIENCE: PART II
Chapter 25: The Earth's History

25.1 The Story in the Rocks Ex. 105
A. 1. Layer G **2.** Layer A **3.** The layers have been pushed up by uplifting and folding. **B.** Students should mention the position of rock layers, radioactive decay, and the study of fossils.

Critical Thinking
Answers include studying the types of rock, the position of rock layers, and the thickness of rock layers in an area.

25.2 Geological Time: Eras Ex. 106
A. Students should circle: **1.** Mesozoic **2.** Cenozoic
3. Precambrian **4.** Paleozoic **B.** The area was originally a sea. It dried up and became land. Then a sea covered the area again.

Critical Thinking
Students should reason that, just as in the past, natural events such as severe climate change or mass extinctions could occur. These events could end the Cenozoic era. A new era would then follow.

25.2 Geological Time: Past Life Ex. 107
A. 1. bacteria; Precambrian **2.** dinosaurs; Mesozoic
3. birds; Cenozoic **4.** humans; Cenozoic **5.** algae; Precambrian **6.** ferns; Paleozoic **7.** flowering plants; Mesozoic **B. 8.** Dinosaurs **9.** Students might reason that the Animal Kingdom developed more because of the appearance of humans. Accept reasonable answers students can support with facts. **10.** Bacteria, algae, flowering plants, and ferns are ancient. Humans and birds are new.

Critical Thinking
Probably not. Some kinds of organisms may not have become fossils. The fossils of some kinds of organisms might have been destroyed during geologic processes. Also, many kinds of organisms probably remain to be found.

25.2 Geological Time: Ordering Eras Ex. 108
a. Precambrian era **b.** Paleozoic era **c.** Mesozoic era
d. Cenozoic era

Critical Thinking
Animals listed will vary.

Chapter 26: The Earth's Oceans

26.1 Features of the Oceans: Water Ex. 109
1. True   **2.** False. The study of the ocean is called oceanography.   **3.** False. The ocean's salinity is the measure of how much salt is in it.   **4.** True   **B. 5.** b   **6.** a   **7.** c

Critical Thinking
Answers should address the fact that most people, animals, and plants need fresh water. So life as we know it would not exist on an Earth with only salt water.

26.1 Features of the Oceans: The Ocean Floor Ex. 110
A. 1. continental shelf   **2.** continental slope   **3.** ocean basin   **4.** mid-ocean ridge   **5.** ocean trench   **B. 6.** Continental shelf   **7.** Continental slope   **8.** Ocean basin

Critical Thinking
Accept answers that include any of the following obstacles: the need to stay under water for a long time to explore, the ocean is very deep, and the ocean contains dangerous creatures. Some students may know about the cold and crushing pressure at great depths that would make exploration difficult.

26.1 Features of the Oceans: Comparing the Ocean Floor to the Land Ex. 111
A. 1. Accept any of the following: mountains (mid-ocean ridges), plains (ocean basin), cliffs (continental slopes), valleys (trenches). Students may also include volcanoes.   **2.** Accept any reasonable answers. Students might say the ocean trenches would be least known because they are the deepest parts of the ocean.   **3.** The continental shelf would be better known because the waters over it are shallow, and the shelf is at the shoreline.   **4.** Along the mid-ocean ridge   **B. 5.** c   **6.** a   **7.** d   **8.** b

Critical Thinking
Accept all reasonable answers, including that mountains on land are worn down by weathering and erosion.

26.2 Waves and Tides: Understanding Waves Ex. 112
A. 1. c   **2.** a   **3.** b   **B. 4.** Arrow should be horizontal and should point toward the shore.   **5.** Arrow should be under the crest of one wave and show circular movement.   **C. 6.** Local <u>winds</u> cause most ocean waves.   **7.** <u>Breakers</u> form as the tops and bottoms of waves move at different speeds near the shore.

Critical Thinking
Answers should reflect an understanding that the ocean water would probably pile up on shore and spill inland.

26.2 Waves and Tides: Looking at Tides Ex. 113
A. 1. coast   **2.** moon   **3.** spring   **4.** low tide   **5.** neap   **6.** gravity   **B. 7.** spring tide   **8.** neap tide

Critical Thinking
Low tide would be better because a large area of coast that is under water at high tide would be visible at low tide.

26.3 Ocean Resources: Ocean Life Ex. 114
1. In polar areas   **2.** Near the equator   **3.** Accept any reasonable answers, such as whales could become trapped in ice or their calves would freeze to death in mid-winter polar areas.   **4.** Whales would find food scarce and the population of whales would eventually decrease.

Critical Thinking
Reasons for yes: important to a few countries' economies, important for some native peoples' livelihoods; also they could be considered resources for tourism, as are some big-game animals in Africa. Reasons for no: they should not be used as resources at all because of their scarcity, their beauty and/or their intelligence; also they are not economically important on a worldwide scale.

26.3 Ocean Resources: How We Use Them Ex. 115
A. Checks should be in front of the following: fish, coral, oil, salt, oxygen from algae, tides (as an energy source), natural gas, metals   **B. 1.** fish   **2.** salt   **3.** oil   **4.** tides (as an energy source)   **5.** natural gas   **6.** metals   **7.** coral   **8.** oxygen from algae

Critical Thinking
Answers will vary. Be sure that students explain the reason for their choices.

Chapter 27: Exploring Space

27.1 The Last Frontier Ex. 116
A. 1. universe   **2.** galaxy   **3.** astronomy   **4.** stars   **B.** The spiral galaxy should be circled.

Critical Thinking
Students might mention the size of galaxies or the numbers of stars they contain. Accept any reasonable groupings.

27.2 The Solar System: The Inner Planets Ex. 117
The map of the solar system should be labeled with Mercury closest to the sun, then Venus, Earth, and Mars.   **1.** Mercury: very hot in day, very cold at night; closest planet to the sun   **2.** Venus: solar system's hottest planet, thick atmosphere that traps heat   **3.** Earth: surface covered mostly with water, has life   **4.** Mars: has two tiny moons, called the "red planet"

Critical Thinking
The sun produces its light and heat by means of nuclear fusion. In nuclear fusion, the sun burns hydrogen.

27.2 The Solar System: The Outer Planets Ex. 118
The map of the solar system should be labeled with Jupiter (the largest planet), then Saturn, Uranus, Neptune, and Pluto.   **1.** Jupiter: has a Great Red Spot,

largest planet in solar system   **2.** Saturn: surrounded by seven rings; has 18 named moons   **3.** Uranus: rolls on its side in orbit, made of solid core surrounded by a gas made up of hydrogen, helium, and methane.
4. Neptune: sometimes changes places with Pluto, has eight moons and several thin rings   **5.** Pluto: surface is always in darkness, may be the escaped moon of Neptune

Critical Thinking
The moons and rings both circle the planets. They may be related to each other if they are made of the same substances. Also, they may be related if they were formed in the same way and at the same time.

27.2 The Solar System: Asteroids, Comets, and Meteors Ex. 119
A. 1. b   **2.** d   **3.** a   **4.** e   **5.** c   **B. 6.** satellite
7. meteor   **8.** asteroid   **9.** comet

Critical Thinking
Most of the objects burn up in the Earth's atmosphere before reaching the ground.

27.3 Space Exploration Ex. 120
A. 1. d   **2.** c   **3.** a   **4.** b   **5.** Accept any choice.
6. Accept all answers that include a reasonable method of finding the answer to the student's question.

Critical Thinking
Accept any answer, but look for a good reason. Mars is the most likely to be explored because of its distance and relatively benign atmosphere compared to Venus.

Classroom Resource Binder Answer Key

UNIT 1 THE WONDERS OF SCIENCE

Chapter 1 What Is Science?

1 Words to Know
A. 1. galaxy 2. matter 3. technology
4. experiment 5. atom B. 6. energy 7. universe
8. observation 9. life science 10. physical science
11. earth science 12. research

2 Practice • From Atoms to Galaxies
A. 1. atom 2. star 3. galaxy 4. universe
B. 5. experiment 6. observation 7. experiment
8. experiment 9. observation 10. observation
11. observation 12. experiment 13. observation
14. experiment 15. observation **Write About Science** Answers will vary. Students should mention a topic they could research and a reason for their interest in the topic.

3 Practice • Science at Work
A. 1. life 2. physical 3. earth 4. earth 5. life
B. 6. False. Technology helps to make life better for people. 7. False. A beam of light inside a CD player plays the music. 8. True **Write About Science** Answers will vary. Students should mention a job related to science and what they like or dislike about the job.

4 Challenge
1–2. Answers will vary. Accept any discovery.
3–4. Answers will vary. Accept any invention.
5. Encourage students to be creative in their discoveries and inventions.

5 Another Way
Physical Science—Topics: energy, matter; Careers: electrician, computer technician; Earth Science— Topics: Earth, stars, weather; Careers: landfill manager, weather person; Life Science—Topics: animals, plants, humans; Careers: zookeeper, landscaper

6 Lab Activity • What Do Scientists Do?
Students' charts should be based on the articles they chose. If time permits, you may want to have students choose one article from each branch of science. **Draw Conclusions** Answers will vary. Students should refer to the work of the scientists in the articles.

7 Science in Your Life • Using Technology
A. 1. e 2. d 3. g 4. a 5. c 6. b 7. f
B. 8. Answers will depend on the object chosen. Encourage students to be creative. 9. Answers will depend on the object chosen. Encourage students to be creative.

8 Chapter 1 • Test A
A. 1. e 2. a 3. d 4. b 5. c B. 6. research
7. experiment 8. observation 9. energy 10. laser
Critical Thinking Answers will vary. Students should suggest conducting a controlled experiment in which all variables except sunlight are controlled. For example, students might grow identical plants under

identical conditions except that one would receive direct sunlight and one would be in the shade. Results will depend on many variables, especially the types of plants used.

9 Chapter 1 • Test B
1. d 2. a 3. b 4. c 5. a 6. c 7. c 8. a 9. c
10. c **Critical Thinking** Answers will vary. Students should suggest conducting a controlled experiment in which all variables except salt concentration are controlled. For example, students might test the freezing point of different saltwater solutions (including one with no salt).

Chapter 2 The Process of Discovery

10 Words to Know
A. 1. measurement 2. unit 3. metric 4. meter
5. liter 6. gram B. 7. h 8. f 9. g 10. b 11. c
12. a 13. e 14. d

11 Practice • The Scientific Method
A. 5, 3, 1, 2, 4 B. 1. experiments 2. charts, graphs
3. procedure 4. method **Write About Science** Answers will vary. Accept any answer student provides that involves the steps in the scientific method.

12 Practice • Measuring in Science
A. 1. mile 2. milliliters 3. ten 4. 90 5. kilograms
B. 6. quart. A quart is not a metric unit of volume.
7. ounce. An ounce is not a metric unit. 8. liter. A liter is not a unit of mass. 9. mile. A mile is not a metric unit of distance. **Write About Science** Answers will vary. Students should give reasons that support their opinions.

13 Practice • Laboratory Science
A. 1. False. Read the instructions for the activity before you get to the lab. 2. False. Food and gum are not allowed in the lab. 3. True 4. False. The safety rules should be followed when working in a lab.
5. True B. 6. laboratory 7. microscope 8. larger
9. balance 10. petri dish 11. Bunsen burner

14 Challenge
1. Answers will vary. Students may suggest filling the egg with a number of different materials, such as seeds or water, and then measuring the volume of those materials. Students may also suggest measuring the volume of the egg that was once in the shell. They may also suggest filling the egg with a solid, such as foam or clay, and measuring the amount of liquid displaced when the egg is submerged. Accept all reasonable answers. 2–4. Answers will depend on the method chosen. 5. Answers will vary. The eggshell is fragile, so filling it with a solid and then using displacement may break the egg. If the egg has any cracks, using water or a liquid that can run out the cracks will not be accurate. Folding up a piece of cloth also will not produce an accurate volume measurement. Accept all reasonable explanations of students' results.

15 Another Way

Length diagram: hectometer, decimeter   Volume diagram: kiloliter, liter, centiliter, milliliter   Mass diagram: kilogram, dekagram, gram, milligram

16–17 Lab Activity • Using a Compound Microscope

11. Answers will vary and will depend on the objects observed. In general, students should say that things appear larger than they really are and that fine details not apparent to the eye alone are shown.
12. Answers will vary. Students should note that the high-power objective provides greater magnification than the low-power objective.   **Draw Conclusions** Answers will vary. Students may say that a microscope makes small things look larger than they are. A scientist can use a microscope to learn about this small world.

18 On-the-Job Science • Medical Lab Technician

1. A. bacilli **B.** cocci **C.** streptococci **D.** spirilla
2. Students should recognize and circle the streptococci, figure C.   **Critical Thinking** Answers will vary. Students should mention that other bacteria in the lab could cause mistakes when a technician looks at a culture under the microscope.

19 Chapter 2 • Test A

A. 1. e **2.** d **3.** a **4.** b **5.** c **6.** f **B. 7.** area
8. volume **9.** microscope **10.** kilograms **Critical Thinking** Answers will depend on the type of work that students suggest.

20 Chapter 2 • Test B

1. a **2.** b **3.** d **4.** c **5.** d **6.** a **7.** b **8.** a **9.** b
10. d **Critical Thinking** Answers will depend on the type of work that students list.

Chapter 3 The Study of Life

21 Words to Know

A. 1. biology **2.** organism **3.** waste **4.** life span
5. genetics **6.** ecology **7.** botany **B. 8.** zoology
9. environment **10.** microbiology **11.** characteristic
12. reproduced

22 Practice • A Home for Life

A. 1. b **2.** c **3.** a **B. 4.** microbiology **5.** ecology
6. botany **7.** genetics **8.** zoology **9.** botany
10. genetics **Write About Science** Answers will vary. Students should give reasons that support their opinions.

23 Practice • What Is Life?

Answers will vary and may include the following characteristics: 1) Plants make their own food. Some animals eat other animals for food. 2) Some animals fly. Some animals swim. 3) All living things grow. Most organisms stop growing. 4) All organisms can reproduce themselves. Plants reproduce using seeds. 5) Some animals respond to the sight or smell of other animals. Garden plants respond to heavy watering by growing deep roots.

24 Challenge

Living things include frog, chipmunk, bird, fox, eagle, rabbits, squirrel, human, trees, and grass. Nonliving things include the sky, fire, tent, camper's clothing, mug, water, mountains, rocks, and snow on the mountain.

25 Another Way

Order may vary: **1.** reproduce **2.** (grow) **3.** move
4. get and use food **5.** respond to the environment
Order may vary: **6.** learn **7.** breathe **8.** (digest food)
9. make their own food

26 Lab Activity • Investigating Mushrooms

Day 2 **1.** Students should see a dark print of the gills. **Draw Conclusions** They fall out so new mushrooms can grow when the spores hit the ground.

27 Science in Your Life • Plan a Flower Garden

1. No. The flashes of light from the car inhibit blooming as the diagram shows. **2.** Answers will vary. Students may suggest putting the plant in a closet or a garage with no windows for 8 hours straight each night. **3.** Students may suggest using two plants in an experiment. One plant could be placed in the dark for 8 hours, and the other plant could always be placed in the light. **Critical Thinking** It is hard to get the plants to bloom again because they require continuous darkness.

28 Chapter 3 • Test A

A. 1. e **2.** a **3.** b **4.** c **5.** d **B. 6.** botany
7. organism **8.** biology **9.** zoology **10.** ecology
Critical Thinking Answers will vary. Answers should be based on the characteristics of life given in the chapter.

29 Chapter 3 • Test B

1. c **2.** a **3.** b **4.** d **5.** b **6.** a **7.** d **8.** c **9.** b
10. d **Critical Thinking** Answers will vary. Answers should be based on the characteristics of life given in the chapter.

Chapter 4 Cells and Life

30 Words to Know

A. 1. cell **2.** cytoplasm **3.** nucleus **4.** vacuole
5. cell membrane **6.** cell wall **7.** chlorophyll
8. chloroplast **9.** DNA **10.** mitochondrion
11. cellular respiration **B. 12.** b **13.** c **14.** a

31 Practice • The Basic Units of Life

A. 1. atom **2.** molecule **3.** cell **4.** universe
B. 5. microscope **6.** cells **7.** matter **8.** living
9. chemical bonds **10.** molecules **11.** elements
12. DNA **Write About Science** Student paragraphs should include the fact that cells are made up of matter, and all matter on Earth is made of atoms.

32 Practice • Understanding Cells

A. 1. d **2.** b **3.** h **4.** c **5.** e **6.** g **7.** a **8.** f
B. 9. both **10.** both **11.** plant **12.** both **13.** both
14. plant **15.** both **16.** plant **Write About Science** Student paragraphs should describe cellular respiration using the words *energy*, *waste*, and *membrane*. Responses should include the fact that cells

use oxygen to release energy. This oxygen gets into the cells through the cell membrane.

33 Challenge
800× 1,200× 3,200×

34 Another Way
1. (sunlight) **2.** (photosynthesis) **3.** (oxygen) **4.** food molecules **5.** (cellular respiration) **6.** (heat) **7.** energy **8.** carbon dioxide or water **9.** water or carbon dioxide

35 Lab Activity • Observing Plant Cells
Draw Conclusions Answers will vary. Students should be able to locate the cell wall, nucleus, vacuole, and chloroplasts. Student responses will vary on which parts were difficult to find. Students should support their responses with examples from the activity.

36 On-the-Job Science • Histologic Technician
1. malaria **2.** normal **3.** sickle-cell anemia **Critical Thinking** Atoms do not change and they do not get diseases. Cells would show signs of diseases, while atoms would not.

37 Chapter 4 • Test A
A. 1. c **2.** a **3.** d **4.** e **5.** b **B. 6.** cell **7.** element **8.** nucleus **9.** respiration **10.** microscope **11.** molecule **12.** digestion **Critical Thinking** Answers will vary. Students should mention that if something is not made up of cells, it is not living.

38 Chapter 4 • Test B
1. d **2.** d **3.** c **4.** a **5.** c **6.** b **7.** b **8.** c **9.** a **10.** d **Critical Thinking** Answers will vary. Students should compare three other cell parts, such as vacuole, nucleus, and cytoplasm, to the parts of a city. Accept all reasonable answers.

Chapter 5 The Kingdoms of Life

39 Words to Know
A. 1. e **2.** c **3.** a **4.** d **5.** f **6.** b **B. 7.** biologist **8.** bacterium **9.** kingdoms **10.** species **11.** protist

40 Practice • Classifying Organisms
A. 1. animal **2.** fungus **3.** protist **4.** plant **5.** animal **6.** fungus **7.** true bacteria **8.** protist **B. 9.** f **10.** c **11.** a **12.** b **13.** d **14.** e **C.** Answers will vary. Students' diagrams should indicate that species is a subset of kingdom. **Write About Science** All plants are many-celled, and they have cell walls. Plants use sunlight and chlorophyll to make food.

41 Practice • Earth's Simplest Organisms
A. 1. yeast. Yeast belong to the Fungus Kingdom. **2.** algae. Algae belong to the Protist Kingdom. **3.** bacteria. Bacteria belong to one of two kingdoms, True Bacteria or Ancient Bacteria. **4.** mushroom. Mushrooms belong to the Fungi Kingdom. **5.** yeast. Yeast belong to the Fungi Kingdom. **B. 6.** False. Fungi are organisms. **7.** True **8.** False. Algae are protists. **9.** True **10.** False. Monerans have DNA. **Write About Science** A microscope helped scientists see smaller groups of organisms. They could group these organisms into more kingdoms.

42 Challenge
1. (live oak) **2.** poplar **3.** shingle oak **4.** red bud

43 Another Way
Animals: mammals, insects, spiders, reptiles, birds, humans Plants: trees, ferns, flowering plants Fungi: yeast, molds, mushrooms Protists: protozoa, algae True Bacteria: blue-green bacteria; Ancient Bacteria: salt marsh bacteria

44 Lab Activity • Classifying Animals
Draw Conclusions Possible answer: All animals with backbones and feathers are birds. Some animals with backbones and no feathers have fur.

45 Science in Your Life • Controlling Bacteria
1. You should wash your hands when they seem dirty, before eating, and after using the bathroom. **2.** You should keep food that can spoil in the refrigerator; cook meat all the way through; and wash utensils, using hot water and soap. **3.** You should throw spoiled food away. **4.** You should wash cuts with alcohol or peroxide, put antibiotic ointment on them, and use a bandage. **Critical Thinking** Answers will vary. Possible student responses include not touching your hair or face while preparing food and using antibacterial soap.

46 Chapter 5 • Test A
A. 1. f **2.** e **3.** a **4.** b **5.** c **6.** d **B. 7.** fungi **8.** bacteria **9.** algae **10.** protozoa **Critical Thinking** Possible answers: Animals: People eat chicken in sandwiches and burritos. Plants: People eat vegetables like carrots or lettuce. Fungi: People eat mushrooms with their pasta. Bacteria: People eat yogurt or cottage cheese.

47 Chapter 5 • Test B
1. c **2.** a **3.** d **4.** b **5.** c **6.** d **7.** c **8.** b **9.** a **10.** c **Critical Thinking** Sausage is made from pigs, which are members of the Animal Kingdom. Peppers are members of the Plant Kingdom. Mushrooms are members of the Fungi Kingdom.

Chapter 6 The Animal Kingdom

48 Words to Know
A. 1. parasite **2.** amphibian **3.** mollusk **4.** vertebrate **5.** crustacean **6.** reptile **7.** insect **B. 8.** warm-blooded **9.** host **10.** mammals **11.** invertebrate **12.** arthropods

49 Practice • From Simple to Complex
A. 1. False; five **2.** True **3.** True **4.** False; Plants **5.** True **6.** False; do **7.** False; many-celled **B. 8.** skin cells **9.** nerve cells **10.** muscle cells **11.** nerve cells **12.** skin cells **Write About Science** Answers will vary. Students may respond that having many different kinds of cells allows animals to do many kinds of jobs and to be more complicated. The flatness of skin cells allows them to cover and protect the body surface. Being long and stringlike allows nerve cells to carry messages throughout the body.

50 Practice • Invertebrates
A. 1. invertebrates **2.** sponges **3.** parasites **4.** hosts **5.** mollusks **6.** sea stars **7.** appendages

B. 8. crustacean. The crab is a crustacean because it has five pairs of legs.   **9.** insect. The ant is an insect because it has three pairs of legs.   **10.** spider. The tick is a spiderlike arthropod because it has four pairs of legs and no antennae.   **Write About Science** Answers will vary. Sponges live in the sea, have a rubbery skeleton with many holes, and filter food out of the water that washes through them. Sea stars live in salt water, usually have five arms and spiny skin, and feed on oysters by pushing their own stomach out of their mouth. Tapeworms live inside other animals, have a ribbonlike body, and eat their hosts' digested food. Earthworms live in the soil, have a segmented body, and use a gizzard for grinding food.

51 Practice • Vertebrates
A. 1. bird, mammal   **2.** fish, amphibian, reptile
3. fish, amphibian, reptile, bird, mammal   **4.** fish, amphibian   **5.** mammal   **B. 6.** The ostrich does not belong. It is a bird; the rest are mammals.   **7.** The dolphin does not belong. It is a mammal; the rest are fish.   **8.** The frog does not belong. It is an amphibian; the rest are reptiles.   **Write About Science**   Answers will vary. The skin of reptiles is covered with hard scales, which keep in moisture. Reptile eggs have a leathery cover that keeps them from drying out. Most amphibians need to keep their skin wet, and amphibian eggs have no shells to retain moisture.

52 Challenge
1. a. Tadpoles have a streamlined body with a tail; frogs have four legs but no tail.   **b.** Tadpoles breathe with gills; frogs breathe with lungs.   **c.** Tadpoles swim in water; frogs hop around on land and swim in water.
2. a. Caterpillars have a wormlike body; butterflies have wings and jointed legs.   **b.** Caterpillars eat leaves; butterflies feed on nectar in flowers.   **c.** Caterpillars crawl; butterflies fly.   **Write About Science**   Possible Answers: Being able to fly allows insects to cover large distances in search of food or good places to lay eggs. Being able to jump around on land allows amphibians to move to wet areas when other areas dry up.

53 Another Way
1. (encrusting sponge)   **2.** (free-standing sponge)
3. (sand dollar)   **4.** sea star or oyster or squid
5. oyster or sea star or squid   **6.** squid or sea star or oyster   **7.** (spider)   **8.** scorpion   **9.** crab or crayfish
10. crayfish or crab   **11.** bee or cockroach
12. cockroach or bee   **13.** (shark)   **14.** trout
15. toad or salamander   **16.** salamander or toad
17. snake or crocodile   **18.** crocodile or snake
19. warbler or sparrow   **20.** sparrow or warbler
21. whale or squirrel   **22.** squirrel or whale

54 Lab Activity • Identifying Mollusks
2. clam   **3.** B: octopus; C: snail; D: slug   **Draw Conclusions**   Answers will vary. Useful characteristics include the presence or absence of a shell, the shape and number of pieces of the shell, and the shape of the body.

55 On-the-Job Science • Pet Store Worker
1. vertebrates: goldfish, dog, turtle, parrot; Invertebrates: tarantula, crayfish   **2.** spiders:

tarantula; birds: parrot; reptiles: turtle; mammals: dog; crustaceans: crayfish; fish: goldfish   **3.** Answers will vary. All of these animals can move around; all must get their own food; and all have cells that do special jobs.   **4.** Answers will vary. Vertebrates have a backbone, and invertebrates do not. Vertebrates are more complicated than invertebrates and have larger brains, more digestive parts, and more reproductive parts.   **Critical Thinking**   The parrot could travel the farthest. It can fly, while the others cannot.

56 Chapter 6 • Test A
A. 1. c   **2.** d   **3.** a   **4.** e   **5.** b   **B. 6.** insects
7. mammals   **8.** crustaceans   **9.** hosts
10. invertebrates   **Critical Thinking**   Answers will vary. They are alike because all are animals without backbones. Differences: arthropods have an outer skeleton, jointed appendages, and a body divided into segments; mollusks have a soft body and usually a hard shell, and they may live on land or in water; spiny-skinned invertebrates have sharp spines on their skin and live only in salt water.

57 Chapter 6 • Test B
1. d   **2.** c   **3.** b   **4.** a   **5.** c   **6.** d   **7.** a   **8.** b   **9.** c
10. a   **Critical Thinking**   Answers will vary. They are alike because all are animals with backbones. Differences: amphibians have wet, slippery skin and four legs, and they lay eggs with no shells; reptiles have dry, scaly skin and either four legs or no legs, and they lay eggs with a leathery cover; birds have feathers, hollow bones, two wings, and two legs, and most of them can fly.

Chapter 7 The Plant Kingdom
58 Words to Know
A. 1. c   **2.** d   **3.** g   **4.** b   **5.** f   **6.** a   **7.** e
B. 8. germination   **9.** egg cell   **10.** pollination
11. photosynthesis   **12.** sperm cell; fertilization
13. fruit   **14.** pollen

59 Practice • Plants as Food Makers
A. 1. True   **2.** True   **3.** False; leaves   **4.** False; carbon dioxide   **5.** False; oxygen   **B. 6.** stem   **7.** leaves
8. chlorophyll   **9.** carbon dioxide   **10.** water
C. 11. Through the roots and stems to the leaves
12. Sunlight, energy, carbon dioxide, water

60 Practice • Plant Reproduction
A. 1. b   **2.** a   **3.** c   **4.** d   **5.** a   **6.** a
B. 7. pollination   **8.** fertilization   **9.** germination
Write About Science   Answers will vary. Accept all reasonable answers.

61 Challenge
1. b   **2.** d   **3.** c

62 Another Way
Answers will vary.

63 Lab Activity • Growing New Plants
Draw Conclusions • Roots always grow downward, and stems always grow upward.   • Leaves grow from stems and need to be above ground to get sunlight in order to make food for the plant.   • Dried beans need a little water and a little light to grow.

64 Science in Your Life • Products From Grasses
1. Corn, oats, rice **2.** Corn, rye, oats, barley, millet
3. Corn, rye, wheat **Critical Thinking** Answers will vary depending on the individual student's diet and taste.

65 Chapter 7 • Test A
A. 1. c **2.** d **3.** a **4.** e **5.** b **B. 6.** food **7.** roots
8. pistil **9.** germination **10.** fruits **Critical Thinking** In a rain forest, water, insects, or other animals would probably transfer pollen. At the North Pole, wind and animals would probably transfer pollen.

66 Chapter 7 • Test B
1. d **2.** a **3.** b **4.** c **5.** a **6.** c **7.** a **8.** d **9.** a
10. b **Critical Thinking** On a tropical island, water, insects, or other animals would probably transfer pollen. In a desert, wind or animals would probably transfer pollen.

Chapter 8 Genetics: The Code of Life

67 Words to Know
A.

```
m   o   e   p   c   l   r   s   d
i   d   k   f   h   i   t   a   v
h   g   e   e   r   g   t   b   f
y   e   o   r   i   p   r   o   j
b   n   t   d   m   t   a   s   y
r   e   c   e   s   s   i   v   e
i   d   l   a   i   e   t   l   h
d   m   u   t   a   t   i   o   n
```

1. hybrid **2.** gene **3.** mutation **4.** trait
5. recessive **B. 6.** offspring **7.** heredity
8. crossbreeding **9.** dominant **10.** chromosome

68 Practice • The Same But Different
A. 1. traits **2.** crossbreeding **3.** hybrid
4. dominant **B. 5.** False. The color of your skin or hair is a physical trait. **6.** False. Genetics is the study of the passing down of traits from parents to offspring. **Write About Science** Mendel was not recognized as a great scientist during his life. Sixteen years after his death, Hugo De Vries, Carl Correns, and Erich Tschermak, three European scientists, credited Mendel as the discoverer of the laws of heredity.

69 Practice • The Building Blocks of Heredity
A. 1. chromosomes **2.** genes **3.** fertilization
4. mutation **B. 5.** False; heredity **6.** True **7.** False; recessive **8.** True **9.** False; harmful

70 Practice • Controlling Heredity
A. 1. b **2.** d **3.** a **B. 4.** GE **5.** SB **6.** E **7.** SB
8. E **Write About Science** Students should

demonstrate their understanding of traits. Coat color; type of fur; keen eyesight, hearing, or smell; strength; speed; tongue color; and retrieving instinct are examples of traits that breeders of dogs, cats, or horses might select.

71 Challenge
1. White fur color **2.** Either black or white fur color
3. White because white is recessive. There would have been no dominant trait to mask it. **4.** Drawings should show a black father mouse and six black babies labeled with a *D*. The white mother mouse and the two white babies should be labeled with an *R*.

72 Another Way
1. mother **2.** (father) **3.** (dominant) **4.** recessive
5. genes **6.** chromosomes **7.** nucleus

73 Lab Activity • Fingerprints
Draw Conclusions • Student fingerprints will vary.
• Fingerprints can be used to identify a person because no two fingerprints are alike.

74 On-the-Job Science • Cattle Breeder
Brangus are a cross between Angus and Brahman; Santa Gertrudes are a cross between Brahman and Shorthorn. **Critical Thinking** Hornless breeds will not be able to use horns to harm other cattle or the breeder.

75 Chapter 8 • Test A
A. 1. e **2.** a **3.** c **4.** d **5.** b **B. 6.** dominant
7. DNA **8.** sex cell **9.** body cell **10.** selective breeding **Critical Thinking** The sex cells of a horse would have 32 chromosomes. The offspring would have 64 chromosomes.

76 Chapter 8 • Test B
1. c **2.** a **3.** b **4.** d **5.** a **6.** b **7.** c **8.** d **9.** d
10. a **Critical Thinking** The sex cells of a grasshopper would have 12 chromosomes. The offspring would have 24 chromosomes.

Chapter 9 Evolution

77 Words to Know
Across: 5. natural selection **6.** paleontology
7. extinct **Down: 1.** fossil **2.** evolution **3.** theory
4. naturalist

78 Practice • Time and Change
A. 1. evolution **2.** extinct **3.** fossils
4. paleontology **5.** bones **6.** ancestor **B. 7.** Two organisms that have had a similar evolution have very similar DNA. **8.** The bones of tigers and lions **Write About Science** Answers will vary. Early horses were much smaller and had shorter teeth than modern horses. They also had four toes instead of one. Drawings should resemble Figure 9-1 in the Student Edition.

79 Practice • Theories of Evolution
A. 1. Jean Baptiste Lamarck **2.** Charles Darwin
3. environment **4.** natural selection **5.** mutation
B. 6. True **7.** False; more **8.** False; helpful **9.** True
10. True **11.** False; harmful **Write About Science** Answers will vary. Lamarck thought that giraffes

lengthened their necks as they began to eat the leaves on trees and that this trait was passed on to the giraffes' offspring. Darwin's theory says that certain giraffes inherited gene combinations that produced longer necks. Those giraffes were more likely to survive and pass on that trait to their offspring.

80 Challenge
1. At the tip of the Yucatán Peninsula in the Gulf of Mexico   2. There is a large crater at that site.   3. The crater was formed at about the same time that the dinosaurs became extinct.   4. Dust and chemicals released into the air by the impact would have blocked sunlight. This lowered the Earth's temperature and would have caused highly acidic rain to fall. 5. The darkness and acidic rain would have caused most plants to die. That would have caused plant-eating dinosaurs to die. Dinosaurs that ate the plant-eaters would then have died.

81 Another Way
1. traits; environment   2. offspring   3. selection 4. food and space

82 Lab Activity • Making Fossil Models
Draw Conclusions • clay; sand   • There are plants. There are animals. There is sea life.   • Answers will vary. The scientist could learn what kinds of plants and animals are living at this time and how large the animals and the plants' leaves are.

83 Science in Your Life • Changing the Course of Natural Selection
1. $90 + 10 = 100$; $10/100 = 10\%$ 2. $100\% \times 10 = 10$ short; $10\% \times 90 = 9$ tall   3. $10 \times 100 = 1{,}000$ short; $9 \times 100 = 900$ tall   4. $800/1{,}000 = .8 = 80\%$ **Critical Thinking**   Having short flowers is a helpful trait. Dandelions with short flowers are less likely to be cut by a lawn mower. Therefore, they are more likely to reproduce.

84 Chapter 9 • Test A
A. 1. fossil   **2.** naturalist   **3.** trait   **4.** ancestor 5. offspring   **B. 6.** d   **7.** e   **8.** b   **9.** c   **10.** a **Critical Thinking**   Answers will vary. Scientists can compare the DNA in different organisms. If the DNA is very similar, the organisms probably evolved from the same ancestor. For example, humans and chimpanzees have very similar DNA.

85 Chapter 9 • Test B
1. c   **2.** a   **3.** d   **4.** b   **5.** a   **6.** c   **7.** b   **8.** a   **9.** b 10. d   **Critical Thinking**   Answers will vary. Scientists can compare the bones in corresponding parts of different animals. If the bones are very similar, the animals have a common ancestor. For example, the bones in a lion's foreleg, a bat's wing, and a dolphin's flipper are very similar.

86 Extra Credit: More About DNA
A. 1. two strands or thin fibers that are attached to each other; sugars and other substances or nitrogen bases   **2.** A, T, C, G; proteins   **B. 3.** TCG   **4.** CAG

Chapter 10 The Human Body
87 Words to Know
A. 1. hormone   **2.** fetus   **3.** calcium   **4.** organ 5. skeleton   **6.** system   **7.** humans   **B. 8.** puberty 9. testes   **10.** menstruation   **11.** tissue   **12.** tendon 13. joint   **14.** ovaries   **15.** uterus

88 Practice • From Cells to Systems
A. 1. cells   **2.** tissues   **3.** organs   **4.** system   **B. 5.** c 6. b   **7.** a   **8.** e   **9.** d   **C. 10.** d   **11.** c   **12.** a   **13.** b **Write About Science**   Answers will vary. Students may point out that our large brains have been the source of countless ideas that have made survival easier for people than it is for other animals. Examples of these ideas include temperature-controlled homes and plumbing that brings water directly to us.

89 Practice • Your Body at Work
A. 1. skeleton   **2.** joints   **3.** calcium   **4.** muscles 5. tendons   **6.** movement   **B. 7.** False. The biceps muscle bends the arm.   **8.** True   **9.** False. Muscles move bones by pulling.   **Write About Science** Answers will vary. If describing how a hand grips something, students should note that messages come from the brain to the spinal cord, through neurons to the hand. The hand muscles then pull the bones, which move. Joints bend. Then the hand grips the object.

90 Practice • Reproduction
A. 1. True   **2.** False; hips, breasts   **3.** False; testes 4. False; menstruation   **5.** True   **6.** True **B. 7.** reproductive   **8.** ovaries   **9.** uterus   **10.** egg cell **Write About Science**   The egg cell is fertilized by the sperm cell, and an embryo is formed. The embryo grows and stretches the uterus. By four months, the embryo, now a fetus, has many human features. Most of its organs are developed and working by seven months. The fetus is ready to be born at about nine months.

91 Challenge
Answers will vary. Possible answers: Human invention: scuba gear   What it does: allows people to breathe under water   Other animal: fish   Body part or special ability: gills   What it does and how: allows fish to breathe under water

92 Another Way
1. (blood)   **2.** heart   **3.** (teeth)   **4.** stomach 5. tendons   **6.** (biceps)   **7.** (rib cage)   **8.** backbone or hip bone   **9.** hip bone or backbone   **10.** (nose) 11. lungs   **12.** ovaries or testes   **13.** (uterus) 14. testes or ovaries   **15.** (brain)   **16.** neurons or spinal cord   **17.** spinal cord or neurons

93 Lab Activity • Fooling Your Senses
1. BC   **2.** No (Both are the same.)   **3.** B; no (Both are the same.)   **4.** Vase or shadows of two faces   **Draw Conclusions**   Students may say that details surrounding what they look at can affect how they see something. This affects their sense of vision.

94 On-the-Job Science • Fitness Instructor
Student heart rates will vary. **6.** Answers will vary.
7. Answers will vary. **Critical Thinking** Answers
will vary. Students may say that on some days they
were more active than on other days.

95 Chapter 10 • Test A
A. 1. c **2.** e **3.** d **4.** b **5.** a **B. 6.** uterus
7. puberty **8.** tendons **9.** ovaries **10.** hormones
Critical Thinking Answers will vary. Sense of taste is
used to detect flavors, while sense of smell detects
scents. These two senses sense different things, but
combined together, they can make the experience of
eating pleasant or unpleasant. These senses are alike
in that sometimes a piece of food seems to smell the
way it tastes and tastes the way it smells.

96 Chapter 10 • Test B
1. a **2.** d **3.** d **4.** c **5.** b **6.** d **7.** a **8.** c **9.** a
10. c **Critical Thinking** The skeletal system
supports the body. The muscular system connects
bones and provides movement. These systems are
alike because they both give shape, strength, and
movement to the body. They are different because the
skeleton is hard bone and muscles are soft tissue.

Chapter 11 Getting Energy Into and Around the Body

97 Words to Know
A. 1. plasma **2.** trachea **3.** platelet **4.** vein **5.** red
blood cell **6.** capillary **7.** artery **B. 8.** g **9.** d
10. c **11.** e **12.** a **13.** f **14.** b

98 Practice • Digestion
A. 1. enzymes **2.** esophagus **3.** stomach **4.** small
intestine **5.** blood **B. 6.** b **7.** a **8.** d **9.** c **10.** a
Write About Science The mouth and enzymes in the
mouth break down the bite of pizza. Then it travels
down the esophagus to the stomach. The muscles and
enzymes in the stomach break down the food even
more. After the stomach, the food moves to the small
intestine and into the blood. The solid waste passes
from the small intestine to the large intestine where it
passes out of the body through the anus.

99 Practice • Respiration
A. 1. nose **2.** trachea **3.** bronchi **4.** air sacs
5. capillaries **6.** bloodstream **B. 7.** c **8.** a **9.** b

100 Practice • Circulation
A. 1. c **2.** d **3.** a **4.** b **B. 5.** oxygen **6.** blood
vessels **7.** clogged **8.** heart attack **C. 9.** c **10.** a
11. d **Write About Science** Students' paragraphs
will vary but should include the terms *heart, artery,
vein, capillary,* and *body cells.* The paragraph should
show the path of the red blood cell as it carries blood
away from the heart to the body cells in an artery and
returns blood to the heart in a vein.

101 Challenge
1. An elephant's heart beats approximately 50,400
times per day (35 beats per minute × 60 minutes per
hour × 24 hours per day). The mouse's heart beats
approximately 763,200 times per day (530 beats per
minute × 60 minutes per hour × 24 hours per day).

2. Shrew: 1,300 beats per minute × 60 minutes per
hour × 24 hours per day × 365 days per year ×
2 years per lifetime = 1,366,560,000 beats   Whale:
20 beats per minute × 60 minutes per hour ×
24 hours per day × 365 days per year × 40 years per
lifetime = 420,480,000 beats   A shrew's heart beats
more times in a lifetime.

102 Another Way
1. heart **2.** lungs **3.** vein **4.** capillary **5.** artery
There should be two arrows pointing *away from the
heart*: one on the left side of the heart (the outline's
left side) pointing from the heart out to the body, and
one pointing from the heart to the lungs. There
should be two arrows pointing *to the heart*: one on the
right side of the heart (the outline's right side) coming
from the body into the heart, and one pointing from
the lungs to the heart.

103 Lab Activity • How Much Blood?
1–2. Student charts will vary.   **Draw Conclusions**
5 L per minute × 60 minutes per hour × 24 hours per
day = 7,200 L of blood pumped per day

104 Science in Your Life • The Activity Pyramid
1–2. Student charts will vary.   **Critical Thinking**
Most of a child's activity would be at the Lifestyle,
Aerobic, and Active levels. An older person's activity
would probably be mostly at the Lifestyle and Rest
levels.

105 Chapter 11 • Test A
A. 1. d **2.** b **3.** a **4.** e **5.** c **B. 6.** stomach
7. small intestine **8.** oxygen **9.** heart **10.** blood
vessels **Critical Thinking** Students might respond
that the heart beats faster during exercise and slower
during sleep.

106 Chapter 11 • Test B
1. a **2.** c **3.** b **4.** a **5.** b **6.** d **7.** c **8.** b **9.** d
10. b **Critical Thinking** Students might respond
that drugs, alcohol, or disease can cause the heart to
beat dangerously fast or slow.

Chapter 12 Staying Healthy

107 Words to Know
A. 1. d **2.** a **3.** c **4.** g **5.** e **6.** b **7.** f
B. 8. defense **9.** nutrition **10.** disease **11.** virus

108 Practice • Fighting Disease
A. 1. b **2.** a **3.** c **4.** a **B. 5.** disease **6.** defense
7. defense **8.** viruses **9.** viruses **Write About
Science** Students should respond that both fleas and
mosquitoes bite humans. The bacteria or protists that
cause the disease are transferred during the bite.

109 Practice • Nutrition
A. 1. The Food Guide Pyramid shows you which
foods in what amounts make up balanced meals.
2. Oils, fats, sweets **B. 3.** cholesterol **4.** water
5. carbohydrate **6.** protein **Write About Science**
Answers will vary. Some students might say that the
Food Guide Pyramid is based on grains and that other
countries have a commonly used grain. Different
countries have their own type of bread or
breadlike food.

110 Practice • Guarding Your Health

A. 1. False. Your heart is a muscle that needs to be exercised. **2.** True **3.** True **4.** False. It is harder for blood to flow through narrow blood vessels. **5.** False. Heart disease is the number one cause of death in the United States. **B. 6.** heart disease **7.** nicotine **8.** exercise, smoking **Write About Science** Answers will vary but should reflect an understanding of the health risk to the lungs and heart.

111 Challenge

1. It can lead to bad health habits such as experimenting with drugs, alcohol, smoking, and poor diet. **2.** For example, if a person's favorite movie star smokes, that person may start smoking to be more like the star. **3.** These conditions create a serious health risk for many people.

112 Another Way

A. 1. immune system or white blood cells **2.** white blood cells or immune system **3.** (defenses) **4.** not smoking or exercising **5.** exercising or not smoking **6.** vitamins or minerals or a healthy diet **7.** minerals or a healthy diet or vitamins **8.** a healthy diet or vitamins or minerals **B.** (in any order) **9.** Eat well **10.** Exercise regularly **11.** Get enough sleep

113 Lab Activity • Controlling Bacteria

Drawing Conclusions Answers will vary depending on the brands of medications used.

114 On-the-Job Science • Cafeteria Attendant

Student charts will vary. **Critical Thinking** Because meat is mostly protein and fat and contains no starch, it would not turn purple.

115 Chapter 12 • Test A

A. 1. b **2.** d **3.** e **4.** a **5.** c **B. 6.** nutrients **7.** Food Guide Pyramid **8.** nicotine **9.** defense **10.** HIV **Critical Thinking** White blood cells would surround the bacteria and try to break them down. Later, the skin would make a scar to heal the cut.

116 Chapter 12 • Test B

1. a **2.** c **3.** d **4.** c **5.** b **6.** b **7.** a **8.** d **9.** a **10.** a **Critical Thinking** Your body could develop heart disease or other kinds of disease related to muscles, blood vessels, or the heart.

Chapter 13 Depending on Each Other

117 Words to Know

A. 1. e **2.** f **3.** d **4.** c **5.** g **6.** b **7.** a **B. 8.** d **9.** b **10.** b **11.** a **C. 12.** food chain **13.** food web **14.** producers **15.** consumers **16.** decomposers

118 Practice • Living Together

A. 1. community **2.** population **3.** community **4.** habitat **5.** ecosystem **B. 6.** c **7.** a **8.** d **9.** a **10.** d **Write About Science** Student responses will vary. Some students may say that each grade, club, or team is a different population. The habitat may be the classroom or a playing field. Student comparisons will vary.

119 Practice • Using Nature's Resources

A. 1. b **2.** d **3.** f **4.** a **5.** g **6.** c **7.** e **B. 8.** False; limited **9.** False; Heat and pressure **10.** True **11.** False; conservation **12.** True **Write About Science** Water is used in life processes, cooking, washing, producing electricity, manufacturing, and transportation. Forests are used for construction, furniture, paper, fuel, and recreation. Fossil fuels are used to power vehicles, factories, and electric power plants. Water can be conserved by having full loads in washing machines or dishwashers. Conserving paper use can help save forests. Walking instead of driving, when possible, would help conserve fossil fuels. Accept all reasonable answers.

120 Challenge

1. Answers will vary. Examples include cans, buckets, and trash cans. **2.** Answers will vary. Examples include bottles, paper towels, and writing paper. **3.** Answers will vary. Examples include newspapers, cereal boxes, junk mail, shrink wrap from boxed products, aluminum and "tin" cans, plastic bottles, glass bottles, and jars. **4.** Answers will vary. **5.** Answers will vary.

121 Another Way

1. b **2.** d **3.** c **4.** a **5.** e **6.** f

122 Lab Activity • A Wormery

Draw Conclusions The worms may or may not be visible on the fourth day. The layers of the wormery will not be as easily seen by the fourth day. The action of the worms mixes the layers together. The worms are important in the food chain because they decompose and absorb matter.

123 Science in Your Life • Recycling Garbage

Student charts will vary. **Critical Thinking** The item could be purchased in a large quantity so that one large container is disposed of rather than several smaller ones.

124 Chapter 13 • Test A

A. 1. e **2.** a **3.** c **4.** f **5.** b **6.** d **B. 7.** natural resources **8.** fossil fuels **9.** solar energy **10.** oxygen **Critical Thinking** The middle link could be a cow, goat, or sheep.

125 Chapter 13 • Test B

1. a **2.** c **3.** a **4.** c **5.** d **6.** c **7.** c **8.** a **9.** b **10.** b **Critical Thinking** Student food chains will vary, but must include both plants and animals.

126 Extra Credit: Water Conservation

1. Taking a bath **2.** Fill the tub less full **3.** About 20 gallons **4.** Washing dishes **5.** Filling the sink instead of leaving the water running; rinsing in a sink full of water instead of under running water

Chapter 14 The Properties of Matter

127 Words to Know
Across: 2. property 3. gas 5. solution 6. density
9. compound 11. mixture Down: 1. physics
2. proton 4. solid 7. electron 8. liquid
10. neutron Unscramble: 12. chemistry

128 Practice • From Molecules to Matter
A. 1. nucleus 2. protons 3. positive 4. neutrons
5. electrons 6. negative B. 7. C 8. P 9. C 10. P
11. P 12. C C. 13. Ca 14. He 15. Zn 16. Ag
17. Al 18. Cu 19. C 20. Hg 21. S 22. Sn
Write About Science Descriptions might include
properties such as color, texture, length, mass, and
composition.

129 Practice • More About Matter
A. 1. air 2. cotton ball 3. comb 4. rock
B. 5. solid 6. solid 7. liquid 8. solid 9. liquid
10. gas 11. liquid 12. gas 13. solid 14. liquid
C. 15. mixture 16. compound 17. solution
18. mixture Write About Science Student
descriptions should indicate that molecules in a solid
vibrate in place. Molecules in a liquid are freer to
move around and slide past each other.

130 Challenge
2. Circle around 5 protons and 6 neutrons; 5 electrons
outside of nucleus 3. Circle around 3 protons and 4
neutrons; 3 electrons outside of nucleus 4. Circle
around 7 protons and 7 neutrons; 7 electrons outside
of nucleus

131 Another Way
1. protons 2. neutrons 3. electrons 4. solid
5. liquid 6. gas 7. ice 8. water 9. steam

132 Lab Activity • Part of the Solution
Draw Conclusions • Students should be able to see
a regular shape and color to the crystals. • Water
evaporates from the solution and crystals form on the
string. Salt produces cube-shaped crystals.

133 On-the-Job Science • Concrete Worker
Yes, it can be done. The reaction of sulfuric acid and
calcium carbonate in concrete is a balanced reaction.
There are the same number of elements before and
after the reaction. Critical Thinking Answers will
vary. Students might say that cars and factories should
be redesigned. Some students might mention using
electric cars, bicycles, or walking instead.

134 Chapter 14 • Test A
A. 1. d 2. c 3. a 4. e 5. b B. 6. gas 7. liquid
8. mixture 9. solid 10. electrons Critical
Thinking It is chemistry because it deals with matter
and how it reacts when it comes into contact with
other matter.

135 Chapter 14 • Test B
A. 1. c 2. b 3. c 4. b 5. b 6. c 7. b 8. a 9. a
10. d Critical Thinking It involves physics because
it deals with energy and how it interacts with matter.

Chapter 15 Energy and Matter

136 Words to Know
Across: 3. condensation 5. electrical 7. heat
8. light 9. fission Down: 1. kinetic 2. potential
3. chemical 4. nuclear 5. energy 6. mechanical
9. fusion

137 Practice • Energy in All Things
1. potential 2. kinetic 3. potential 4. kinetic
5. kinetic 6. kinetic 7. potential 8. kinetic

138 Practice • The Different Forms of Energy
A. 1. c 2. f 3. a 4. e 5. b 6. d B. 7. nuclear
fission 8. nuclear fusion 9. nuclear fusion
10. nuclear fission Write About Science Answers
will vary. Check student answers for scientific
accuracy. Sample answer: I used light energy to be
able to see. I could see how to get ready for school,
how to go to school, and I could read books.

139 Practice • Changing Matter Using Energy
A. 1. physical change 2. chemical change
3. chemical change 4. chemical change 5. physical
change 6. physical change B. In general, student
answers will reflect that physical changes can be
reversed and chemical changes cannot. The vase can
be glued together, and the building could be rebuilt.
The most obviously reversible change is melted ice
refreezing. C. 7. melting 8. freezing
9. evaporation 10. condensation

140 Challenge
Check student graphs for accuracy. Write About
Science Oxygen is a gas at room temperature and
above. It must be cooled to a very low temperature in
order for it to change from a gas to a liquid. The
temperature at which it changes from a gas to a liquid
is the same as its boiling point.

141 Another Way
1a. (Natural gas) 1b. (22%) 2a. Oil 2b. 40%
3a. Coal 3b. 22% 4a. Nuclear power 4b. 7%
5a. Water and other renewable resources 5b. 9%
6. oil 7. 84%

142 Lab Activity • Is Energy Absorbed or
Released?
Student tables will vary. Draw Conclusions
• Bubbles formed. • Rise • Energy was released
because the temperature before the chemical change
was lower.

143 Science in Your Life • Calories and Energy
1. 60; 480 2. 108 3. Playing basketball because it
uses more calories than walking does 4. 40 5. 21
Critical Thinking Burning involves the changing of
chemical energy into heat energy. When the body
uses calories, the chemical energy in the calories also
is changed into heat energy.

144 Chapter 15 • Test A
A. 1. energy 2. potential 3. kinetic 4. light
5. heat B. 6. b 7. d 8. e 9. a 10. c Critical
Thinking Melting is changing from a solid to a
liquid, and freezing is changing from a liquid to
a solid.

145 Chapter 15 • Test B
1. b **2.** d **3.** b **4.** c **5.** d **6.** d **7.** c **8.** a **9.** c
10. b **Critical Thinking** Evaporation is changing from a liquid to a gas. Condensation is changing from a gas to a liquid.

Chapter 16 Force and Motion

146 Words to Know
A. 1. f **2.** e **3.** h **4.** b **5.** a **6.** g **7.** d **8.** c
B.

```
e  g  l (f  o  r  c  e) m  t  i  e  x  i  n  f
l  b  i  r  a  g  r  p  w  o (w  r  t  n  g  r
(l  u  b  r  i  c  a  n  t) b  e  s  o  e  e  e
d  s  e  c  h  k  i (m  o  t  i  o  n) r  l  m
e  r  t  t  d  s  l  c  e  a  g  i  f  t  z  y
r  p (f  r  i  c  t  i  o  n) h  j  a  i  k  g
z  i  e  p  w (g  r  a  v  i  t  y) l  a  l  o
(c  e  n  t  r  i  p  e  t  a  l  f  o  r  c  e)
```

147 Practice • What Is Force?
A. 1. c **2.** a **3.** d **4.** b **5.** c **6.** a **B. 7.** b **8.** d **9.** c **10.** a **Write About Science** Mass is the total amount of matter in an object. Mass never changes, as long as the amount of matter remains the same. Weight is a measure of the pull of gravity on an object. Weight increases when the pull of gravity increases and decreases when the pull of gravity decreases. An example of mass would be a person having the same mass on the moon as on Earth. An example of weight would be that person weighing less on the moon as on Earth because the moon has less gravity.

148 Practice • Inertia and Motion
A. 1. False. Sir Isaac Newton figured out the law of inertia. **2.** True **3.** False. An object at rest shows a complete lack of motion. **4.** False. A large rock rolling down a hill has more inertia than a small rock. **5.** False. Motion is the change in the position or place of an object. **6.** True **B. 7.** inertia **8.** rest **9.** motion **10.** force **11.** matter **12.** mass

149 Challenge
1. 40 miles per hour **2.** 60 miles/1 hour; 60 miles per hour **3.** 10 miles/5 hours; 2 miles per hour **4.** 5 miles/1 hour; 5 miles per hour **5.** 150 miles/3 hours; 50 miles per hour **6.** 100 yards/100 seconds; 1 yard per second **Write About Science** When talking about very high speeds, larger units of distance and smaller units of time are usually used. An example includes the speed of light, which is expressed in units of miles or kilometers per second. When talking about very slow speeds, smaller units of distance and larger units of time are used. For example, the rate of continental drift is expressed in inches or centimeters per year.

150 Another Way
Technically, all the forces apply to each picture, but some are more clearly illustrated than the others.
1. centripetal **2.** gravity **3.** gravity **4.** friction **5–6.** inertia and friction **7–8.** friction and gravity

151 Lab Activity • Applying Force
Measurements will vary depending on the size of the washers and the thickness of the rubber band. Sample data is shown below.

Washers	Total Mass Hanging From Paper Clip (in grams)	Length of Rubber Band (in cm)
0	0	7.6 cm
1	19	8.0 cm
2	38	8.4 cm
3	57	8.8 cm
4	76	9.2 cm
5	95	9.6 cm

Draw Conclusions The more washers that are added, the longer the rubber band stretches.

152 On-the-Job Science • Truck Driver
1. $243 \times 2 = 486$ feet **2.** $666 \times 2 = 1,332$ feet **3.** $366 \times 3 = 1,098$ feet **4.** $431 \times 3 = 1,293$ feet **Critical Thinking** There is less friction on a snow-covered road because tires make no contact with the road, only the slippery snow. On a wet road, tires make some contact with the road and some contact with the slippery water.

153 Chapter 16 • Test A
A. 1. force **2.** gravity **3.** weight **4.** fluid friction **5.** centripetal force **B. 6.** d **7.** c **8.** a **9.** e **10.** b **Critical Thinking** Answers will vary. Examples of fluid friction include soap suds sliding with water down the drain; a boat moving on the water; and a plane, ball, or other object sailing through the air. Examples of sliding friction include walking on the floor or on ice, dragging something across the floor, and playing a game such as shuffleboard. Examples of rolling friction include the movement of bikes or any other wheeled vehicles, playing games such as bowling or billiards, and seeing something roll across a table or other flat surface.

154 Chapter 16 • Test B
1. c **2.** a **3.** d **4.** b **5.** b **6.** c **7.** a **8.** d **9.** b **10.** b **Critical Thinking** Answers will vary. Paragraphs should describe the force that sets an object in motion, the inertia that keeps it in motion, and the friction that must be overcome or eventually will bring the object to a stop.

Chapter 17 Machines at Work

155 Words to Know
A. 1. load **2.** work **3.** mechanical advantage **4.** effort force **5.** machine **6.** resistance force **B. 7.** c **8.** e **9.** g **10.** d **11.** a **12.** b **13.** f

156 Practice • All Kinds of Work

A. 1. work **2.** speed or direction **3.** direction or speed **4.** force **5.** simple machines **B. 6.** c **7.** a **8.** b **9.** a **10.** b **Write About Science** Paragraphs will vary but should reflect the following: (1) Effort force is the force applied by the rider. (2) Resistance force could be a combination of friction, gravity, and wind. (3) The load is the combination of the weight of the bike and the rider.

157 Practice • Simple and Compound Machines

A. 1. e **2.** d **3.** a **4.** b **5.** b **6.** c **7.** e **8.** b **B. 9.** True **10.** False. A wedge is two inclined planes back to back. **11.** False. A compound machine is made of two or more simple machines. **Write About Science** A can opener is made up of a lever, wheels and axles, and a wedge. The lever squeezes the blade, which is one wheel and axle, into the lid. Another wheel and axle turns the can, while the wedge cuts the lid off. A bicycle is made up of wheels and axles and levers. The wheels and axles allow the rider to pedal the bicycle and the bicycle to move. The brakes are levers that squeeze together to stop the wheels of the bicycle.

158 Challenge

1. a. 609 **b.** 580 **c.** Shawna **2. a.** 6 **b.** 12 **c.** It would double the amount of work.

159 Another Way

1. seesaw **2.** nutcracker **3.** baseball bat **4.** flagpole **5.** doorknob **6.** screw

160 Lab Activity • Why Is the Screw a Simple Machine?

3. An inclined plane **5.** A screw **Draw Conclusions** A screw is an inclined plane wrapped around a cylinder.

161 Science in Your Life • Machines as Tools

1. shovel **2.** lever or wedge **3.** wedge or lever **4.** faucet **5.** screw **6.** flagpole **7.** pulley **8.** wheelbarrow **9.** wheel and axle or lever **10.** lever or wheel and axle **11.** clippers **12.** lever or wedge **13.** wedge or lever **Critical Thinking** The flagpole makes work easier by changing the direction of the force. It does so by allowing a worker to pull down in order to raise something.

162 Chapter 17 • Test A

A. 1. machines **2.** resistance force **3.** gravity **4.** mechanical advantage **5.** wedge, screw **6.** pulley **B. 7.** a **8.** c **9.** d **10.** b **Critical Thinking** Answers will vary, but simple machines may include wedges (saw, nail, wood screw, chisel), levers (hammer, paintbrush), screws (drill, vise, wood screw). Compound machines may include a power drill, a belt sander, and a power saw.

163 Chapter 17 • Test B

1. c **2.** a **3.** b **4.** d **5.** b **6.** a **7.** b **8.** a **9.** c **10.** b **Critical Thinking** Answers will vary, but simple machines may include wedges (saw, nail, wood

screw, chisel), levers (hammer, paintbrush), screws (drill, vise, wood screw).

164 Extra Credit: Fishing Machines

1. Pulley **2.** Class 1 levers **3.** Screw **4.** Wedge **5.** Fishing rods, net **6.** Reels, anchor pulley

Chapter 18 Heat, Light, and Sound

165 Words to Know

1. insulator **2.** amplitude **3.** wavelength **4.** conduction **5.** convection **6.** radiation **7.** vacuum **8.** prism **9.** spectrum

166 Practice • Heat and Matter

A. 1. atoms **2.** kinetic **3.** total **4.** average **B. 5.** b **6.** c **7.** a **8.** d **9.** b **Write About Science** When warm air meets cold air, the cold air pushes under the warm air and the warm air rises. A convection current is formed. No, the same thing does not happen in space because there is no air.

167 Practice • Light

A. 1. b **2.** c **3.** a **B. 4.** False. The wavelength is the distance from the crest or trough of one wave to the crest or trough of the next wave. **5.** False. The number of wave cycles that pass through a point in one second is a wave's frequency. **6.** True **C. 7.** bent **8.** white light **9.** reflects **10.** prism

168 Practice • Sound

A. 1. True **2.** False. When your vocal cords vibrate, the surrounding air vibrates. **3.** False. The result of vibrating vocal cords is a sound wave. **B. 4.** amplitude **5.** sound wave **6.** vibrate **Write About Science** You would see the explosion because light waves travel through the vacuum of space. You would not hear the explosion because sound waves cannot travel through a vacuum.

169 Challenge

1. Yes, the boy can hear the ticking just as well as the girl can because the tube traps the sound waves and keeps them from spreading out and losing energy. **2.** No, the girl must use the cups and string to allow the sound waves of the boy's whisper to travel from one cup to the other. **3.** They both trap sound waves, preventing them from losing energy. Thus, the sound remains loud enough to hear, even at a distance.

170 Another Way

1. convection **2.** radiation **3.** refraction **4.** conduction **5.** reflection **6.** sound waves **Write About Science** Heat and sound travel through solids by moving molecules. Heat travels through a solid by means of conduction. In conduction, warm molecules pass their heat along by bumping into cooler molecules. Sound waves travel through a solid when molecules pass their vibrations along to one another.

171 Lab Activity • Sound and Vibrations

2. The thinner rubber band makes a high sound; the wider rubber band makes a low sound. **Draw Conclusions** • The wider rubber band produced a lower sound because it produced sound waves with a lower frequency. • Yes. Faster vibrations make sound waves with higher frequencies. Holding the rubber band in different places made the amount of rubber band vibrating shorter or longer. A shorter length of rubber band vibrates faster than a longer length does.

172 On-the-Job Science • Bar Codes
The bar code identifier would be most helpful in distinguishing between the canisters of flour and sugar; the canisters of brown rice and white rice; the two boxes of cereal; and the hand soap and dish soap. **Critical Thinking** Bar codes can be used to identify each book at the library. They can also be used on people's library cards. That way, when a person checks out a book, his or her library card can be scanned into the computer along with the book being checked out. This is a good way to keep track of the library's books.

173 Chapter 18 • Test A
A. 1. c **2.** a **3.** e **4.** b **5.** d **B. 6.** total **7.** convection **8.** vacuum **9.** amplitudes **10.** absorbed **Critical Thinking** It is harder to see colors in dim light because less light is reflected off the objects.

174 Chapter 18 • Test B
1. c **2.** a **3.** c **4.** b **5.** d **6.** c **7.** a **8.** d **9.** b **10.** a **Critical Thinking** An object appears white when it reflects all the colors in the spectrum. An object appears black when it absorbs all the colors in the spectrum. White could be considered a color because all the colors are being reflected. Therefore, all the colors can be seen. Black probably is not a color because no colors are being reflected. Therefore, no color can be seen.

Chapter 19 Electricity and Magnetism

175 Words to Know
Across: 3. fuse **6.** discharge **9.** static **10.** insulator **11.** battery **Down: 1.** generator **2.** conductor **4.** electricity **5.** circuit **7.** field **8.** magnet

176 Practice • All Charged Up
A. 1. False. Electricity is caused by the movement of electrons. **2.** True **3.** False. Things that have opposite charges attract each other. **B. 4.** static electricity **5.** thunder **6.** discharge **7.** neutral **8.** electricity **9.** lightning **Write About Science** Electrons from the atoms in the sweater rub off onto the atoms in the balloon. The sweater now has fewer electrons than protons. It will have a positive charge. The balloon will have more electrons than protons. It will have a negative charge. The negatively charged balloon is attracted to the positively charged sweater. Static electricity holds them together.

177 Practice • Electrical Currents
A. 1. electrical insulator **2.** electrical conductor **3.** electrical insulator **4.** electrical insulator **5.** electrical conductor **6.** electrical insulator **7.** electrical conductor **B. 8.** electrons **9.** chemical **10.** electrical **11.** generator **12.** mechanical or heat

13. heat or mechanical **Write About Science** Electrical wiring is usually made from metal coated with rubber or plastic. The metal part conducts electricity. The rubber or plastic coating acts as an insulator to protect people from the electricity running through the wire inside.

178 Practice • Electrical Circuits
A. 1. circuits **2.** filament **3.** open **4.** closed **5.** overloaded **B. 6.** False. Electrons move from the negative end of a battery to the positive end. **7.** True **8.** False. Electrons cannot flow through a circuit without a source of energy.

179 Practice • Magnetism
A. 1. magnet **2.** poles **3.** magnetic field **4.** repel **5.** attract **B. 6.** False. Lodestones are attracted to each other and to iron. **7.** True **8.** False. Iron, nickel, and cobalt are three elements with strong magnetism. **9.** True **10.** True **Write About Science** Iron and steel become magnetized when a magnet touches then for a long time. This means their electrons have lined up. This suggests that magnets affect iron and steel by changing the position of their electrons.

180 Challenge
1. parallel **2.** series **3.** series **4.** parallel **5.** parallel **6.** series

181 Another Way
A. 1. d **2.** c **3.** f **4.** e **5.** b **6.** a **B. 7.** 6 **8.** 2 **9.** 5 **10.** 3 **11.** 4 **12.** 1

182 Lab Activity • Observing Magnetic Fields
Draw Conclusions If the like poles of the magnets face each other, the two magnetic fields will remain separate. (Iron filings will line up between the north and south poles of each magnet.) If the opposite poles of the magnets face each other, the magnetic fields will combine. (Iron filings will line up between the north pole of one magnet and the south pole of the other.)

183 Science in Your Life • Using Electricity
1. 5,108 kWh **2.** 4,624 kWh **3.** 5,109 kWh **4.** $430 **5.** $370 **6.** $60 **Critical Thinking** Answers will vary. A buyer must weigh the initial cost of an appliance against the long-term cost of using the appliance.

184 Chapter 19 • Test A
A. 1. e **2.** d **3.** a **4.** c **5.** b **B. 6.** fuse **7.** static electricity **8.** battery **9.** circuit **10.** magnetic field **Critical Thinking** First, a cloud builds up a lot of electrons. This gives it a large negative charge. The electrons in the cloud are attracted to something on the ground with a positive charge. The electrons then jump to that object with a discharge of electricity. This causes a large flash of light and a loud boom.

185 Chapter 19 • Test B
1. c **2.** a **3.** d **4.** b **5.** a **6.** c **7.** b **8.** d **9.** b **10.** a **Critical Thinking** Clothes in the dryer stick together because one of the pieces of clothing builds

up a lot of electrons. This gives it a negative charge. The electrons in one piece of clothing are attracted to another piece of clothing with a positive charge. When the pieces of clothing are pulled apart, the electrons from one jump to the other with a discharge of electricity. This causes tiny sparks and crackling noises.

Chapter 20 Energy Resources

186 Words to Know
A. 1. turbine **2.** geyser **3.** nuclear reactor **4.** solar collector **5.** hydroelectric energy **6.** geothermal energy **7.** radioactive **B. 8.** e **9.** c **10.** g **11.** b **12.** a **13.** d **14.** f

187 Practice • Fossil Fuels
A. 1. a **2.** c **3.** b **4.** a **B. 5.** fossil fuels **6.** less **7.** gasoline **8.** insulation **Write About Science** Stories will vary. Make sure students' stories reflect the understanding that staying warm requires energy and that insulation helps save energy by keeping heat in and cold out.

188 Practice • Other Energy Resources
A. 1. False. A nuclear reactor splits atoms to produce energy. **2.** True **3.** True **4.** False. Solar energy causes little pollution. **5.** False. A turbine is a machine with blades that turn when moving water hits the blades. **B. 6.** steam **7.** generators **8.** geothermal **9.** ocean

189 Challenge
1. F **2.** O **3.** F **4.** F **5.** F **6.** F **7.** O **8.** F **9.** F **10.** O **11.** F **12.** O **13.** O **14.** F **15.** O

190 Another Way
1. Energy source: steam; Benefit: no pollution; Problem: not available everywhere **2.** Energy source: the sun; Benefit: unlimited or clean; Problem: expensive **3.** Energy source: nuclear fission; Benefit: tremendous amounts of energy; Problem: Wastes pollute. **4.** Energy source: wind; Benefit: does not pollute; Problem: Locations are limited.

191 Lab Activity • Absorbing Solar Energy
Students charts will vary. **Draw Conclusions** • oil • water • This happened because there are more particles in oil than in water.

192 On-the-Job Science • Nuclear Reactor Operator
1. (260°C) **2.** 270°C **3.** 275°C **4.** 280°C **5.** 285°C Students' arrows on the gauges should point to the temperatures above.

193 Chapter 20 • Test A
A. 1. d **2.** c **3.** a **4.** b **B. 5.** plastics, gasoline **6.** radioactive **7.** nuclear fusion **8.** solar **9.** hydroelectric **10.** winds, tides, hot rocks **Critical Thinking** For tidal energy locations, students should select places that are located on an ocean. For solar energy locations, students should select places where there is more sunlight and the sky is clear.

194 Chapter 20 • Test B
1. c **2.** a **3.** b **4.** c **5.** d **6.** a **7.** d **8.** d **9.** a **10.** a **Critical Thinking** Solar energy is made by using solar collectors to turn the energy from the sun into heat energy. Energy from ocean tides uses the rise and fall of ocean water to produce energy. Answers to the second part of the question will vary, depending on where students live. Accept reasonable answers that take into account the availability of the energy source mentioned.

Chapter 21 Planet Earth

195 Words to Know
A. 1. longitude **2.** latitude **3.** equator **4.** orbit **5.** prime meridian **6.** globe **B. 7.** crust **8.** mantle **9.** core **10.** axis **11.** continent

196 Practice • Spaceship Earth
A. 1. b **2.** a **3.** d **4.** a **B. 5.** planets **6.** spaceship **7.** third **8.** pull **Write About Science** The Earth is like a spaceship because it travels through space and has people on it. It has air, water, and food to support people. Accept other reasonable similarities.

197 Practice • Features of the Earth
A. 1. c **2.** b **3.** e **4.** a **5.** d **B. 6.** False. The Earth revolves around the sun in about one year. **7.** True **8.** False. Because the Earth spins from west to east, the sun rises in the east. **9.** False. The Earth's outer mantle moves like thick molasses. **10.** True **Write About Science** Continents: Africa, Asia, Antarctica, Australia, Europe, North America, South America; Facts: They are all large landmasses. Asia has the highest and the lowest points on Earth. Mountains, plains, deserts, and islands are found on or near the surface of the continents. Oceans: Arctic, Atlantic, Indian, Pacific; Facts: They are all connected. They are all made of salt water.

198 Practice • Dividing Up the Earth
A. 1. 24 **2.** 15 **3.** 15 **4.** 1 **5.** 4 **B. 6.** c **7.** b **8.** a **9.** d **10.** b **Write About Science** Jet lag happens because your body is used to sleeping at a certain time every day. When you travel to a different time zone, your body's "clock" no longer matches the time of day. For example, suppose you live in the Eastern time zone and your usual bedtime is 11 P.M. If you were to travel to the Pacific time zone, which is three hours behind the Eastern time zone, you might feel like going to bed at 8 P.M.

199 Challenge
1. 1.002 **2.** Globe 1: 1.006. Globe 2: 1.007. Ball: 1.002 **3.** The ball has a roundness ratio of 1.002, which is closest to the Earth's ratio. **4.** 1.0

200–201 Another Way
2. Asia, South America, Africa **3.** Europe, Africa **4.** Arctic Ocean **5.** The western boundary is about 127 degrees west longitude; the eastern boundary is about 60 degrees west longitude. **6.** About 58 degrees south latitude, 67 degrees west longitude **7.** Africa **8.** Accept any figure between 20 and 25. **9.** Australia

202 Lab Activity • Making a Model of the Earth
Draw Conclusions • A model can turn a concept into something you can see and hold. This often makes the concept easier to understand. • Accept any reasonable answers for what students learned about the Earth by making a model of its layers.

203 Science in Your Life • Topographic Maps
1. Parallel lines **2.** Numbers will vary. The number on the contour line tells you how high the land is at that point. **3.** School. The elevation of the school is over 1,250. The elevation of the airport is about 500. **4.** Difficult. You would be walking up a steep hill. **Critical Thinking** If a bicyclist wanted to avoid steep terrain, he or she could use a topographic map to plan the route.

204 Chapter 21 • Test A
A. 1. b **2.** c **3.** a **4.** d **B. 5.** core **6.** crust **7.** rotation **8.** revolution **9.** latitude **10.** longitude
Critical Thinking Rotation is one complete turn of a planet on its axis. Revolution is one full orbit of a planet around the sun. Planets used as examples will vary.

205 Chapter 21 • Test B
1. b **2.** a **3.** b **4.** c **5.** d **6.** b **7.** a **8.** b **9.** c **10.** c **Critical Thinking** Lines of latitude run east and west around the globe and measure distances north and south of the equator. Lines of latitude are parallel to one another. This means they never touch. Lines of longitude run north and south around the globe. They measure distances east and west of the prime meridian. All the lines of latitude and longitude cross at the North and South poles. Spots on the Earth will vary.

Chapter 22 The Earth's Crust

206 Words to Know
A. 1. f **2.** g **3.** d **4.** e **5.** b **6.** a **7.** c
B. 8. glacier **9.** erosion **10.** metamorphic **11.** weathering **12.** soil **13.** sedimentary **14.** igneous **15.** granite

207 Practice • Plate Tectonics
A. 1. crust **2.** plates **3.** earthquakes **4.** trench **5.** mountains **B. 6.** b **7.** c **8.** b **9.** b **10.** d
Write About Science Answers should include the idea that many small earthquakes could show increased activity leading to a larger one.

208 Practice • Rocks and Minerals
a. pumice **b.** obsidian **c.** basalt **d.** granite **Write About Science** Granite forms underground. Movement in the Earth's crust could have pushed it to the surface, or weathering and erosion could have removed soil and rock above it.

209 Challenge

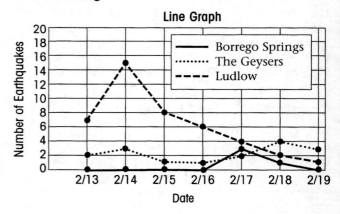

1. Ludlow **2.** Borrego Springs **3.** Monday, 2/14 **4.** Saturday, 2/19

210 Another Way
1. plate movements **2.** earthquakes **3.** trenches or mountains **4.** mountains or trenches **5.** volcanoes

211 Lab Activity • Identifying Minerals
Samples from top to bottom of chart: sulfur, milky quartz, talc, magnetite, hornblende **Draw Conclusions** • Minerals often share properties. Looking at several properties lets you identify minerals by finding a property they do not share. • You can identify minerals by examining their color, hardness, and specific gravity. Some students may say that the feel of a mineral or its habitat can also help to identify it.

212 On-the-Job Science • Geologist
Igneous: granite, obsidian Sedimentary: sandstone, coal Metamorphic: marble, slate **Critical Thinking** The Earth's crust would contain more granite because 95 percent of the Earth's crust is made of igneous rock.

213 Chapter 22 • Test A
A. 1. plate tectonics **2.** mantle **3.** geologist **4.** earthquake **5.** volcano **6.** lava **7.** metamorphic
B. 8. c **9.** a **10.** b **Critical Thinking** Movements in the Earth's crust can bury sedimentary rock deposits. The sedimentary rock can then be heated and squeezed deep in the crust, changing it to metamorphic rock.

214 Chapter 22 • Test B
1. d **2.** a **3.** a **4.** d **5.** a **6.** c **7.** b **8.** c **9.** c
10. b **Critical Thinking** Erosion or weathering and deposits of broken down rock into compacted layers can cause igneous rock to become sedimentary rock.

Chapter 23 The Earth's Atmosphere

215 Words to Know
1. mesosphere **2.** atmosphere **3.** barometer **4.** precipitation **5.** dew point **6.** cirrus cloud **7.** stratosphere **8.** stratus cloud

216 Practice • Air All Around Us

A. 1. troposphere **2.** stratosphere **3.** mesosphere **4.** ionosphere **5.** thermosphere **B. 6.** ionosphere **7.** troposphere **8.** thermosphere **9.** stratosphere **10.** mesosphere **Write About Science** Answers should note that special clothing is needed to supply the astronaut with oxygen and keep the astronaut warm.

217 Practice • Properties of Air

Caption 1: Caption should indicate that the land heats up faster than the ocean. **Caption 2:** Caption should indicate that air over the land becomes warm and rises. **Caption 3:** Caption should indicate that the cool air over the ocean rushes in toward land.

218 Practice • Water and Air

A. 1. precipitation **2.** frozen **3.** snow **4.** hail **5.** sleet **B. 6.** b **7.** a **8.** b or c (Accept either answer or both.) **9.** c **10.** a **11.** c **12.** b **Write About Science** Water enters the air by evaporating off the ground, lakes, oceans, rivers, plants, and animals. Water falls from the atmosphere in different forms: rain, snow, sleet, and hail.

219 Challenge

1. c **2.** a **3.** b **Write About Science** Airplane travelers experience a change in air pressure just like mountain climbers. The popping is the body's way of adjusting to the change in air pressure.

220 Another Way

1. troposphere **2.** stratosphere **3.** mesosphere **4.** ionosphere **5.** thermosphere **6.** cirrus clouds or stratus clouds **7.** stratus clouds or cirrus clouds **8.** frozen **9.** hail **10.** rain

221 Lab Activity • Wind Systems

Draw Conclusions • The balloon inflated. • Heat from the hair dryer warmed the air inside of the bottle. The air molecules spread out, and the air became less dense. It moved upward into the balloon. • The change would not have occurred without heating the bottle. Without a source of heat, the air molecules would have kept their original position. • The hair dryer represents the sun. The air in the bottle represents air in the atmosphere. As the sun warms air, the air rises. Cool air takes its place. This moving air is wind.

222 Science in Your Life • Wind Chill Temperature

Student drawings will vary. **Critical Thinking** Students should explain how each part of their design helps stop heat loss.

223 Chapter 23 • Test A

A. 1. d **2.** a **3.** e **4.** b **5.** c **B. 6.** precipitation **7.** air pressure **8.** dew point **9.** humidity **10.** barometer **Critical Thinking** Cumulus and stratus clouds are both made of water droplets. Cumulus clouds are big, puffy low-altitude clouds that usually signal good weather. Stratus clouds are low-lying gray clouds that often signal rainy weather.

224 Chapter 23 • Test B

1. b **2.** c **3.** d **4.** a **5.** c **6.** a **7.** b **8.** d **9.** c **10.** b **Critical Thinking** Cirrus clouds are made of ice crystals, while cumulus clouds are made of water droplets. Cirrus clouds are feathery high-altitude clouds. They are bright white and usually seen in the mountains. Cumulus clouds are big, puffy low-altitude clouds that usually signal good weather.

Chapter 24 Weather and Climate

225 Words to Know

1. typhoon **2.** hurricane **3.** cyclone **4.** tornado **5.** c **6.** d **7.** a **8.** g **9.** e **10.** b **11.** f

226 Practice • Air on the Move

A. 1. Density. These make up the weather. **2.** Water front. These form where air masses meet. **3.** Lava flows. These happen at cold fronts. **4.** Telescope. These are used by meteorologists to forecast the weather. **B. 5.** It is a huge body of air that moves from place to place. **6.** Clouds and precipitation are common. **7.** It forms when a cold front overtakes a warm front. **8.** They use computers to collect and process data and to make models of weather systems. Computers also help meteorologists make maps to forecast weather.

227 Practice • Storms

A. Red should shade the tropical areas of the Atlantic; blue should shade the tropical areas of the Pacific; green should shade the central part of the United States in the Mississippi Valley and the Great Plains. **B. 1.** False. Hurricanes get energy from warm, tropical ocean water. **2.** True **3.** False. Wind is air that moves from high pressure to low-pressure areas. **4.** True **Write About Science** Accept either choice as long as it is supported reasonably. Hurricanes may be considered more dangerous because their effects can last for days and cover wide areas. Severe flooding also may occur. Tornadoes may be considered more dangerous because they are extremely violent and often strike with less advance warning than hurricanes do.

228 Practice • The Earth's Climate Zones

1–4. Polar Climate: huge icebergs; polar bears; short, cool summers; much of ground always frozen **5–8.** Temperate Climate: wool winter coats, summer T-shirts; leaves fall in autumn; greatest climate change between seasons; not the coldest or hottest climate **9–12.** Tropical Climate: outdoor swimming all year; longest growing season for crops; no cold winter; world's hottest climate **Write About Science** Answers will vary, but students must offer reasons for their choice. For example, some students might think it is harder to live in a polar climate because the cold and snow make it hard to keep warm and get around. Other students might think a tropical climate is harder because the heat makes outdoor activity difficult.

229 Challenge

1. High pressure **2.** The weather in New York should be clear and dry because it is in an area of high pressure. **3.** An area in between **4.** Cloudy skies; rain just passed. The weather should clear within the next day or so. **5.** Answers will vary according to location. **6.** Answers will vary according to location. Note that weather systems move from west to east. Places in or east of high-pressure areas can expect clear weather. Places in or east of low-pressure areas can expect stormy weather.

230 Another Way

1. warm front **2.** rain **3.** sunny **4.** cold front **5.** snow **6.** Kansas City **7.** It will become rainy.

231 Lab Activity • The Greenhouse Effect

Draw Conclusions • The thermometer in the bags has a higher temperature. The plastic bags help to hold in the heat. • The temperatures went down. The temperature of the thermometer in the open changed more. The temperature dropped more quickly. This happens because there was no plastic bag around it to help hold in heat. • The gases in the plastic bags let in sunlight, but they trap heat inside next to the thermometer. This is similar to the atmosphere, which lets in sunlight but traps heat radiated from the ground.

232 On-the-Job Science • Meteorologist

1. It is hot all year. **2.** It is cold in winter and warm in summer. **3.** City A **4.** City B

233 Chapter 24 • Test A

A. 1. c **2.** d **3.** e **4.** b **5.** a **B. 6.** warm **7.** temperate **8.** thunderstorms **9.** wind **10.** stormy **Critical Thinking** Answers should reflect the understanding that changes in temperature and precipitation occur at fronts. The location of a front tells forecasters what the weather in front of and behind the front will be as it passes.

234 Chapter 24 • Test B

1. d **2.** c **3.** a **4.** c **5.** c **6.** a **7.** b **8.** a **9.** b **10.** a **Critical Thinking** Answers should reflect the understanding that these systems determine weather in an area. Lows bring stormy weather, and highs bring clear weather.

Chapter 25 The Earth's History

235 Words to Know

Across: 2. Precambrian **4.** geological **5.** Cenozoic **6.** uplifting **7.** Paleozoic **Down: 1.** Mesozoic **3.** radioactive

236 Practice • The Story in the Rocks

1. The layer on the bottom (layer A) is the oldest. Layers of rock that have not been shifted by uplifting and folding are arranged by age, with the oldest at the bottom and the youngest at the top. **2.** Rock B is older. The amount of the radioactive element used for dating in the rock decreases as the rock ages and the element decays. So, the rock with less of the element is older. **Write About Science** Rocks are often the

only evidence of ancient life or the Earth's past environments.

237 Practice • Geological Time

1. Cenozoic **2.** Precambrian **3.** Mesozoic **4.** Paleozoic **5.** Paleozoic **6.** Precambrian **7.** Precambrian **8.** Paleozoic **9.** Mesozoic **10.** Cenozoic **11.** Precambrian **12.** Paleozoic **13.** Cenozoic **14.** Mesozoic **Write About Science** Answers will vary. Accept all reasonable responses including those based on speculation in the text concerning new ice ages, pollution that will cause climate shifts, or an asteroid or comet strike that will wipe out many or most life forms.

238 Challenge

1. b **2.** I. A. and B. Details can include: longest geological era; some granite and marble from this era; few fossils; signs of early plant life and bacteria as well as fossil worm tunnels have been found II. A. and B. Details may include: Age of Invertebrates and Marine Life; fossils of jellyfish, sponges, snails, seaweed, and ferns found; many coal beds formed; the Earth was warm and wet with many swamps where giant ferns grew; mountain ranges such as the Appalachians formed III. A. and B. Details may include: Age of Reptiles; flowering plants replaced ferns; many kinds of dinosaurs lived; the Earth was dry at start of era; many volcanic eruptions; Sierra Nevadas and Coast Ranges of California formed; dinosaurs became extinct by end of era IV. A. and B. Details may include: Age of Mammals and Birds; several ice ages; humans appeared

239 Another Way

Sequence of colors in the graph from bottom to top: green, red, black, blue **1.** Cenozoic **2.** Mesozoic **3.** Paleozoic **4.** Precambrian **5.** Cenozoic **6.** Mesozoic **7.** Precambrian **8.** Paleozoic

240 Lab Activity • Uplifting and Folding

Draw Conclusions • Students should see folds of various types. • Predictions will vary. • The clay layers were pushed together and folded by the wooden blocks the way rock layers are pushed together and folded by movements in the Earth's crust.

241 Science in Your Life • Going on Dino Digs

1. B **2.** D **3.** C **4.** A **Critical Thinking** We can guess what dinosaurs ate by their teeth, claws, and body structure. We might also guess what they ate by where they lived.

242 Chapter 25 • Test A

1. uplifting **2.** radioactive dating **3.** geological eras **4.** extinctions **5.** Precambrian **6.** Paleozoic **7.** Mesozoic **8.** Cenozoic **9.** Africa **10.** sun **Critical Thinking** Charts should reflect the idea that there were bacteria and simple plants and animals in the Precambrian era. Life forms became more complex in the Paleozoic era, with the appearance of more types of invertebrates, marine life, and large ferns.

243 Chapter 25 • Test B
1. b **2.** a **3.** b **4.** d **5.** c **6.** d **7.** c **8.** b **9.** d
10. c **Critical Thinking** Charts should reflect the idea that the Mesozoic era was the Age of Reptiles when dinosaurs were dominant and when flowering plants replaced ferns. Birds and mammals, including humans, appeared in the Cenozoic era. Humans became dominant and remain dominant today.

Chapter 26 The Earth's Oceans

244 Words to Know
A. 1. c **2.** a **3.** d **4.** b **B. 5.** tide **6.** mid-ocean ridge **7.** seismic sea wave **8.** continental shelf **9.** undertow **10.** ocean basin **11.** continental slope

245 Practice • Features of the Ocean
A. 1. shallow water, people swimming from shore **2.** signs of sea-floor spreading, magma seeping out **3.** no light, very deep water **4.** mostly flat sea floor, trenches **B.** Dead Sea, Atlantic Ocean, Mississippi River **C.** wave, Gulf Stream, Gulf Stream system
Write About Science Some students may think exploration of the ocean is more important because it is here on Earth and affects life on our planet. Other students may think exploration of outer space is more exciting and teaches us a lot about the universe. Accept all reasonable answers.

246 Practice • Waves and Tides
A. 1. low tide; the water is as low as it gets close to shore **2.** high tide; the water is as high as it gets close to shore **B. 3.** b **4.** c **C.** The Gulf Stream is a warm current that starts in the warm waters of the Gulf of Mexico. It runs northeastward along the East Coast of the United States and Canada. At Newfoundland, it moves eastward across the Atlantic toward Europe. The current passes northwest of Ireland, warming the air there. This makes the climate of Ireland warmer than other areas, such as eastern Canada, at the same latitude. **Write About Science** You should build it at high tide. The water reaches farthest up the shore at high tide. If you build the castle above the high tide line, ocean waves will not reach it. If you build the castle above the waves at low tide, the waves will destroy it as the ocean moves up the beach at high tide.

247 Practice • Ocean Resources
A. 1. shellfish or fish **2.** fish or shellfish **3.** natural gas **4.** copper or nickel **5.** nickel or copper **6.** muscle relaxers from sea snails **B. 7.** True **8.** True **9.** False. In some places, people remove the salt from the ocean to make drinking water. **10.** False. Algae in the ocean produce most of the oxygen in the air we breathe. **Write About Science** Accept all reasonable answers. For example, as we use up the resources that we can easily reach on land, resources that are harder to reach on the ocean floor will become more important to us.

248 Challenge
1. Because the whales and seals eat the same foods, when the whales are removed, there is much more food for the seals. With more food, the fur seal population increases. **2.** Accept all answers that are supported with reasons. Some students will think that the fishers must sacrifice now to save the fish stocks for the future. Others will think that the fishers should be allowed to keep fishing if there is no other way to make a living, but might offer a solution such as limiting the amount of fish that each fisher can take each day. **3.** Students should reason that the eggs and young of many bird and marine species in the area would be killed. For the near future, there will be fewer animals, fish, and shellfish in the marsh and in nearby ocean waters. If the waters are severely poisoned, the area could be lifeless, or nearly so, for a long time.

249 Another Way
A. The Gulf Stream extends from the Gulf of Mexico to the area of Newfoundland. The Gulf Stream system includes this area plus the North Atlantic Current that flows from Newfoundland eastward to western Europe. **B. 1.** spring tide **2.** neap tide

250 Lab Activity • Making a Cold-Water Current
Draw Conclusions • Water drops from the lid into the aluminum pan. • The water no longer tastes salty at the end of the lab. When the water boiled, it evaporated. It condensed on the underside of the cooler lid, then dripped into the aluminum pan. The salt was left behind in the pot. • People could find a way to evaporate large amounts of ocean water inexpensively. The salt would be left behind. This could create a supply of fresh water.

251 On-the-Job Science • Underwater Photographer
1. Answers can include giant clam, sponge, octopus, sea star, sea anemone, sea horse, clown fish, butterfly fish **2.** Many types of fish live near coral reefs, so there would be good fishing near them. **3.** The corals are the foundation of the reef. Breaking off pieces would probably destroy the coral. It would also disturb plants or animals that live on or around the reef by changing their habitat or disturbing their food supply.

252 Chapter 26 • Test A
A. 1. sea-floor spreading **2.** surface **3.** salinity **4.** density **5.** salt water **B. 6.** False, shelf **7.** True **8.** False, earthquakes **9.** False, high tides **10.** True **Critical Thinking** Planet Ocean would be a good name because most of the Earth's surface is covered by water, and most of the Earth's species live in the ocean. Accept all other reasonable answers.

253 Chapter 26 • Test B
1. d **2.** a **3.** a **4.** a **5.** c **6.** b **7.** a **8.** c **9.** d **10.** b **Critical Thinking** Students should mention the resources we get from the ocean, such as fish and shellfish for food, mineral resources such as oil and natural gas, and substances that can be made into medicines. Accept any other reasonable answers. The chapter does not mention other important functions of the ocean, such as moderating the Earth's climate,

but accept any of these other functions if students are aware of them.

Chapter 27 Exploring Space

254 Words to Know
Across: **1.** meteor **2.** asteroids **5.** meteoroid **6.** comet **7.** Way **Down: 1.** meteorite **2.** astronomy **3.** satellite **4.** sunspot

255 Practice • The Last Frontier
A. 2, 3, 1 **B.** Some students might think that spending a lifetime on such a trip would be too high a price to pay for the experience. Others might think the adventure and experience of seeing another solar system would be worth the time spent. Accept all reasonable answers. **Write About Science** Accept all reasonable answers, but make sure students explain the reasons for their responses.

256 Practice • The Solar System
A. 1. Mercury **2.** Venus **3.** Earth **4.** Mars **5.** Jupiter **6.** Saturn **7.** Uranus **8.** Neptune **9.** Pluto **B. 10.** False. The sun is a star at the center of the solar system. **11.** True **12.** False. Comets form glowing tails when they get near the sun. **Write About Science** Students should build their responses around information from the text that compares the two planets. Mars is much colder, has an atmosphere in which people could not breathe without spacesuits, has no water, has red soil, has no known life, and has two moons in its sky.

257 Practice • Space Exploration
A. 1. a. *Sputnik I* launches; **b.** *Gemini* program begins; **c.** *Apollo* program begins; **d.** space shuttle program begins **2. a.** Yuri Gagarin becomes first person to travel in space; **b.** Alan Shepard becomes first American launched into space; **c.** John Glenn orbits the Earth; **d.** Neil Armstrong lands on the moon **3. a.** *Explorer 1* goes into orbit; **b.** *Pioneer 10* takes first pictures of Jupiter; **c.** *Voyager 1* takes first pictures of Uranus; **d.** *Mars Pathfinder* sends images and data from Mars **B.** Answers should include the idea that the United States had to develop spacecraft that could reach the moon. Astronauts had to test techniques that would be needed for a moon trip, such as space walks and the joining of spacecraft in orbit. Scientists also needed to find out how being in space would affect the health of astronauts. **Write About Science** The space shuttle was the first reusable spacecraft. Earlier spacecraft could be used only once. The space shuttle lifts off like a rocket, but it lands like an airplane.

258 Challenge
1. The sun is blocked out by the moon except for a halo around the moon's edge, and the sky is black as night. **2.** The Earth's shadow **3.** There would be no solar eclipses because there would be no moon to cast a shadow on Earth. **4.** Solar eclipses in the day; lunar eclipses at night

259 Another Way
1. Jupiter: largest planet; fifth planet; ball of hydrogen liquid wrapped in clouds; little if any solid surface; 16 named moons; rings; Great Red Spot **2.** Mars: fourth planet; atmosphere mostly carbon dioxide; no water; colder than any place on Earth **3.** Uranus: seventh planet; made of a solid core surrounded by a gas made up mostly of hydrogen, helium, and methane; axis runs sideways instead of up and down; 20 moons; thin rings **4.** Saturn: sixth planet; no solid surface; rocky core surrounded by liquid hydrogen and helium clouds; seven main rings; 18 named moons **5.** Earth: third planet; about same size as Venus; mostly covered with water; has life **6.** Mercury: side facing sun very hot; side facing away from sun very cold; life as we know it could not exist there **7.** Pluto: usually farthest planet from the sun; orbit sometimes crosses that of Neptune; one moon **8.** Neptune: eighth planet; thick gas clouds around a liquid layer; rocky/dense core; several thin rings **9.** Venus: positioned between Mercury and Earth; hotter than Mercury

260 Lab Activity • Exploring the Moon
Draw Conclusions • Features should be harder to see as students look away from the terminator. • Answers will vary depending on the features observed. The features look different as the moon moves in orbit and the angle of sunlight shining on its surface changes.

261 Science in Your Life • Observing Satellites
1. Students should spot at least one satellite. **2.** Answers will vary depending on location, but students should have good luck in the eastern sky after sunset and in the western sky before sunrise. **3.** Answers will vary, but students should be able to spot the movement of the satellites against the background of the rest of the objects in the sky. **Critical Thinking** Check the location and movement of a satellite. Note the time. Then check about 90 minutes later to see if you spot the object in the same spot.

262 Chapter 27 • Test A
A. 1. True **2.** False, nine **3.** False, star **4.** True **5.** False, small **B. 6.** oxygen **7.** comets **8.** moon **9.** outer **10.** asteroids **Critical Thinking** Similarities: Both orbit the sun; both rotate on their axes; both are rocky inner planets; both have soil; both have water in some form; both have at least one moon; both have carbon dioxide in the atmosphere. Differences: The Earth is closer to the sun; Mars is colder than the Earth; the Earth has liquid water, and Mars does not; Mars has two moons, and the Earth has only one; the Earth has oxygen in the atmosphere, and Mars does not; the Earth has life, and Mars probably does not.

263 Chapter 27 • Test B
1. b **2.** d **3.** b **4.** a **5.** b **6.** d **7.** d **8.** a **9.** c **10.** b **Critical Thinking** Similarities: Both orbit the sun; both rotate on their axes; both are rocky inner planets; they are about the same size; both have

carbon dioxide in the atmosphere.   Differences: Venus is hotter than the Earth; the Earth has liquid water, and Venus does not; the Earth has a moon and Venus does not; the Earth has oxygen in the atmosphere, and Venus does not; Venus has much more carbon.

264 Extra Credit: Phases of the Moon
A. Parts listed should be colored in: full moon: none; waxing gibbous: left one-quarter; first quarter: left half; waxing crescent: left three-quarters; new: all; waning crescent: right three-quarters; last quarter: right half; waning gibbous: right one-quarter
B. 1. Revolution around the Earth   **2.** Three weeks
3. Waxing crescent, first quarter, waxing gibbous
4. Waning gibbous, last quarter, waning crescent
5. The moon spins on its axis at the same rate it orbits the Earth. This means the same side of the moon always faces us.

TEST PREPARATION TAB

Diagnostic Test

Answer	Lesson Correlation
A.	
1. scientific method	2.1
2. meter	2.2
3. life	3.2
4. biology	3.1
5. cells	4.1
6. molecule	4.1
7. kingdoms	5.1
B.	
8. False. Grouping organisms by their type is called classification.	5.1
9. True	6.2
10. True	6.3
11. False. The green substance that plants use in photosynthesis is called chlorophyll.	7.1
12. False. Roots are plant parts that soak up water and minerals.	7.1
13. False. Inherited traits are passed from parent to offspring.	8.1
14. True	9.1
15. False. The process of change in a species over time is called evolution.	9.1
16. True	10.1
C.	
17. nervous system	10.1
18. lungs, trachea	11.2
19. artery	11.3
D.	
20. h	12.2
21. i	13.1
22. g	13.2
23. c	14.2
24. e	14.2
25. a	15.1
26. f	16.1
27. b	16.1
28. j	17.1
29. k	18.1
30. d	18.3
E.	
31. current	19.2
32. fossil	20.1
33. sun	20.2
34. year	21.2
35. water	21.2
36. erosion	22.2
37. rock	22.2
F.	
38. True	23.1
39. True	23.1
40. False. The place where two air masses meet is a front.	24.1
41. False. Uplifting and folding causes layers of the Earth's crust to switch places.	25.1
42. False. The main difference between ocean water and fresh water is that ocean water has more salt.	26.1
43. False. The galaxy in which we live is the Milky Way.	27.1
44. False. The sun is average in size compared to other stars.	27.2
45. True	27.2
G.	
46. b	13.2
47. c	13.2
48. d	13.2
49. a	23.3

Critical Thinking
50. Water pollution can break a food chain by killing some of the living parts of the chain. If a food chain is broken, all of the living things in it are hurt. Populations of plants and animals can disappear.   13.2

Unit 1 Test

1. b		2.3
2. c		2.3
3. d		2.3
4. c		2.3
5. b		1.2
6. d		1.2
7. b		2.1
8. b		2.2
9. a		1.1
10. d		1.1
11. a		2.2
12. d		2.3
13. c		2.2
14. d		1.2
15. c		1.2

Advantages: It is easy to convert from one unit to another because they are all based on ten. It is easy to share information with others because most countries use metric units. Disadvantages: Americans are not used to these units and would have to learn them. 2.2

Unit 2 Test

1.	c	3.1
2.	c	3.2
3.	d	4.2
4.	a	4.2
5.	c	5.1
6.	d	5.1
7.	c	6.1
8.	b	6.2
9.	d	6.3
10.	b	8.1
11.	c	8.2
12.	b	9.2
13.	c	7.2
14.	d	7.2
15.	b	7.2

Critical Thinking
Reasons given will vary somewhat but should include one of the following: Invertebrates' body structures are simpler, yet more varied than those of vertebrates. This makes invertebrates able to live in more places than vertebrates, such as inside the bodies of other animals. Invertebrates also reproduce faster, in general, so they can adapt to changing environments more easily. Because of the more complicated body structures of vertebrates, their needs are also more complicated and more difficult to fill. Vertebrates, in general, need more space to live and more time to grow into adulthood than invertebrates do. 6.2, 6.3

Unit 3 Test

1.	d	11.3
2.	c	10.1
3.	a	10.1
4.	b	10.2
5.	c	10.3
6.	a	11.1
7.	c	11.2
8.	d	12.2
9.	d	13.2
10.	a	13.2
11.	d	13.2
12.	a	11.3
13.	a	12.2
14.	d	12.3
15.	c	13.1

Critical Thinking
The heart pumps blood throughout the body. This circulation of blood is important because blood brings food and oxygen to all body cells. Blood also carries wastes from cells. Living things can't continue to live without these two processes. 11.3

Unit 4 Test

1.	b	15.1
2.	a	15.1
3.	d	16.1
4.	a	15.2
5.	c	14.1
6.	d	14.2
7.	a	14.2
8.	d	15.2
9.	b	14.2
10.	d	16.1
11.	a	16.1
12.	c	17.2
13.	b	17.1
14.	d	17.1
15.	b	17.2

Critical Thinking
Answers will vary, but students' responses should reflect an understanding of the following concepts: 1) Physical changes include such changes as things breaking, crushing, grinding, melting, freezing, drying, or dissolving; 2) Chemical changes include such things as eggs cooking, milk souring, things burning, or iron rusting; 3) Change of one form of energy into another includes such things as electricity changing into heat, light, or kinetic energy in household appliances; batteries changing chemical energy into light, as in flashlights, or into sound, as in radios, and a windmill changing kinetic energy of wind into mechanical energy. 15.3

Unit 5 Test

1.	d	18.2, 18.3
2.	a	18.2
3.	c	18.3
4.	c	18.2
5.	d	18.1
6.	a	19.1
7.	a	19.3
8.	b	19.1
9.	c	19.4
10.	d	19.4
11.	b	20.1
12.	a	20.2
13.	b	20.2
14.	b	20.2
15.	a	20.2

Critical Thinking

Descriptions will vary, but students' answers should reflect an understanding of the following concepts: 1) The colors of the fireworks are related to the wavelength of the light rays. 2) The sounds of the explosions are related to frequency and amplitude. Very loud explosions have greater amplitude. High-pitched sounds have higher frequency. Low-pitched sounds have a lower frequency.   18.2, 18.3

Unit 6 Test

1.	c	21.1
2.	b	21.2
3.	c	21.2
4.	d	21.2
5.	c	22.1
6.	d	22.1
7.	c	24.2
8.	a	24.1
9.	a	24.3
10.	d	24.3
11.	d	24.2
12.	a	23.1
13.	d	23.1
14.	a	23.1
15.	c	23.1

Critical Thinking

In the Northern Hemisphere, the farther south you travel, the closer you get to the equator, where it s warm year-round. In the Southern Hemisphere, the farther south you go, the closer you get to the South Pole, where it is cold year-round.   24.3

Unit 7 Test

1.	c	25.2
2.	c	25.2
3.	a	25.2
4.	c	25.2
5.	a	25.2
6.	c	26.1
7.	c	26.1
8.	c	26.1
9.	b	26.2
10.	b	26.2
11.	d	27.1
12.	c	27.2
13.	a	27.2
14.	b	27.2
15.	b	27.2

Critical Thinking

The two most important features are liquid water and a mild temperature. Life on Earth began in the water. In addition, all life on Earth depends on water. The temperature of Earth is warm enough so organisms do not freeze, and cool enough so they do not burn up.   25.1, 25.2

Final Exam

1.	c	2.1
2.	a	2.2
3.	b	3.2
4.	b	3.1
5.	d	4.1
6.	a	4.1
7.	c	5.1
8.	d	5.1
9.	b	6.2
10.	c	6.3
11.	a	7.1
12.	c	7.1
13.	d	8.1
14.	d	9.1
15.	c	9.1
16.	b	10.1
17.	d	10.1
18.	c	11.2
19.	a	11.3
20.	c	12.2
21.	a	13.1
22.	d	13.2
23.	a	14.2
24.	b	14.2
25.	a	15.1
26.	b	16.1
27.	a	16.1
28.	c	17.1
29.	b	18.1
30.	d	18.3
31.	c	19.2
32.	d	20.1
33.	a	20.2
34.	b	21.2
35.	a	21.2
36.	c	22.2
37.	a	22.2
38.	c	23.1
39.	d	23.1
40.	c	24.1
41.	a	25.1
42.	a	26.1
43.	c	27.1
44.	b	27.2
45.	d	27.2
46.	b	13.2
47.	c	13.2
48.	a	13.2
49.	b	23.3

Critical Thinking

50. One possible answer is that pollution in the water can move to distant locations by way of rivers, streams, and underground water flow. In this way, water pollution affects people in more than one area.   13.2

VISUALS TAB

V1 Animal Cell and Plant Cell
1. cell wall 2. cell membrane 3. vacuole
4. nucleus 5. cytoplasm 6. chloroplast
7. mitochondria

V2 Parts of an Insect
1. antennae 2. thorax 3. wings 4. legs 5. head
6. legs 7. abdomen

V3 Parts of a Fish
1. caudal fin 2. dorsal fins 3. scales 4. anal fin
5. pelvic fin 6. pectoral fin 7. gills

V4 Parts of a Leaf
1. fine vein 2. petiole 3. blade 4. large vein

V4 Parts of a Flower
1. pistil 2. petal 3. stamen 4. ovary

V5 The Brain and Nervous System
1. cerebrum 2. cerebellum 3. brain stem 4. brain
5. spinal cord 6. fibers made of neurons

V5 The Eye
1. retina 2. cornea 3. iris 4. pupil 5. lens
6. optic nerve

V6 The Skeleton
1. skull 2. collarbone 3. upper arm bone 4. wrist
bones 5. ankle bones 6. shoulder blade 7. rib
8. backbone 9. hip bone 10. thigh bone

V6 Arm Muscles
1. muscle 2. tendon 3. bone

V7 The Digestive System
1. mouth 2. epiglottis 3. liver 4. gall bladder
5. large intestine 6. small intestine 7. esophagus
8. stomach 9. pancreas 10. rectum 11. anus

V8 The Respiratory System
1. nose 2. mouth 3. larynx 4. trachea 5. right
lung 6. diaphragm 7. air sacs 8. bronchus
9. bronchioles 10. left lung

V9 The Circulatory System and Heart
1. right atrium 2. right ventricle 3. left atrium
4. valve 5. left ventricle 6. arteries 7. veins
8. heart 9. artery 10. capillary 11. vein

V10 The Water Cycle
1. clouds 2. condensation 3. river 4. ocean
5. rain 6. water vapor 7. evaporation 8. trees

V10 The Oxygen/Carbon Dioxide Cycle
1. oxygen 2. carbon dioxide

V11 Model of the Atom
1. neutron 2. proton 3. electron 4. nucleus
5. electron cloud

V11 Features of a Wave
1. frequency = wavelengths per second
2. wavelength 3. crest 4. amplitude 5. trough

V12 The Layers of the Earth
1. crust 2. outer mantle 3. inner mantle 4. outer
core 5. inner core

V13 The Earth's Tectonic Plates
1. North American plate 2. Eurasian plate
3. Caribbean plate 4. Philippine plate 5. Pacific
plate 6. African plate 7. Pacific plate 8. Australian-
Indian plate 9. Nazca plate 10. South American
plate 11. Antarctic plate

V14 The World's Climate Zones
1. North Pole 2. Tropic of Cancer 3. Equator
4. Tropic of Capricorn 5. South Pole 6. polar zone
7. temperate zone 8. tropical zone 9. temperate
zone 10. polar zone

V15 The Ocean Floor
1. continent 2. mid-ocean ridge 3. ocean floor
4. plate 5. magma

V16 The Solar System
1. Sun 2. Mercury 3. Venus 4. Earth 5. Mars
6. asteroid belt 7. Jupiter 8. Saturn 9. Uranus
10. Neptune 11. Pluto

Notes

1-800-321-3106
www.pearsonlearning.com

ISBN 0-130-23436-2

90000

9 780130 234360

PACEMAKER®

General
Science

Third Edition

WORKBOOK

GLOBE FEARON

Pearson Learning Group

REVIEWERS
We thank the following educators, who provided valuable comments
and suggestions during the development of this book:

Philip Altshuler, River Ridge Middle/High School, New Port Richey, Florida
Anthony Arbino, Woodward High School, Cincinnati Public Schools, Cincinnati, Ohio
Shirley Johnson-Young, Memorial Middle School, Houston, Texas
Martha Kelly, Belleville Middle School, Belleville, New Jersey
Dorie Knaub, Downey Unified School District, Downey, California

Subject Area Consultants:
Gregory L. Vogt, Ed.D., Aerospace Education Specialist, Oklahoma State University. Dr. Vogt has degrees in General Science, Earth Science, and Aerospace Education. He taught science in the Milwaukee Public Schools, helped design and run the Discovery World Museum of Science, Economics, and Technology also in Milwaukee, and is now part of the Teaching From Space Program at NASA's Johnson Space Center in Houston, Texas.
Dr. Lisa K. Wagner, Director of Education/Associate Professor South Carolina Botanical Garden, Clemson University, Clemson, South Carolina
Pacemaker Curriculum Advisor: Stephen C. Larsen, formerly of the University of Texas at Austin

Executive Editor: Eleanor Ripp
Supervising Editor: Stephanie Petron Cahill
Lead Editor: Maury Solomon
Editor: Theresa McCarthy
Production Editor: Laura Benford-Sullivan
Assistant Editor: Kathy Bentzen
Designers: Susan Brorein, Jennifer Visco
Market Manager: Katie Kehoe-Erezuma
Research Director: Angela Darchi
Cover Design: Susan Brorein, Jennifer Visco
Editorial, Design and Production Services: Navta Associates
Electronic Composition: Linda Bierniak, Phyllis Rosinsky, Jeff Wickersty

About the Cover: Science is the study of everything in the universe, from the Earth's moon to the farthest galaxies, from the motion of atoms to the forces on a roller coaster. The images on the cover of this book show areas of life science, physical science, and Earth science. In life science, you study living things, such as plants and animals. In physical science, you study motion and forces, such as those affecting a roller coaster. In Earth science, you study things on Earth and in space, such as oceans and moons. You also learn about the skills and tools used to carry out scientific investigation, such as the microscope.

ISBN: 0-130-23437-0
Printed in the United States of America

11 12 V036 12 11

1-800-321-3106
www.pearsonlearning.com

Contents

A Note to the Student

This workbook is to be used along with your *Pacemaker®* *General Science* textbook. Each exercise is linked to a lesson in your textbook.

In this workbook, you will be asked to demonstrate what you have learned in a lesson and perhaps even apply it to new situations. Some of the ways you can demonstrate your new knowledge is by matching vocabulary to correct definitions, determining whether statements are true or false, correcting statements to make them true, completing fill-in sentences, and answering questions about a diagram or chart.

Your critical thinking skills are challenged when you answer the questions at the bottom of each exercise page. Critical thinking—or, to put it another way, thinking critically—means putting information to use. For example, suppose you are in a supermarket. You want to buy a can of soup, but you are uncertain about which brand to choose. As you read the ingredients listed on the label, you might review the list of ingredients. Perhaps you check the vitamin and sodium content. You may also look at the price. Then you evaluate the information and make a choice. You have just used your critical thinking skills. You have processed information and used it in a new, meaningful way.

Your textbook is a wonderful source of knowledge. By studying it, you will learn a great deal of information about the three different areas of science: life science, physical science, and Earth science. However, the real value of that information will come when you know how to put your knowledge to use by thinking critically.

▶1.1 From Atoms to Galaxies

A. Match each term below with its definition. Write the correct letter on the line.

_____ **1.** universe

_____ **2.** galaxy

_____ **3.** science

_____ **4.** observation

_____ **5.** atom

_____ **6.** research

a. the study of nature and the universe

b. the careful study of something

c. using books and doing experiments to study a subject

d. the smallest part of a substance that can still be recognized as that substance

e. all that exists

f. a group of billions of stars

B. Read the following sentences. If the sentence is a process, write *yes* on the line. If it is not, write *no*.

_____ **7.** The Earth is round.

_____ **8.** Scientists learn about stars by using telescopes.

_____ **9.** A biologist takes notes on a plant's growth.

_____ **10.** An earth scientist weighs a piece of rock.

_____ **11.** Lava is from volcanoes.

_____ **12.** If you place a ball on a hill, it will roll down.

_____ **13.** A physical scientist places three balls at the top of a hill to see which ball will roll fastest.

_____ **14.** The ocean is full of salt water.

CRITICAL THINKING

Choose an example of a technology developed in the last ten years. Some examples are the Internet, digital TV, and cell phones. On a separate sheet of paper, describe how the new technology helps people.

1.2 Science at Work: Science as Solution   Exercise 2

A. Match each subject below with the kind of scientist who would study it. Write the correct letter on the line. Each scientist can be used twice.

_____ **1.** machines   **a.** life scientist

_____ **2.** mountains   **b.** physical scientist

_____ **3.** behavior of geese **c.** earth scientist

_____ **4.** mushrooms

_____ **5.** storms

_____ **6.** heat

B. Group the scientists below according to their branch of science. Write the number that is next to each scientist's name in the correct box below.

Earth Science	Physical Science	Life Science

7. Thomas Edison invented the lightbulb and many other things.

8. Caroline Herschel made telescopes and studied stars.

9. J. Tuzo Wilson explained why the continents move.

10. Marie Curie discovered the element radium.

11. Jane Goodall studied the behavior of chimpanzees.

12. T. Theodore Fujita developed a scale for classifying tornadoes.

13. Charles Drew showed that blood plasma could be stored longer than whole blood and could be given to a person of any blood type.

CRITICAL THINKING

Explain how a science-related career could combine two or more branches of science. Write your answer on a separate sheet of paper.

▶1.2 Science at Work: Making the Right Choices   Exercise 3

A. The director of the National Science Foundation has a budget of about $4,000,000,000. Read the following descriptions of projects that different scientists wrote. Then decide which are the most worthwhile to receive money. Write the amount of money you will give to each project on the line next to its description. You do not have to give money to all the projects.

Budget

$_____ **1.** I would like to do a project that studies how farmers can grow wheat that is healthier for people to eat.

$_____ **2.** In this project, I will look into the possibilities of life in other parts of the universe.

$_____ **3.** My project will study why people are overweight today.

$_____ **4.** This study will show how newborn babies are affected by cigarette smoke.

$_____ **5.** I would like to study ways to make faster jets.

$_____ **6.** My project is looking for a cure for sleepwalking.

$_____ **7. TOTAL BUDGET** (should equal $4,000,000,000)

B. Explain why you divided the money the way you did. Which projects did you feel were the most important and why?

_____

_____

_____

_____

_____

_____

CRITICAL THINKING

What project would you like to add to this list and why? Write your answer on a separate sheet of paper.

2.1 The Scientific Method: The Five Steps — Exercise 4

A. On the lines below, number the five steps of the scientific method in their correct order.

_____ **1.** Perform experiments.

_____ **2.** Draw conclusions and report the results.

_____ **3.** Describe the problem.

_____ **4.** Suggest an answer.

_____ **5.** Gather information.

B. Scientists observe the world around them. Then they make an educated guess, or hypothesis, about what they see. Next, they run experiments to see if their hypothesis is correct. Below are three hypotheses. For each one, describe an experiment that would test it.

6. Danny has two lawn mowers. He thinks the red lawn mower cuts grass faster than the blue one.

Experiment: _____

_____

7. Maria thinks that taking the bus to school takes longer than walking to school.

Experiment: _____

_____

8. Dawn thinks planting grass on a hillside will stop soil from washing away.

Experiment: _____

_____

CRITICAL THINKING

List three different ways to report the results of an experiment. Write your answer on a separate sheet of paper.

2.1 The Scientific Method: Using the Five Steps   Exercise 5

You are doing a study that uses the scientific method. The problem is: *Do people learn better in rooms that have windows?*

1. **Gather information.** Talk with the members of your family. Ask: *Do you think you learn better in a room that has windows?* Write what they say below.

   _____

   _____

   _____

2. **Suggest a good answer to the problem.** Decide on a hypothesis. Do windows make a difference in learning? Explain your answer.

   _____

   _____

   _____

3. **Test the hypothesis by performing an experiment.** Discuss how you could design an experiment to test whether people learn better in rooms that have windows. On the lines below, describe how you would do your experiment.

   _____

   _____

   _____

4. **Report the results.** Carry out the experiment in your classroom. Discuss your results with the class. Was your hypothesis correct?

   _____

CRITICAL THINKING

Most experiments lead to the discovery of new problems. Based on the results of your experiment, what new problems might turn up that you could design an experiment for? Write your ideas on a separate sheet of paper.

2.2 Measuring in Science:
Comparing Metric and Nonmetric Units

Exercise 6

A. Complete each sentence with the correct word or phrase. Use the table to help you.

Length	Volume	Weight
1 foot = 30.5 cm	1 quart = .95 liter	1 gram = .04 ounce
1 yard = .91 meter	1 gallon = 3.79 liters	1 kilogram = 2.2 pounds
1 kilometer = .62 mile		

1. A liter is a _____ than a quart.
   (a) little less   **(b)** lot less   **(c)** little more

2. A gallon is _____ four liters.
   (a) a little less than   **(b)** a little more than   **(c)** exactly the same as

3. A kilogram is about _____ as much as a pound.
   (a) half   **(b)** four times   **(c)** two times

4. A meter is close to the same length as a _____.
   (a) foot   **(b)** yard   **(c)** kilometer

B. To change the miles below into kilometers, multiply by 1.6. For example, 8 miles is 12.8 kilometers (8 × 1.6 = 12.8).

5. We have 10 miles left to go.   _____ kilometers

6. It is 6 miles from here to Orlando.   _____ kilometers

7. A marathon race is about 26 miles long.   _____ kilometers

8. The United States is about 3,000 miles across.   _____ kilometers

CRITICAL THINKING

Many people in the United States are not familiar with the metric units of measurement. What could you do to become more familiar with metrics? Write your answer on a separate sheet of paper.

Name _____ Date _____

2.2 Measuring in Science:
Changing Values Using Metrics

A. Below are pictures of items that measure the amounts given. Change each measurement to an equivalent metric unit. Use the table to help you.

Length	Mass	Volume
1 millimeter $= \frac{1}{1,000}$ m	1 milligram $= \frac{1}{1,000}$ gram	1 milliliter $= \frac{1}{1,000}$ liter
1 centimeter $= \frac{1}{100}$ meter	1 kilogram $= 1,000$ grams	
1 kilometer $= 1,000$ meters		

1.

2 kilograms = _____ grams

2.

1,500 milliliters = _____ liters

3.

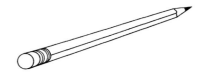

17 centimeters = _____ millimeters

4.

2.5 kilometers = _____ meters

B. Some metric units are much larger than others. For example, a meter is 1,000 times larger than a millimeter. Think about which metric unit would be best for measuring each item below. Write the names of the metric units on the lines.

5. mass of a person   _____

6. length of a football field   _____

7. volume of a glass of milk   _____

CRITICAL THINKING

On a separate sheet of paper, describe or draw four items and their metric measurements. Choose one item each for length, area, volume, and mass. Do not use the items shown above.

Name _____   Date _____

Consider a career as a scientist who runs a lab. Then answer
the questions below.

1. In what field of science would you like to work? Circle one.

life   physical   earth

2. What do you want to study in that field? Be as specific as possible.

_____

_____

3. How will the topic you picked to study help people?

_____

_____

4. Describe the laboratory you would use. Explain where it is and what
kinds of things are in it.

_____

_____

_____

_____

5. If you needed someone to help you in your research, what kind of
person would you hire? Write three questions that you would ask
a person who is interested in the job.

_____

_____

_____

CRITICAL THINKING

On a separate sheet of paper, list three safety rules from page 26 of
your textbook. After each rule, write why you think it is important to
follow that rule.

3.1 A Home for Life: Earth's Position

A. If the Earth moved a little *closer* to the sun, what would happen to each thing listed below?

1. The ice caps at the North Pole and the South Pole would

   _____

2. The oceans would _____

3. Leaves and plants would _____

4. The soil would _____

B. If the Earth moved a little *farther away* from the sun, what would happen to each thing listed below?

5. The lakes would _____

6. The ice caps would _____

7. Leaves and plants would _____

8. Animals would _____

CRITICAL THINKING

Science fiction deals with the possible effects of science on the world sometime in the future. The stories are made up, though they are based on ideas from science. Write a brief science fiction story about being on Earth during a warming or cooling period. Describe the world and what you see and do in it. What does this different Earth look, sound, smell, and feel like? Write your story on a separate sheet of paper.

Name_____ Date_____

A. Write the name of the science field that fits each picture below. Choose terms from the box.

| botany   zoology   genetics   microbiology   ecology |

1. _____   2. _____   3. _____

4. _____   5. _____

B. Match each kind of scientist below with a field of study. Write the correct letter on the line.

_____ **6.** botanist

_____ **7.** ecologist

_____ **8.** zoologist

_____ **9.** geneticist

_____ **10.** microbiologist

a. studies animals

b. studies organisms too small to be seen with the eye alone

c. studies plants

d. studies how features of organisms are passed along to offspring

e. studies interactions between organisms and their environment

CRITICAL THINKING

What are two different fields of life science? For each one, write what might be studied, where it would be studied, and what tools would be used. Write your answer on a separate sheet of paper.

▶ 3.2 What Is Life? Characteristics of Life   Exercise 11

Use the picture below and information from your textbook to
answer the questions about the characteristics of life. Name
two organisms for each question. Choose terms from the box.

fox
frog
duck
insect
waterlilies
trees
fish
eagle
bushes
mouse

1. Which animals are moving away from danger?

_____

2. Which animals are moving to get food?

_____

3. Which plants have the easiest time getting sunlight?

_____

4. Which animals walk?

_____

5. Which animals fly?

_____

6. Which animals swim?

_____

CRITICAL THINKING

Which of the above questions could apply to you? Write a brief
paragraph that explains your answer. Use a separate sheet of paper.

Name _____ Date _____

Use the table to answer the questions below.

1. For each living or nonliving thing listed in the table, answer the questions across the top of the table. Write *yes* or *no* in each box for your answers.

Living or nonliving thing	Gets and uses food?	Moves?	Grows?	Reproduces?	Responds to environment?	Is it alive?
housefly						
grass						
rock						
pine tree						
computer						
crab						
shrub						
squirrel						
glass						

2. Which things are organisms?

_____

_____

3. Name one thing that is *not* an organism. Explain why it is not.

_____

_____

CRITICAL THINKING

Choose an organism that is not on the chart. Explain how it has all five characteristics of life. Write your answer on a separate sheet of paper.

4.1 The Basic Units of Life

Exercise 13

A. Match each term below with its definition. Write the correct letter on the line.

_____ **1.** chemical bond

_____ **2.** cell

_____ **3.** molecule

_____ **4.** element

a. the smallest, most basic unit of life

b. matter that is made of only one kind of atom

c. a force that holds atoms together

d. two or more atoms that are joined by chemical bonds

B. Label the parts of the microscope using the terms from the box.

| eyepiece | stage | coarse adjustment knob |
| objectives | mirror | fine adjustment knob |

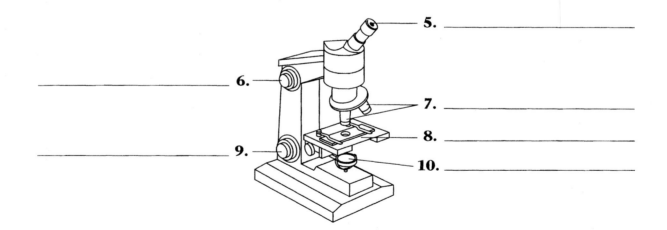

5. _____

6. _____

7. _____

8. _____

9. _____

10. _____

CRITICAL THINKING

If you were looking for signs of life on another planet, what elements would you look for? Explain your answer on a separate sheet of paper.

Name _____   Date _____

▶ 4.2 Understanding Cells: Parts of Cells   Exercise 14

Label the cells using the terms from the box. Some terms can
be used more than once.

vacuole	cell membrane	cytoplasm	chloroplast
mitochondrion	cell wall	nucleus	

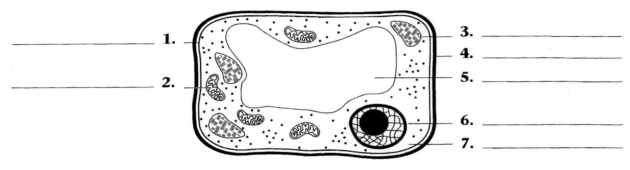

_____   1. ─

_____   2. ─

3. _____
4. _____
5. _____

6. _____
7. _____

Plant Cell

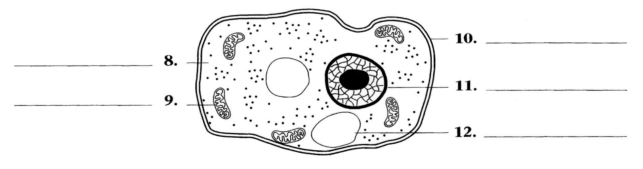

_____   8. ─

_____   9. ─

10. _____

11. _____

12. _____

Animal Cell

13. What is one activity plants do that animals do not? What cell part do
they use to do that?

_____

CRITICAL THINKING

What might cause a cell to become larger or smaller in size? Write
your answer on a separate sheet of paper.

Name_____ Date_____

Write check marks in the correct box in the chart below to show whether the cell part is found in an animal cell, a plant cell, or both. Then describe the job each part does.

Cell part	Animal cell	Plant cell	Job
1. Cell membrane			
2. Nucleus			
3. Chlorophyll			
4. Cytoplasm			
5. Mitochondria			
6. Vacuoles			
7. Chloroplasts			
8. Cell wall			

CRITICAL THINKING

On a separate sheet of paper, explain what the following equation means.

FOOD MOLECULE + OXYGEN = ENERGY + WATER + CARBON DIOXIDE

▶ 4.2 Understanding Cells: DNA

**Write *true* or *false* on the lines below each sentence. If the
sentence is false, rewrite it to make it true.**

1. DNA molecules are smaller than most other molecules found in cells.

_____

_____

2. Watson and Crick described the structure of a DNA molecule.

_____

_____

3. A DNA molecule contains a code that controls the activities of a cell.

_____

_____

4. The vacuole in a cell contains DNA.

_____

_____

5. Thousands of cells make up a DNA molecule.

_____

_____

6. A DNA molecule has the shape of a ball.

_____

_____

CRITICAL THINKING

Make a list of at least ten human characteristics that you think are
controlled completely or partly by a person's DNA. Name two
characteristics that you think are not controlled by DNA. Write your
lists on a separate sheet of paper.

5.1 Classifying Organisms: Species   Exercise 17

You have been sent to another planet to explore. You find a
living creature. You must send a message back to Earth
describing what you have found. After studying the creature,
you find the following to be true:

> It is many-celled. It has chloroplasts in its cells. Its
> cells do not have walls. It can move around on its
> own. It has no true nuclei in its cells.

1. Write a message to send back to Earth saying what kingdom of life, if
   any, the creature belongs to. If you need help, look at the chart on page
   65 of your textbook. Explain your answer.

   _____

   _____

   _____

   _____

2. You are asked to send a drawing of the creature back to Earth. Draw a
   picture of the creature below. Label its body parts.

3. Since you discovered the new creature, you get to name it. Create a
   name for the new creature. Explain why you chose this name.

   _____

   _____

CRITICAL THINKING

Pet dogs come in a wide range of sizes and shapes. They are all able to
reproduce with each other. Do they all belong to the same species?
Explain why or why not. Write your answer on a separate sheet of paper.

5.1 Classifying Organisms:
The Kingdoms of Life

A. Look at the pictures below. Write the name of the kingdom in which each organism belongs.

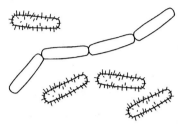

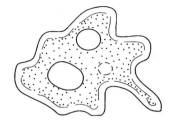

1. _____   2. _____

3. _____   4. _____   5. _____

B. Answer the following questions on the lines below. If you need help, look at the chart on page 65 of your textbook.

6. Why is a mushroom not considered a plant?

_____

7. How are bacteria different from protozoa?

_____

8. Why can human bodies not make their own food using sunlight?

_____

CRITICAL THINKING

Why would grouping organisms into kingdoms based on size not be
a good idea? Write your answer on a separate sheet of paper.

5.2 Earth's Simplest Organisms: Identifying Simple Organisms

Exercise 19

A. Decide what type of organism each set of statements describes. Write *bacterium, alga, protozoan,* or *fungus* on the line. Some terms can be used more than once.

1. I am a one-celled organism with a nucleus. I can make my own food.

   _____

2. I break down dead matter to get my food. My cells have nuclei and cell walls. _____

3. I am a one-celled organism. I do not have a nucleus. _____

4. I am a one-celled organism with a nucleus. I am animal-like. _____

5. I am a one-celled organism and absorb my food. I have a nucleus.

   _____

6. I am a plantlike organism and live in the ocean. I can make my own food. _____

B. Replace the underlined term to make the sentence true. Write the correct term on the line.

7. The DNA of bacteria is found in the <u>nucleus</u>. _____

8. Algae and protozoa are two types of <u>fungi</u>. _____

9. Molds belong in the <u>Plant Kingdom</u>. _____

10. Mushrooms cannot make their own food because they do not have <u>cell walls</u>. _____

CRITICAL THINKING

Suppose you discovered a one-celled organism. How would you decide if it was a bacterium, a protist, or a fungus? Write your answer on a separate sheet of paper.

5.2 Earth's Simplest Organisms: Friends or Enemies?

Exercise 20

A. Describe one way that each of these organisms can help people.

1. bacteria _____

_____

2. protists _____

_____

3. fungi _____

_____

B. Describe one way that each of these organisms can harm people.

4. bacteria _____

_____

5. protists _____

_____

6. fungi _____

_____

CRITICAL THINKING

A friend tells you that she once got very sick from an infection. The infection was caused by bacteria. She says she wishes she could destroy all bacteria. Do you think that would be a good thing to wish for? Explain why or why not on a separate sheet of paper.

▶6.1 From Simple to Complex

Read the list of "Characteristics of Living Things" below. Decide which organisms shown in the pictures have each characteristic. Write the letter below each organism on the correct lines. There can be more than one answer for each characteristic. The first one is done for you.

a.

b.

c.

Characteristics of Living Things

_a, b, c_   **1.** It can grow.

_____   **2.** It is made of specialized cells.

_____   **3.** It does not have specialized cells.

_____   **4.** It can reproduce.

_____   **5.** It can move from place to place.

_____   **6.** It cannot move from place to place.

_____   **7.** It gets food from other organisms.

_____   **8.** It can make its own food.

_____   **9.** It can respond to the environment.

CRITICAL THINKING

Sea squirts are organisms that live in the ocean. They move around when they are young, but they grow in one place when they are adults. They filter small bits of food out of the water. Their bodies are made of specialized cells. Are sea squirts plants, protists, monera, animals, or fungi? Write your answer on a separate sheet of paper. Explain your reasoning.

6.2 Invertebrates: Grouping by Type   Exercise 22

Complete the chart below. Place each of these animals in the correct column.

ant	crab	lobster	roundworm	snail
bee	crayfish	mite	sand dollar	spider
butterfly	earthworm	mosquito	scorpion	squid
clam	flea	octopus	sea star	tapeworm
cockroach	grasshopper	oyster	slug	tick

1. Worms	2. Mollusks	3. Spiny-Skinned Invertebrates	4. Arthropods

CRITICAL THINKING

If you found an animal with a hard outer covering, how would you decide if it was a mollusk or an arthropod? On a separate sheet of paper, write a paragraph to explain your answer.

Name_____ Date_____

A. Label each invertebrate below with one of these terms: *sponge, worm, mollusk,* or *spiny-skinned.* You will need to use some labels twice.

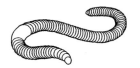　　　　

1. _____　　2. _____　　3. _____

　　　　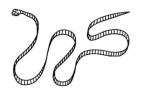

4. _____　　5. _____　　6. _____

B. Match each invertebrate below with its habitat. Write the correct letter on the line. Some items may have more than one answer. Some answers will be used more than once.

Invertebrate	Habitat
_____ **7.** earthworm	**a.** water
_____ **8.** sand dollar	**b.** land
_____ **9.** slug	**c.** inside a host
_____ **10.** snail	
_____ **11.** sponge	
_____ **12.** tapeworm	

CRITICAL THINKING

Think of a kitchen item that has the same function as the crop of an earthworm. Think of another item that has the same function as the gizzard of an earthworm. On a separate sheet of paper, write the names of the kitchen items. Describe their functions.

6.2 Invertebrates: Arthropods   Exercise 24

A. Each sentence below is false. Replace the underlined term and rewrite the sentence to make it true.

1. An arthropod is an animal with an <u>inner</u> skeleton.

   _____

2. Arthropods have jointed <u>heads</u>.

   _____

3. <u>Spiders</u> are the largest group of arthropods.

   _____

4. An insect's body has <u>two</u> main parts.

   _____

5. Insects have feelers, which are called <u>parasites</u>.

   _____

6. A crustacean's front pair of legs are called <u>walking legs</u>.

   _____

B. Complete the chart below with the correct numbers. The first one is done for you.

	Insects	Spiders	Crustaceans
Number of body segments	7. 3	9.	11.
Number of pairs of legs	8.	10.	12.

CRITICAL THINKING

On a separate sheet of paper, name three ways you can tell insects, spiders, and crustaceans apart.

▶ 6.3 Vertebrates: Organizing Major Groups   Exercise 25

A. Here is a branching diagram that organizes foods into different groups. It shows foods found in each group.

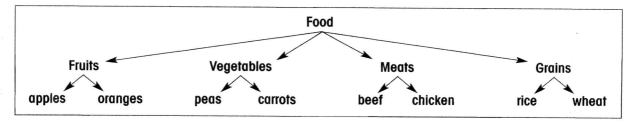

Make a branching diagram of the animal kingdom. Show *vertebrates*, *invertebrates*, and the kinds of animals that go into those two major groups.

The Animal Kingdom

B. Make a branching diagram of vertebrates. Show *cold-blooded* and *warm-blooded* vertebrates and the kinds of animals that go into those two major groups.

Vertebrates

CRITICAL THINKING

Which type of animal would find it easier to live in extreme kinds of weather—a cold-blooded animal or a warm-blooded animal? Explain your answer on a separate sheet of paper.

▶6.3 Vertebrates: Characteristics   Exercise 26

A. Match each vertebrate group below with its
characteristics. Write the correct letter on the line.

_____ **1.** fish

_____ **2.** amphibian

_____ **3.** reptile

_____ **4.** bird

_____ **5.** mammal

a. covered with feathers; has hollow bones

b. covered with scales; has lungs

c. covered with scales; has fins and gills

d. covered with hair; feeds young with mother's milk

e. has wet, slippery skin and two pairs of legs

B. Choose one of the vertebrates pictured below. Then
answer the questions that follow.

6. Which vertebrate did you choose? _____

7. What group of vertebrates does it belong to? _____

8. Is it cold-blooded or warm-blooded? _____

9. What is its body covered with? _____

CRITICAL THINKING

Crocodiles were once endangered. With the help of new laws and
environmental groups, the number of crocodiles has increased again.
Do you think it was right to help them? Why or why not? Explain
your answer on a separate sheet of paper.

▶ 7.1 Plants as Food Makers: Food From Plants   Exercise 27

A. Here is a recipe for carrot cake. Write *P* next to the six
ingredients that come from plants. Write *A* next to the one
ingredient that comes from an animal. Write *N* next to the
three ingredients that do not come from living things.

Carrot Cake
Mix together:

_____ **1.** 1 cup whole wheat flour

_____ **2.** 1 teaspoon baking soda

_____ **3.** 1 teaspoon baking powder

_____ **4.** 1 teaspoon salt

Mix and add:

_____ **5.** $\frac{2}{3}$ cup vegetable oil

_____ **6.** 2 beaten eggs

_____ **7.** 1 cup sugar

Add and blend in well:

_____ **8.** 1 cup chopped walnuts

_____ **9.** $1\frac{1}{2}$ cups grated carrots

_____ **10.** 1 teaspoon grated lemon rind

Bake in a greased and floured pan about 30 minutes at 325°F.

B. List four ingredients you found that come from plants.
Next to each one, write what part of the plant it comes
from. Use reference books or the Internet if you need
help. The first one is done for you.

11. _wheat flour (seed)_____   **12.** _____

13. _____   **14.** _____

CRITICAL THINKING

On a separate sheet of paper, explain the following statement:
"All animals depend on plants."

Name _____ Date _____

A. Each sentence below is false. Replace the underlined term and rewrite the sentence to make it true.

1. The <u>leaf</u> is the part of a seed plant from which a new plant can grow.

   _____

   _____

2. Most of a plant's chlorophyll is found in its <u>seeds</u>.

   _____

   _____

3. Plants make sugar using sunlight, water, chlorophyll, and <u>oxygen</u>.

   _____

   _____

B. Label the parts of the plant below using these words: *root*, *leaf*, and *stem*. Then, on the lines below, write what job or jobs each part does.

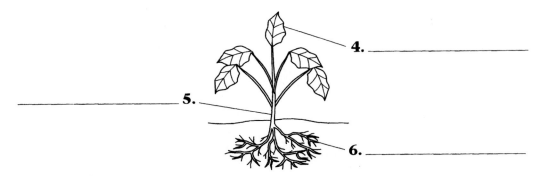

4. _____

5. _____

6. _____

7. root: _____

8. leaf: _____

9. stem: _____

CRITICAL THINKING

How do you think life on Earth would be different without chlorophyll? Write your answer on a separate sheet of paper.

7.2 Plant Reproduction: Pollination   **Exercise 29**

A. Label the parts of the flower below using these words:
petal, *pistil*, *stamen*, *pollen*, and *ovary*.

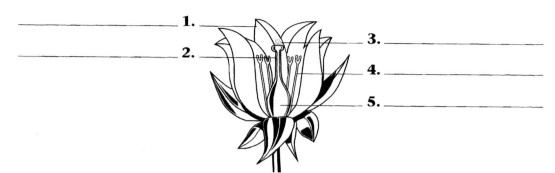

_____ **1.** ___
_____ **2.** ___
3. _____
4. _____
5. _____

B. For each "if" below, circle the letter of the best ending for
each sentence. Then, on the line, write why you chose
your answer.

6. If the pistil of a flower were not sticky, then
   (a) pollination would not occur as easily.
   (b) sperm cells would travel down the pistil more slowly.
   (c) the plant would produce more nectar.

   This is because _____

7. If all the flowers were picked off an apple tree in the spring, then
   (a) the tree could not carry on photosynthesis.
   (b) the tree might not bear fruit.
   (c) the tree could not get oxygen.

   This is because _____

8. If the pollen from one flower lands only on the stamen of
   another flower, then
   (a) fertilization occurs.
   (b) pollination occurs.
   (c) pollination does not occur.

   This is because _____

CRITICAL THINKING

How do you think flower petals attract insects? Write your answer on
a separate sheet of paper.

7.2 Plant Reproduction:
Producing Seeds and Fruit

A. The names of the three processes involved in plant
reproduction and growth are in the box. Write the
processes in the order in which they occur in a plant.
Then, next to each process, describe what happens during
that process.

fertilization	germination	pollination

1. _____   _____

   _____

2. _____   _____

   _____

3. _____   _____

   _____

B. Study the shape of each fruit below. Then, on the lines,
write a sentence explaining how the fruit and seed is most
likely carried away from the parent plant.

4.    _____

   Fruit — Seed
   Maple   _____

5.   _____

   Burr   _____

CRITICAL THINKING

Design a fruit that would help the seeds be carried away easily by the
wind, water, an animal, or some other way. Draw your fruit and seeds
on a separate sheet of paper. Describe how the design helps carry the
fruit and seeds away to a place where the seeds can grow best.

▶ 8.1 The Same But Different   Exercise 31

A. The steps below describe Gregor Mendel's research with breeding pea plants. Number the steps in their correct order. Write the numbers on the lines.

_____ **1.** Hybrid offspring were produced.

_____ **2.** Mendel took the pollen from a tall pea plant.

_____ **3.** Mendel concluded that tallness in pea plants is a dominant trait.

_____ **4.** Mendel used the pollen to pollinate a short pea plant.

_____ **5.** The hybrids were all tall.

B. On the line below each organism shown, describe one of the organism's traits.

 Bacterium    Protist

6. _____   **7.** _____

 Mushroom   Plant

8. _____   **9.** _____

C. Match each term below with its definition. Write the correct letter on the line.

_____ **10.** dominant

_____ **11.** crossbreeding

_____ **12.** offspring

a. a new organism that results from reproduction

b. a trait in an organism that shows no matter the effect of its partner trait

c. the matching of parents with different traits to produce offspring with new traits

CRITICAL THINKING

Mendel crossbred the hybrid tall plants described in Part A above. Some of the offspring were short. On a separate sheet of paper, explain why this happened.

8.2 The Building Blocks of Heredity: Genes   Exercise 32

A. Write the following words on the lines below, in order, from the largest to the smallest thing: *gene, nucleus, chromosome, cell.*

1. _____   2. _____

3. _____   4. _____

B. Draw and label illustrations showing two of the things listed above. You can create your own idea of what a chromosome or gene looks like.

5. [blank box]   6. [blank box]

C. Answer the following questions on the lines below.

7. What is a change in an organism's genetic code called?

_____

8. What is an example of a harmful mutation?

_____

9. What is an example of a helpful mutation?

_____

10. What makes egg cells and sperm cells different from other body cells?

_____

CRITICAL THINKING

How do organisms pass down mutations to their offspring? Write your answer on a separate sheet of paper.

8.2 The Building Blocks of Heredity: Producing Offspring

A. Complete the chart below. Write the correct number of chromosomes in each blank box.

Animal	Number of chromosomes in body cells	Number of chromosomes in sex cells
1. horse	64	
2. frog		13
3. grasshopper	24	
4. alligator		16
5. dog	78	

B. Each sentence below is false. Replace the underlined term and rewrite the sentence to make it true.

6. During fertilization, a <u>body cell</u> joins with an egg cell.

_____

7. A <u>number</u> code is found in an organism's genes.

_____

8. An animal gets <u>all</u> of its chromosomes from its mother.

_____

9. A sperm cell is a <u>body</u> cell.

_____

10. Sex cells reproduce by dividing <u>once</u>.

_____

CRITICAL THINKING

Why is it important that the sex cells of an organism have half the number of chromosomes that are found in the organism's body cells? Write your answer on a separate sheet of paper.

▶8.3 Controlling Heredity

Read each story below. Think about whether the environment or genetics caused the ending in the story. Then circle the word *environment* or *genetics*. Explain your choice.

1. Christina brought home a strong, healthy tomato-plant seedling. She placed the plant in a shady part of the garden. She only remembered to water it about once a week. The plant lived, but it did not produce any tomatoes.

   Environment / Genetics

   Why? _____

   _____

2. Annie's parents met in high school on the track team. Her father was the city's fastest long-distance runner. Her mother was the city's champion high jumper. Annie hated sports, though. The only exercise she got was in gym class. Even so, she was one of the fastest runners and best jumpers in gym class.

   Environment / Genetics

   Why? _____

   _____

3. Bob and Hiroko both entered a garden club contest for growing roses. Bob worked just as hard as Hiroko did. He used the same soil and fertilizer. He watered his roses just the right amount. However, Hiroko got some special seeds from her grandmother to grow her roses. They turned out to be the most beautiful roses in the contest.

   Environment / Genetics

   Why? _____

   _____

CRITICAL THINKING

On a separate sheet of paper, list three human traits that are affected by both genetics and the environment. Explain how both can affect these traits.

▶9.1 Time and Change: Paths of Evolution   Exercise 35

This is the evolutionary tree of life. It shows how different kinds of organisms may have evolved from the very first organisms.

Evolutionary Tree of Life

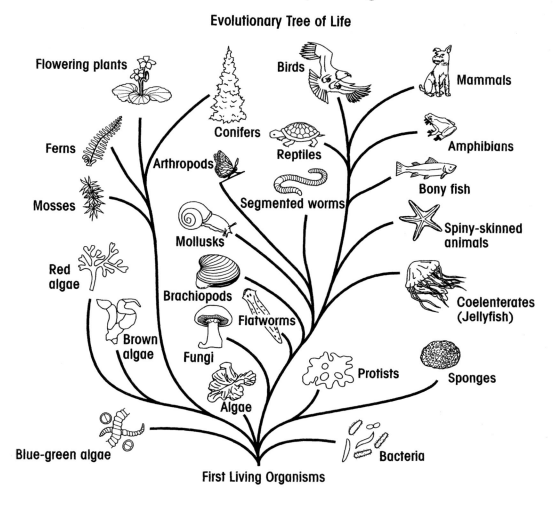

1. Use a pencil to trace the path of evolution from the first living organism to bony fish.

2. In another color pencil, trace the path of evolution from the first living organism to arthropods.

3. Circle the part of the path that fish and arthropods have in common.

CRITICAL THINKING

Notice that algae and plants are both on the left side of this tree. Also notice that the algae branch off just below the branch that leads to plants. What do these facts tell you about the evolution of these organisms? Write your answer on a separate sheet of paper.

▶9.1 Time and Change: Exercise 36
Relationships Among Organisms

Use the evolutionary tree of life on page 35 to answer the
questions below.

1. What were the two earliest organisms? _____

   _____

2. What were the earliest plants? _____

3. Which five animals on this tree are vertebrates? _____

   _____

4. Where on the tree would vertebrates appear? _____
   Write *vertebrates* on the branch that shows where these organisms
   first evolved.

5. Which two plants on this tree are seed plants? _____

   _____

6. Where on the tree would seed plants appear? _____
   Write *seed plants* on the branch that shows where these organisms
   first evolved.

7. Find the fungi on this tree. Which kinds of organisms, if any,
   evolved from fungi?

   _____

8. Which evolved first, sponges or segmented worms? _____

9. Which evolved first, mollusks or reptiles? _____

10. Which evolved first, conifers or mosses? _____

CRITICAL THINKING

According to the evolutionary tree of life, which of today's organisms
did the first living organisms most look like? How do you know this?
Write your answer on a separate sheet of paper.

9.2 Theories of Evolution: Darwin's Theory   Exercise 37

A. What are the four main ideas that make up Charles Darwin's theory of natural selection? Write the ideas on the lines below.

1. _____
   _____

2. _____
   _____

3. _____
   _____

4. _____
   _____

B. Read each sentence. Decide which of Darwin's main ideas above it describes. Write *1*, *2*, *3*, or *4* on the line.

_____ **5.** Two tiger kittens had strong running muscles, just like their mother.

_____ **6.** A pine tree dropped thousands of pine cones full of seeds.

_____ **7.** Hawks fought over places in the field to hunt.

_____ **8.** Insects that lived on the forest floor looked a lot like twigs.

_____ **9.** A plum tree seedling was as healthy as its parent tree.

_____ **10.** The garden was crowded with weeds and tomato plants.

_____ **11.** A salmon laid hundreds of eggs.

CRITICAL THINKING

According to Jean Baptiste Lamarck's theory of evolution, what should parents do if they want their children to be born with musical talent? Why? Write your answer on a separate sheet of paper.

Name _____ Date _____

Each drawing below shows an organism with a mutation. Its
label describes the mutation. Explain how each mutation
would be helpful or harmful to the organism. Write your
answers on the lines below.

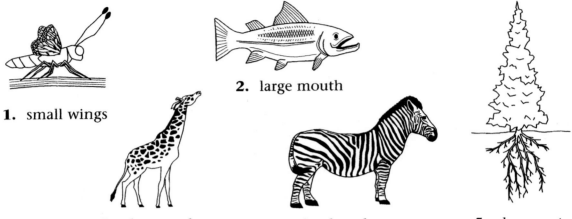

1. small wings

2. large mouth

3. short neck   **4.** short legs   **5.** deep roots

1. _____

_____

2. _____

_____

3. _____

_____

4. _____

_____

5. _____

CRITICAL THINKING

If a male animal had a mutation that kept it from making any sperm
cells, would you expect the animal to pass on this trait to offspring?
Explain why or why not on a separate sheet of paper.

▶10.1 From Cells to Systems: The Basic Plan   Exercise 39

A. Match each term with its definition. Write the correct letter on the line.

_____ **1.** organ

_____ **2.** system

_____ **3.** cell

_____ **4.** tissue

a. a group of similar cells that work together to do a job

b. a building block of life

c. a body part made up of one or more kinds of tissue

d. a group of organs working together

B. Circle any four parts of the body listed in the box. Write each one on a line below and the body system it belongs to. Describe the function of each system. One word is already done for you.

heart	brain	lungs	ovaries
skin	stomach	backbone	biceps

5. _biceps/muscular system. The muscular system allows movement.___

6. _____

7. _____

8. _____

9. _____

CRITICAL THINKING

Organs work together to perform a task. Organs working together form a system. What other examples of different things working together as a system can you think of? Write your answer on a separate sheet of paper.

Name _____ Date _____

A. Label the parts of the brain, using these terms: *cerebrum,*
cerebellum, and *brain stem.*

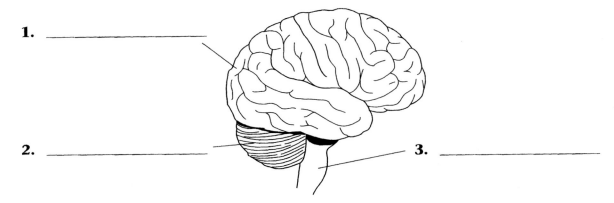

1. _____

2. _____   3. _____

B. Think of a place you would like to visit. It could be a beach,
a forest, or a mountaintop. Write the name of the place in
the center of the topic web below. Then fill in the topic web,
using sense words that describe this place. Write two terms
under each of the sense words.

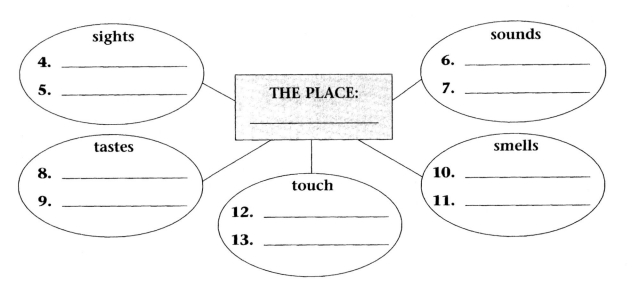

sights
4. _____
5. _____

sounds
6. _____
7. _____

THE PLACE:
_____

tastes
8. _____
9. _____

touch
12. _____
13. _____

smells
10. _____
11. _____

CRITICAL THINKING

Pick one of the five senses. Now think about how life would be if that
sense were much stronger than normal. If you could see great
distances or hear things from far away, how would your life be
different? Write your answer on a separate sheet of paper.

Name_____ Date_____

A. Read the list below of parts of the body. Decide which ones belong to the skeletal system and which belong to the muscular system. Write *skeletal* or *muscular* next to each one.

1. voluntary muscle _____

2. biceps _____

3. skeleton _____

4. joints _____

5. skull _____

6. leg bone _____

7. tendon _____

8. rib cage _____

B. Each body system does one or more jobs. Write *skeletal* or *muscular* next to each job below.

9. This system makes the heart beat involuntarily. _____

10. This system holds the body up. _____

11. This system allows your arm to bend. _____

12. This system helps you swallow food. _____

13. This system moves your legs, arms, and other body parts. _____

14. This system protects important organs such as the brain

and heart. _____

CRITICAL THINKING

Choose one of the following bones: the skull, the backbone, or the hip bone. Describe how you think its shape is related to what it does. Write your answer on a separate sheet of paper.

▶ 10.3 Reproduction   Exercise 42

**Write *true* or *false* next to each sentence below. If the sentence
is false, replace the underlined term and rewrite the sentence
to make it true.**

1. During <u>adulthood</u>, the reproductive system develops. _____

   _____

2. <u>Hormones</u> cause physical changes in the body. _____

   _____

3. Females release one egg each month from their <u>uterus</u>. _____

   _____

4. <u>An ovary</u> will begin to develop when an egg cell is fertilized by a

   sperm cell. _____

   _____

5. A fetus develops inside the mother's <u>uterus</u>. _____

   _____

6. A human fetus usually takes <u>48</u> weeks to fully develop. _____

   _____

7. The <u>support</u> system controls the release of sperm cells and egg cells. _____

   _____

8. A young mammal in between fertilization and birth is called a <u>fetus</u>. _____

   _____

9. Menstruation stops in women at about the age of <u>30</u>. _____

   _____

CRITICAL THINKING

Why do you think women's ovaries stop releasing egg cells later in life?
Write your answer on a separate sheet of paper.

▶11.1 Digestion: The Digestive System

A. Label each part of the digestive system on the diagram
below. Use terms from the box.

large intestine	small intestine	mouth
stomach	anus	esophagus

1. _____

2. _____

3. _____

4. _____

5. _____

6. _____

B. Describe the function of each labeled part on the lines below.

7. _____

8. _____

9. _____

10. _____

11. _____

12. _____

CRITICAL THINKING

What might happen if your digestive system worked faster? How
would your life change? For example, how would your eating habits
be different? Write your answer on a separate sheet of paper.

11.1 Digestion: Breaking Down Food   Exercise 44

**Describe what happens to a piece of food as it passes through each
of the organs listed below. Include as much detail as possible.**

1. mouth _____

_____

_____

2. esophagus _____

_____

_____

_____

3. stomach _____

_____

_____

_____

4. small intestine _____

_____

_____

_____

5. large intestine _____

_____

_____

_____

CRITICAL THINKING

How is the digestive system like an assembly line in reverse? Write
your answer on a separate sheet of paper.

11.2 Respiration: The Respiratory System   **Exercise 45**

A. Match each organ below with its function. Write the correct letter on the line.

_____ **1.** larynx

_____ **2.** trachea

_____ **3.** bronchi

_____ **4.** air sacs

a. carries air to the bronchi; also called the windpipe

b. passes air from the throat to the windpipe

c. tiny pockets that fill with air from the bronchi and pass it to the lungs

d. two tubes that carry air into the lungs

B. Write *true* or *false* next to each sentence below. If the sentence is false, rewrite the sentence to make it true by replacing the underlined term.

5. <u>Digestion</u> gets oxygen to the cells. _____

_____

6. When you breathe in, you take in air through your mouth

or <u>nose</u>. _____

_____

7. <u>Carbon dioxide</u> in the air passes through the air sacs into

your blood. _____

_____

8. The oxygen in the air comes from <u>animals</u>. _____

_____

CRITICAL THINKING

How is respiration in animals similar to respiration in plants? Do a comparison chart on a separate sheet of paper.

11.2 Respiration: Exchanging Oxygen and Carbon Dioxide

A. Fill in each sentence below with a term from the box.

air sacs	oxygen	carbon dioxide	cells

1. Blood from the body contains _____ when it enters the lungs.

2. Blood contains _____ when it leaves the lungs.

3. The exchange of carbon dioxide and oxygen happens in

   the _____.

4. Carbon dioxide is produced in the body's _____.

B. The diagram below shows how oxygen and carbon dioxide are exchanged in the air sacs of the lungs. The sentences below describe what happens in the air sacs. Read the sentences. Then write the letter of the sentence that best describes what happens at that place. Write your answers on the lines.

a. Blood leaves the air sac and goes to the body.

b. Oxygen passes into the blood, and carbon dioxide passes out of the blood.

c. Blood from the body enters the air sac.

d. Air containing oxygen enters the air sac.

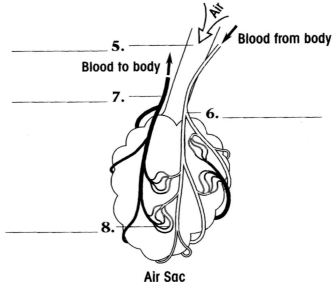

_____ **5.** _____

Blood to body

_____ **7.** _____

6. _____

Air

Blood from body

_____ **8.** _____

Air Sac

CRITICAL THINKING

Why is it good that air can enter your body through either your nose or your mouth? Write your answer on a separate sheet of paper.

▶11.3 Circulation: The Circulatory System   Exercise 47

A. Label each part of the circulatory system shown on the
diagram below. Use terms from the box.

capillaries	heart	vein	artery

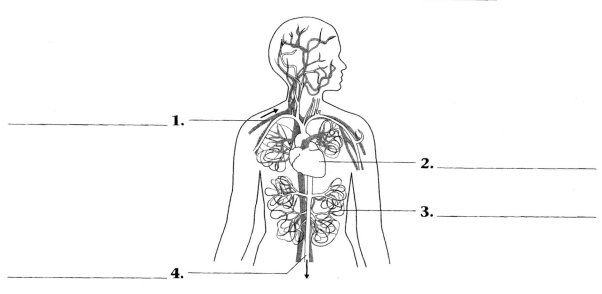

_____ **1.**

2. _____

3. _____

_____ **4.**

B. Use the diagram to answer the questions below.

   5. What organ pumps blood through the body?

   _____

   6. Which type of blood vessel carries blood to the heart?

   _____

   7. Which type of blood vessel carries blood away from the heart?

   _____

   8. What do capillaries do?

   _____

CRITICAL THINKING

On a separate sheet of paper, list and describe the four parts of blood.

Name _____ Date _____

A. Use the drawings of the heart and artery to answer the questions below.

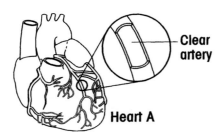
—Clear artery

Heart A

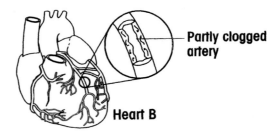
—Partly clogged artery

Heart B

1. In which heart would the artery have higher blood pressure? Why?

_____

_____

2. Change the drawing of Heart A to show what might happen to give this person a heart attack. How would this change give the person a heart attack?

_____

_____

B. Draw a circle around each healthy practice below. Put an X through each unhealthy practice. Tell why each practice is healthy or unhealthy. Write your answers on the lines below.

3.

4.

5.

_____   _____   _____

_____   _____   _____

_____   _____   _____

CRITICAL THINKING

List five "heart-healthy" foods. Tell why each one is "heart-healthy." Write your answer on a separate sheet of paper.

Name _____ Date _____

A. On the lines below each picture, describe what is happening. Tell which picture or pictures show a way disease is spread. Which show a way to prevent the spread of disease?

1.    **2.**    **3.**

_____ _____ _____

_____ _____ _____

_____ _____ _____

_____ _____ _____

B. Complete each sentence with a term from the box.

diseases	bacteria	DNA
white blood cells	viruses	

4. The Plague of the 1300s was caused by _____.

5. The common cold, AIDS, and the Plague are examples of _____.

6. If harmful organisms get into your body, _____ try to destroy them.

7. Polio, chicken pox, colds, and the measles are caused by _____.

8. Viruses are often made mostly of _____.

CRITICAL THINKING

Why do you think it is easier to get the flu when your body is already fighting off a cold? Write your answer on a separate sheet of paper.

Name _____ Date _____

A. Match each section of the Food Guide Pyramid with its food group. Write the correct letter on the line.

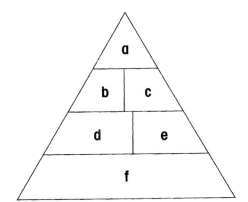

_____ **1.** vegetable group

_____ **2.** fats, oils, and sweets group

_____ **3.** bread, cereal, rice, and pasta group

_____ **4.** fruit group

_____ **5.** meat, poultry, fish, dry beans, eggs, and nuts group

_____ **6.** milk, yogurt, and cheese group

B. Use the foods in the box below to create a balanced meal for each day on the menu chart. Look at the Food Guide Pyramid on page 177 of your textbook if you need help.

macaroni and cheese	carrot cake	rice
hot turkey sandwich	milk	collard greens

Monday	Tuesday	Wednesday
fish sticks	**7.**	beef tacos
8.	mashed potatoes	green salad
oatmeal cookies	milk	custard with apples
9.	carrot, raisin, and pineapple salad	milk
10.	**11.**	**12.**

CRITICAL THINKING

The school cook asks you to plan the meals for Thursday and Friday. You can choose anything you want, as long as you balance the meals. Use the Food Guide Pyramid as a guide. Write your plan on a separate sheet of paper.

12.3 Guarding Your Health

A. Make a list of what you consider to be the top three health problems facing the United States today. Explain why each is a big problem.

1. _____

_____

2. _____

_____

3. _____

_____

B. Suggest one way each problem you chose can be fought.

4. _____

_____

_____

5. _____

_____

6. _____

_____

CRITICAL THINKING

If you were asked to speak on national television about health care, what would you say? Write a speech telling what you think are the nation's three biggest health problems and how these problems can be fought. Write your speech on a separate sheet of paper.

13.1 Living Together

A. The drawings below show the steps in which a pond changes into a forest. Number the steps on the lines in the order in which they occur.

1.

2.

_____   _____

3.

4.

_____   _____

B. Match each term below with its example. Write the correct letter on the line.

_____	**5.** resource	**a.**	all the gorillas in a rain forest
_____	**6.** ecosystem	**b.**	water
_____	**7.** population	**c.**	all the organisms in a desert
_____	**8.** recycling	**d.**	a bird's nest in a tree
_____	**9.** community	**e.**	all the organisms, water, soil, and air in a desert
_____	**10.** habitat	**f.**	breathing air in and out

CRITICAL THINKING

What organisms and other things might you find in an ocean ecosystem, such as a coral reef or the shallow water near the shore? Write your answer on a separate sheet of paper.

▶13.2 Using Nature's Resources:
Food Chains and Webs

A. Study the picture below. Read what the people are saying. Then complete the chart with the names of three producers, consumers, and decomposers that are found in this part of the forest. Some of the organisms may be too small to see.

Producers	Consumers	Decomposers
1.	4.	7.
2.	5.	8.
3.	6.	9.

B. Fill in the food chain below. Use terms from the box.

snake	grass	hawk	mouse

10. _____ ⇨ 11. _____ ⇨ 12. _____ ⇨ 13. _____

gets eaten by   gets eaten by   gets eaten by

CRITICAL THINKING

A freshwater food web may be made up of water plants, frogs, minnows, bass, insects, and turtles. The minnows eat the water plants and insects. The bass eat the frogs and minnows. The frogs eat the insects. The insects eat the water plants. The turtles eat the frogs. What might happen to the community if the frogs suddenly disappeared? Write your answer on a separate sheet of paper.

Name _____   Date _____

13.2 Using Nature's Resources: Water and Air   Exercise 54

A. Look at the drawings of two different kinds of cycles.
Choose the correct title for each one from the box. Write
the titles above the drawings. Then draw arrows to show
the flow of each cycle.

Water Cycle	Oxygen and Carbon Dioxide Cycle

1. _____   2. _____

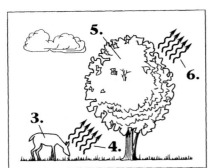   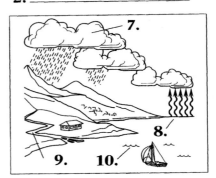

B. Choose the term from the box that matches each step in
the cycles above. Write the term on the line.

photosynthesis	oxygen	evaporation
cellular respiration	ocean	condensation
river	carbon dioxide	

3. _____   7. _____

4. _____   8. _____

5. _____   9. _____

6. _____   10. _____

CRITICAL THINKING

Both processes on the drawings you labeled use the sun's energy.
Explain how. Write your answer on a separate sheet of paper.

Name _____ Date _____

13.2 Using Nature's Resources: Natural Resources and Conservation

A. Match each natural resource below with the way people use it. Write the correct letter on the line.

_____ **1.** wood   **a.** growing crops

_____ **2.** fossil fuel   **b.** making paper

_____ **3.** plants   **c.** eating food

_____ **4.** air   **d.** driving cars

_____ **5.** soil   **e.** inflating tires

B. For each item listed below, decide how it could be reused. Write your idea on the line.

6. lumber from old buildings that have been torn down

_____

7. chunks of concrete from torn-up roads and sidewalks

_____

8. steel from old cars

_____

9. grass clippings, leaves, and other lawn wastes

_____

10. old tires

_____

11. plastic from bottles and other containers

_____

CRITICAL THINKING

What are four things you can do to conserve natural resources? Write your answer on a separate sheet of paper.

Name _____   Date _____

14.1 From Molecules to Matter:
Elements and Physical Science

A. Complete the table below with the names and symbols of
elements. You may use the Periodic Table of Elements in
the Appendix of your textbook.

Name of Element	Symbol of Element	Name of Element	Symbol of Element
1. aluminum		**5.**	H
2. carbon		**6.**	Hg
3.	Cl	**7.** sulfur	
4. copper		**8.**	Sn

B. Read each job description below. Decide the branch of
physical science in which each job would be done. Write
physics or *chemistry* on the line.

9. Doing research in nuclear energy _____

10. Gathering water samples from the deep ocean to find

out what elements they contain _____

11. Carrying out experiments to find out how electrical energy is changed

into mechanical energy _____

12. Finding out how different household chemicals affect a new material

used for kitchen counters _____

CRITICAL THINKING

Study the diagram below. On a separate sheet of paper, write two
sentences that describe what the diagram shows about the study of
physical science.

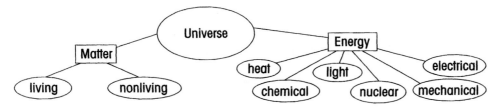

▶14.1 From Molecules to Matter: The Atom   Exercise 57

A. Label the parts of the atom with the terms from the box.

electron	neutron	nucleus	proton

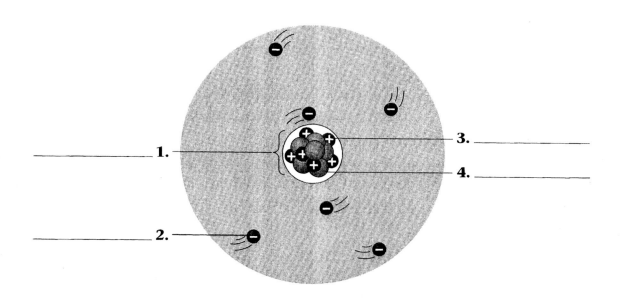

1. _____
2. _____
3. _____
4. _____

B. Use the diagram above and the Periodic Table of Elements in the Appendix of your textbook to answer these questions.

5. How many electrons are in the atom? _____

6. Which element is the atom? _____

C. Match each particle with its charge. Write the correct letter on the line.

_____ 7. proton   **a.** no charge

_____ 8. neutron   **b.** negative charge

_____ 9. electron   **c.** positive charge

CRITICAL THINKING

How can you remember the parts of the atom and what their charges are? List your ideas on a separate sheet of paper.

▶14.2 More About Matter: Properties   Exercise 58

A. Find an example of each item in the chart below. Then complete the chart. Be as descriptive as you can.

Item	Color	State	Odor	Shape
metal wire	1.	2.	3.	4.
milk	5.	6.	7.	8.
air	9.	10.	11.	12.
paper	13.	14.	15.	16.
perfume	17.	18.	19.	20.
pencil	21.	22.	23.	24.

B. Tell something you could do to change the properties of each item. Then describe the properties of the item after the change.

Item	How to change properties	Properties after the change
metal wire	25.	26.
milk	27.	28.
air	29.	30.
paper	31.	32.
perfume	33.	34.
pencil	35.	36.

CRITICAL THINKING

Not all solutions are liquids. For example, bronze is a solid solution made up of copper and tin. Give an example of another solution that is not a liquid. Write your answer on a separate sheet of paper.

Name_____ Date_____

▶14.2 More About Matter: Vocabulary Practice   Exercise 59

A. Read each sentence below. If the underlined term is used correctly, write *correct* on the line. If the term is used incorrectly, choose the correct term from the box, and write that term on the line.

compound	density	solution
protons	solid	

1. A substance that is formed when the atoms of two or more elements join together chemically is called a <u>solution</u>. _____

2. A <u>mixture</u> is two or more elements or compounds that are mixed together but not chemically joined. _____

3. The three states of matter are <u>density</u>, liquid, and gas. _____

4. A chemical connection between elements in a compound is called a <u>bond</u>. _____

5. A bowling ball has a greater <u>compound</u> than a volleyball. _____

B. Identify each picture below, using these terms: *compound*, *mixture*, or *solution*. You can use more than one term for an answer. Write the term or terms on the line.

6.

water

7.

salad

8.

lemonade

_____   _____   _____

CRITICAL THINKING

On a separate sheet of paper, draw a water balloon that is only half-filled with water. Label the solid, liquid, and gas parts of the water balloon.

▶ 15.1 Energy in All Things   Exercise 60

A. Complete each sentence with a term from the box.

energy	kinetic	matter	mass	potential	work

1. Energy is the ability to do _____ or make heat.

2. Energy powers all _____ in the world.   .

3. Without _____, nothing would move.

4. Energy has no _____.

5. Stored energy is _____ energy.

6. Energy of movement is _____ energy.

B. Write *kinetic* or *potential* to identify the kind of energy in each item listed below. Write your answer on the line.

_____ 7. a book lying on your desk

_____ 8. a coat falling from your locker

_____ 9. food stored in the root of a plant

_____ 10. a bus turning a corner

_____ 11. a waterfall

_____ 12. water behind a dam

_____ 13. a cat chasing a toy

_____ 14. a batter swinging a bat

CRITICAL THINKING

A car is driving slowly down the street. Does the car have kinetic energy, potential energy, or both? Explain your answer on a separate sheet of paper.

Name _____ Date _____

A. Look at each picture. Decide whether it represents *light*, *electrical*, *chemical*, *mechanical*, *heat*, or *nuclear energy*. Write the form of energy on the line below the picture.

1.
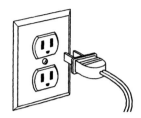
_____

2.

_____

3.
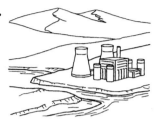
_____

4.

_____

5.

_____

6.

_____

B. Think of one way you have used each of the following forms of energy this week. Write your answers in complete sentences on the lines.

7. heat _____

8. mechanical _____

9. light _____

10. chemical _____

11. electrical _____

CRITICAL THINKING

Typing on a computer keyboard involves mechanical energy. Does it involve chemical energy also? Explain your answer on a separate sheet of paper.

Name _____   Date _____

A. Look for all the forms of energy being used in the picture.
List them on the lines below.

_____

_____

_____

B. Write a paragraph that describes the scene above. Include
all the ways energy is being used.

_____

_____

_____

_____

_____

_____

CRITICAL THINKING

How does energy change form in your everyday life? Give an
example of this and the forms of energy involved. Write your answer
on a separate sheet of paper.

15.3 Changing Matter Using Energy: Matter and Heat Energy

A. Label the arrows in the diagram below to show what process is taking place. Use the words *condensation, evaporation, freezing,* and *melting*. The first arrow is labeled for you.

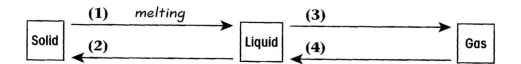

B. The drawings below show H_2O molecules as they change from a *solid* to a *liquid* to a *gas*. Number the drawings in their correct order from 5 to 7, beginning with the solid.

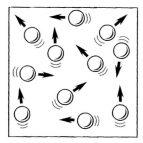   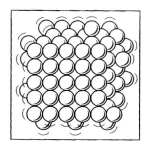   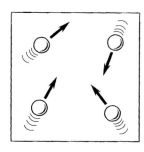

_____   _____   _____

C. Answer these questions.

8. Why does dew form on the grass in the morning?

_____

_____

9. What happens to dew as the weather warms up? Why?

_____

_____

CRITICAL THINKING

Why do beads of water often form on the outside of a glass of ice-cold lemonade on a warm day? Write your answer on a separate sheet of paper.

▶ 15.3 Changing Matter Using Energy   Exercise 64

A. Write *physical change* or *chemical change* on the line to describe what is happening to each item on the list.

_____ **1.** A piece of paper is being cut.

_____ **2.** A candle is burning.

_____ **3.** Food is being digested.

_____ **4.** A piece of stale bread is crumbling.

_____ **5.** A shirt is being folded.

_____ **6.** Cookies are baking.

_____ **7.** Iron is rusting.

_____ **8.** Tree roots are breaking concrete.

_____ **9.** Acid rain is dissolving statues.

_____ **10.** A peach is rotting.

B. Answer these questions.

11. When a car burns gasoline in order to run, which change takes place, a physical change or a chemical change?

_____

12. Matter cannot be destroyed. It just changes form. When gasoline is burned to run a car, what sign of that change can you see?

_____

13. What physical change happens to a car if it crashes into a tree?

_____

CRITICAL THINKING

What is one physical change and one chemical change that has affected your life in some way in the past 24 hours? Write your answer on a separate sheet of paper.

▶16.1 What Is Force? Mass and Weight   Exercise 65

Weight is the measure of the force of gravity on an object. The stronger the force, the greater the weight. The closer something is to the center of the Earth, the greater its weight will be.

Mass is the amount of matter in an object. An object's mass will stay the same wherever that object is. Use this information to write answers to the following problems.

1. You have two golf balls that are exactly the same mass. You take one to the top of a mountain and weigh it. You weigh the other at sea level. Will they weigh the same?

   _____

2. If yes, why? If no, which one will weigh more? Explain your answer.

   _____

   _____

3. You and your friend have the same mass on Earth. Would you both have the same mass on the moon? Explain your answer.

   _____

   _____

   _____

4. An American quarter weighs more in the United States than it does at the equator. What does this tell you about the shape of the Earth?

   _____

   _____

   _____

CRITICAL THINKING

How was it possible for astronauts on the moon to pick up rocks that were too heavy to be picked up by people on Earth? Write your answer on a separate sheet of paper.

16.1 What Is Force?
Friction and Centripetal Force

A. Identify the kind of friction shown in each picture below. Choose from *rolling friction*, *sliding friction*, and *fluid friction*.

1. _____   2. _____   3. _____

B. Circle the word or phrase that best completes each sentence.

4. Two rough surfaces rubbing against each other produce _____ two smooth surfaces do.

   (a) less friction than   (b) more friction than

   (c) the same amount of friction as

5. A bird flying through the air has to overcome _____ friction.

   (a) rolling   (b) sliding   (c) fluid

6. Grease and graphite are two kinds of _____.

   (a) forces   (b) masses   (c) lubricants

7. Oil is added to a car to reduce the _____ of its moving parts.

   (a) friction   (b) centripetal force   (c) weight

8. Centripetal force causes moving objects to go in a _____ path.

   (a) straight   (b) curved   (c) short

9. Light objects fall at the same speed as heavy objects unless _____ causes one to fall more slowly.

   (a) gravity   (b) centripetal force   (c) friction in the air

CRITICAL THINKING

Why do you think tires have treads? Think of a "new and improved" tire tread. Draw a sketch of it on a separate sheet of paper. Explain why you think it is a good design.

Name ______________________ Date ______________________

16.2 Inertia and Motion: Forces in Sports **Exercise 67**

Gravity, friction, inertia, centripetal force, and motion all play a big part in our lives. How do these forces affect playing sports? Answer these questions.

1. How does gravity affect a baseball that is hit into the air?

____

2. What would happen to a fly ball if there were no gravity?

____

3. Why does a ball that is hit on the ground eventually come to a stop?

____

4. When you swing a baseball bat, what force makes the bat move in a curved path?

____

5. What makes a skier go downhill?

____

6. Why do skiers often put a lubricant on the bottom of their skis?

____

7. What makes a boat come to a stop after the motor has been shut off?

____

8. What force makes big football players harder to stop than small ones?

____

CRITICAL THINKING

You are being sent on a mission to the moon. You are in charge of physical fitness for a team of astronauts. You have been asked to create a sport that can be played on the moon, where there is much less gravity than on Earth. Describe your sport on a separate sheet of paper.

Name _____   Date _____

▶ 17.1 All Kinds of Work   Exercise 68

A. Match each term below with its definition. Write the correct letter on the line.

_____ **1.** effort force

_____ **2.** work

_____ **3.** mechanical advantage

_____ **4.** resistance force

_____ **5.** load

a. a measure of how helpful a machine is

b. an object to be moved

c. what happens when a force moves something through a distance

d. a force applied when doing work

e. a force that must be overcome when doing work

B. For each picture below, identify the effort force, resistance force, and load. The effort force and load are shown in the picture. The resistance force is either *gravity* or *friction*. Write your answers on the lines. The first one is partly done for you.

Picture 1

  6. Effort force: _pulling_____

  7. Resistance force: _____

  8. Load: _sack of cement_____

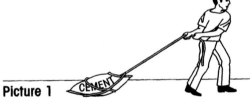

Picture 1

Picture 2

  9. Effort force: _____

  10. Resistance force: _____

  11. Load: _____

Picture 2

Picture 3

  12. Effort force: _____

  13. Resistance force: _____

  14. Load: _____

Picture 3

CRITICAL THINKING

Describe work you did recently, and draw a picture of it on a separate sheet of paper. Identify the effort force, resistance force, and load.

▶ 17.2 Simple and Compound Machines: Identifying Simple Machines

Exercise 69

Label each picture below with the name of a simple machine. Choose one of these terms: *inclined plane, lever, pulley, screw, wedge, wheel and axle.*

1. _____

2. _____

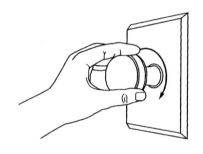

3. _____

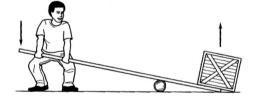

4. _____

5. _____

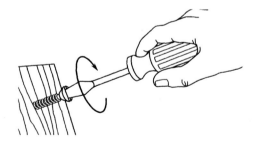

6. _____

CRITICAL THINKING

Which picture above shows a wheel and axle as well as an inclined plane? How do the wheel and axle help make the work easier? Write your answer on a separate sheet of paper.

17.2 Simple and Compound Machines: Exercise 70
Designing Machines to Solve Problems

For each problem below, design a machine to do the work. It
can be a simple machine or two or more simple machines
that work together to make a compound machine. Either
draw and label the machine or describe it in words. Identify
each simple machine used.

1. Tracey is supposed to clean her room every Saturday morning. She
wants to find a way to do this without getting out of bed.

2. Carlos is supposed to help his father work on the roof. Carlos's job
is to get things his father needs up to the roof. Carlos does not want
to keep going up and down the ladder.

3. Florence's family is moving. She is supposed to move all the small
boxes to the truck. From her window, she sees a set of stairs leading
to the truck.

CRITICAL THINKING

What are some large, worldwide problems that can be solved by
using machines? How could machines help? Write your answer on a
separate sheet of paper.

Name _____ Date _____

A. Complete each sentence with a term from the box.

1. Heat is the _____ kinetic energy of a
   substance.

2. Temperature is the measure of the _____
   kinetic energy of the atoms and molecules in a substance.

3. As a substance's temperature increases, the speed of its
   _____ increases.

4. A cup of hot cocoa has a higher _____
   than the Pacific Ocean.

temperature
particles
average
total

B. Study the pictures below. Then answer the questions.

A. 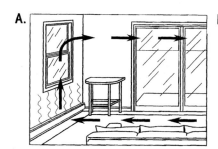   B. 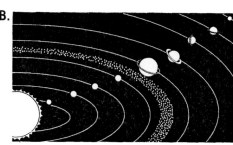   C.

5. In Picture A, why is the air rising to the ceiling?

   _____

6. In Picture B, in what form does the energy from the sun travel to
   the planets?

   _____

7. In Picture C, why is the metal handle on the pan hot?

   _____

CRITICAL THINKING

Why does the Earth's surface get warmer when sunlight strikes it?
Write your answer on a separate sheet of paper.

Name_____ Date_____

18.1 Heat and Matter: Heat on the Move Exercise 72

A. Below are descriptions of things people do to get warm. On the first line below each description, write whether heat moved through a *solid, liquid,* or *gas* to reach the person. Then, on the second line, write the word *conduction, convection,* or *radiation* to describe how the heat was passed along.

1. Randy held a warm towel to his face.

_____   _____

2. Ali added some hot water to his bath.

_____   _____

3. Judith stood in the rays of the sun.

_____   _____

4. Alicia hugged her dog.

_____   _____

5. Sue turned on the heater in her car.

_____   _____

B. In the picture below, the arrows show convection currents in the water. Write the labels *warm water* and *cool water* to describe the currents.

6. _____   7. _____

CRITICAL THINKING

How does warming a bottle of milk in a pot on a stove involve both convection and conduction? Write your answer on a separate sheet of paper.

Name _____ Date _____

A. Label the parts of the three waves below. Use the terms in the box.

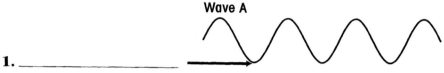

| crest | amplitude | wavelength | trough |

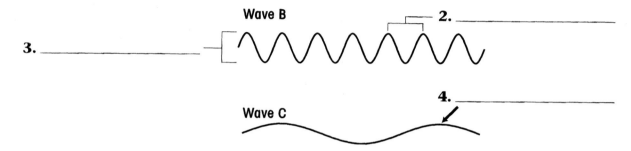

Wave A

1. _____

Wave B

2. _____

3. _____

Wave C

4. _____

B. Use the diagrams of the waves above to answer these questions.

5. Which of the waves has the most energy? _____

6. Which of the waves would produce the least light? _____

7. Which of the waves has the highest frequency? _____

8. Which of the waves would make the loudest sound? _____

9. If Waves B and C were light waves, which one could be ultraviolet light? _____

10. If Waves B and C were light waves, which one could be infrared light? _____

CRITICAL THINKING

You can make small waves in water by dropping a marble into a pan of water. How can you increase the amplitude of the waves that are produced? Write your answer on a separate sheet of paper.

Name _____ Date _____

A. Complete each sentence with a term from the box.

refraction	spectrum	amplitude
reflection	wavelength	

1. When white light passes through a prism, it separates into

   a _____ .

2. The bending of light as it passes from air to water is an example

   of _____ .

3. Increasing the energy of a wave will increase its _____ .

4. The bouncing of light off an object is _____ .

5. The _____ of visible light determines its color.

B. Study the diagrams below. Then answer these questions.

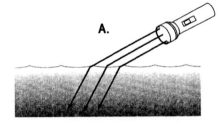
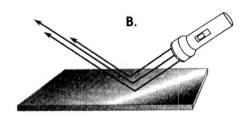

6. Which diagram shows the reflection of light, A or B? _____

7. Which diagram shows the refraction of light, A or B? _____

8. What kind of surface are the light rays striking in Diagram B?

   _____

9. What causes light to refract?

   _____

CRITICAL THINKING

What would happen to the light rays in Diagram B if the surface they
were hitting was black? Write your answer on a separate sheet of paper.

18.3 Sound: Comparing Sound and Light   Exercise 75

**A. On the line next to each phrase below, write *light*, *sound*, or
light or sound to tell which form(s) of energy are described.**

1. a form of energy _____

2. travels through a vacuum _____

3. travels in waves _____

4. travels slowest through a gas _____

5. caused by matter that vibrates _____

6. travels faster through a liquid than through a solid _____

7. has amplitude, wavelength, and frequency _____

8. determines the color of an object _____

9. has amplitude that can vary _____

10. causes tiny bones in the ear to vibrate _____

**B. Match the first part of the sentence on the left with the part
of the sentence on the right that best completes it. Write the
correct letter on the line.**

_____ 11. Looking at your reflection in a
mirror is similar to

_____ 12. Putting more logs on a fire to
make it brighter is similar to

_____ 13. Drawing the blinds to block out
the sunlight is similar to

a. wearing earplugs to
protect your ears from
loud sounds.

b. hearing an echo.

c. banging a drum harder to
make it louder.

CRITICAL THINKING

Why can sound waves travel faster through a liquid than through
a gas? Write your answer on a separate sheet of paper.

▶18.3 Sound: How Sound Travels

A. The steps below describe how you can hear your friend's voice. Number the steps in the order in which they occur. Write the numbers 1 to 6 on the lines.

_____ Air molecules next to your friend's throat vibrate.

_____ You can hear your friend's voice.

_____ Your friend's vocal cords vibrate.

_____ Sound waves enter your ear.

_____ Tiny bones in your ear vibrate.

_____ Sound waves move through the air.

B. Study the pictures below. On each picture, draw an arrow pointing to the part of the instrument that is vibrating. Then write its name. Use a term from the box.

bar	string	drumhead

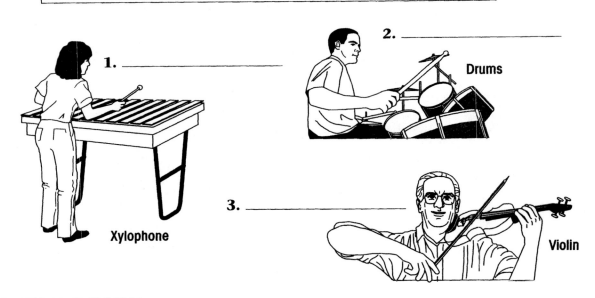

1. _____

Xylophone

2. _____

Drums

3. _____

Violin

CRITICAL THINKING

In the past, people who could not hear well sometimes used a funnel to hear better. They held the narrow end of the funnel against the opening of their ear. How do you think the funnel helped them to hear better? Write your answer on a separate sheet of paper.

19.1 All Charged Up: Static Electricity   Exercise 77

A. Match each term below with its definition. Write the correct letter on the line.

_____ **1.** electricity

_____ **2.** neutral

_____ **3.** discharge

_____ **4.** repel

_____ **5.** static electricity

_____ **6.** negatively charged

_____ **7.** positively charged

a. having too few electrons

b. having extra electrons

c. having no charge

d. push away or push apart

e. a form of energy caused by the movement of electrons

f. caused when objects with opposite charges are attracted to each other

g. the throwing off of static electricity

B. Draw a sketch that shows how lightning occurs. Draw plus signs (+) on the parts of your sketch that have a positive charge. Draw minus signs (−) on the parts that have a negative charge.

CRITICAL THINKING

Should people try to use lightning as a source of energy? Explain why or why not. Write your answer on a separate sheet of paper.

Name _____ Date _____

A. What are six things you use electricity for each week?
Write these on the lines below.

1. _____   4. _____

2. _____   5. _____

3. _____   6. _____

B. Look at your list of six things. Choose three of them.
What job does each of these things do? How did people
do these jobs before they had electricity to use? Write your
answers on the lines.

7. _____

_____

_____

_____

8. _____

_____

_____

_____

9. _____

_____

_____

_____

CRITICAL THINKING

Electricity has always existed in nature. However, people have only
learned how to control it in the last hundred years. On a separate
sheet of paper, list two ways that people would have known of
electricity 150 years ago.

19.2 Electrical Currents

A. Rewrite each sentence, using the correct term for the underlined term. Choose a term from the box.

insulator	metals	electrons	electrical

1. All <u>plastics</u> are excellent electrical conductors.

_____

2. Electricity does not travel easily through an electrical <u>conductor</u>.

_____

3. A battery changes chemical energy into <u>mechanical</u> energy.

_____

4. A generator can be used to start the flow of <u>protons</u>.

_____

B. List three household items that would be good conductors.

5. _____   **7.** _____

6. _____

C. List three household items that would be good insulators.

8. _____   **10.** _____

9. _____

CRITICAL THINKING

Electrical currents are sometimes used in medical devices. For example, pacemakers are used to regulate heartbeat. The pacemaker is implanted under the skin. A battery inside the pacemaker produces a small electrical current. The current flows through wires to the heart muscle. How do you think the electrical current is prevented from affecting the other parts of the body that the wires touch? Write your answer on a separate sheet of paper.

Name _____ Date _____

A. Use the terms from the box to label the diagram of the circuit below.

battery	light bulb	switch

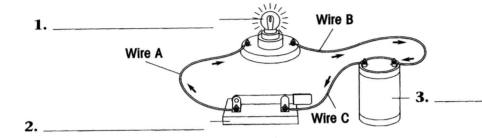

1. _____

2. _____

3. _____

B. Use the diagram above to answer the questions below.

4. What do the arrows show? _____

_____

5. What do you think would happen to this circuit if you cut one of
the wires? Why?

_____

_____

6. What do you think would happen if you removed the battery and
connected Wire B to Wire C? Why?

_____

_____

7. Where in this circuit is energy lost? How is it lost? _____

_____

CRITICAL THINKING

Some fires start when electrical circuits become overloaded. How do
you think a circuit could become overloaded at home? Write your
answer on a separate sheet of paper.

▶19.4 Magnetism   Exercise 81

Write *true* or *false* on the line below each sentence. If the sentence is false, rewrite it to make it true.

1. If you smash a magnet with a hammer, it will still keep its magnetism.

   _____

   _____

2. When a piece of metal becomes magnetized, the electrons line up.

   _____

   _____

3. A magnet is any solid substance that attracts wood or plastic.

   _____

   _____

4. If you let a magnet swing freely on a string, one end will always point toward the north.

   _____

   _____

5. The like poles of magnets attract each other, and the opposite poles repel each other.

   _____

   _____

CRITICAL THINKING

If you were lost, how could a compass help you find your way? Write your answer on a separate sheet of paper.

20.1 Fossil Fuels: How Are They Used?   Exercise 82

A. In the chart below, list ten activities that you did within a
24-hour period. Next to each activity, identify the source
of the fuel that was used to do the activity.

Activity	Fuel
1.	
2.	
3.	
4.	
5.	
6.	
7.	
8.	
9.	
10.	

B. Answer these questions.

11. How many of the activities that you listed above used fossil fuels as
their fuel source?

_____

12. Name one activity that used fossil fuels that could be done using
solar energy instead.

_____

13. Name one activity that used fossil fuels that could have been done
using only the energy your body produces from food.

_____

CRITICAL THINKING

How do you think people's activities will be affected if the world runs
out of fossil fuels? Write your answer on a separate sheet of paper.

20.1 Fossil Fuels: Saving or Wasting? Exercise 83

A. Write *save* next to each practice that would help save fossil fuels. Write *waste* next to each practice that would waste fossil fuels.

1. insulating homes _____

2. riding in a bus instead of driving a car _____

3. buying products packaged in cardboard _____

4. packing groceries in reusable cloth bags _____

5. joining a car pool _____

6. driving a bigger car _____

7. recycling motor oil _____

8. leaving the heat on when you are not home _____

9. wearing a sweater instead of turning up the heat _____

10. using throwaway plastic cups for drinking _____

B. Look over the practices that you have marked *save*. Then answer these questions.

11. Which practice do you think is the best way to save fossil fuel?

_____

12. How does this practice save fossil fuel?

_____

_____

CRITICAL THINKING

Many modern cooking devices, such as microwave ovens, cook food fast. How does this help save fossil fuels and also improve our lives? Write your answer on a separate sheet of paper.

▶ 20.2 Other Energy Resources: Producing Energy

Write *true* or *false* on the line below each sentence. If the sentence is false, rewrite it to make it true.

1. A nuclear reactor is a device that splits atoms to produce energy.

_____

_____

2. A dam traps moving water to produce nuclear energy.

_____

_____

3. A machine with blades that can be turned is a geyser.

_____

_____

4. A solar collector changes sunlight into heat energy.

_____

_____

5. The source of geothermal energy is heat contained in rocks deep inside the Earth.

_____

_____

6. The fuel used in nuclear fission is seawater.

_____

_____

CRITICAL THINKING

People around the world get energy from different sources. Why do you think this is so?

Name _____ Date _____

20.2 Other Energy Sources: Advantages and Disadvantages

A. On the chart below, write one advantage and one disadvantage of each energy source.

Energy Source	Advantage	Disadvantage
dams	1.	2.
nuclear fission	3.	4.
tides	5.	6.
wind	7.	8.
sunlight	9.	10.
hot rocks inside the Earth	11.	12.
nuclear fusion	13.	14.

B. Answer these questions.

15. Which energy source do you think would be best to use where you live?

_____

16. Why do you think this is a good energy source in your area?

_____

17. What is one energy source that you think would not work where you live?

_____

18. Why do you think it would not work?

_____

CRITICAL THINKING

Which energy source listed in the chart do you think will be the most important energy source in the future? Why? Write your answer on a separate sheet of paper.

Name _____   Date _____

A. Match each term below with its definition. Write the correct letter on the line.

_____ **1.** orbit

_____ **2.** gravity

_____ **3.** Earth

_____ **4.** solar system

   a. the sun and all the planets and other objects that circle around it

   b. a closed, curved path

   c. the third planet from the sun

   d. a strong pull that keeps planets and other objects in orbit around the sun

B. The illustrations below show how scientists think the Earth and the rest of the Milky Way galaxy were formed. Put the illustrations in the order from earliest to latest formation. Write the correct number (1, 2, or 3) on the line.

      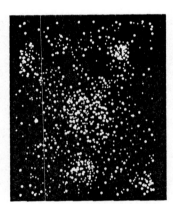

5. _____   **6.** _____   **7.** _____

CRITICAL THINKING

The sun's gravity holds the Earth in orbit around the sun. The Earth's gravity holds the moon in orbit around the Earth. The sun's gravity cannot pull the moon away from the Earth. The Earth and the moon are closer to each other than are the moon and the sun. What can you infer from these facts about gravity? Write your answer on a separate sheet of paper.

▶21.2 Features of the Earth:
The Earth's Surface

Exercise 87

Use a set of colored pens or pencils. Follow the directions below.

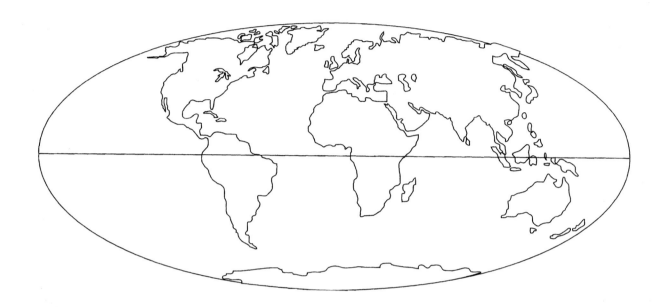

1. The Earth is called the "water planet." From space, it is a blue-green color. Color the water on the map blue.

2. Use the key to color in each of the seven continents.

dark green	= Africa	orange	= South America
yellow	= Antarctica	purple	= North America
gray	= Asia	pink	= Europe
red	= Australia		

3. Label the Indian, Arctic, Atlantic, and Pacific oceans.

4. Label the poles and the equator.

CRITICAL THINKING

A traveler is taking a trip around the world. He can go by land or by sea or by a combination of both. Use the map above and mark the route you think he would take. Why did you choose that route? Write your answer on a separate sheet of paper.

21.2 Features of the Earth:
Land, Layers, and Seasons

Exercise 88

A. Write *true* or *false* on the line below each sentence. If the sentence is false, replace the underlined term with a term from the box to make it true.

<table>
<tr><td>core</td></tr>
<tr><td>mantle</td></tr>
<tr><td>continent</td></tr>
<tr><td>equator</td></tr>
</table>

1. Each of the Earth's seven large landmasses is called a <u>sphere</u>.

   _____

   _____

2. An imaginary line called the <u>axis</u> circles the Earth halfway between the North and South poles.

   _____

3. The center of the Earth is called the <u>mantle</u>.

   _____

4. The continents and ocean floor are part of the Earth's <u>crust</u>.

   _____

B. The diagram below shows the Earth as it orbits the sun. Decide which season it is in the Northern Hemisphere when the Earth reaches each of the four positions. Write the correct answers on the lines.

6. _____

5. _____

7. _____

8. _____

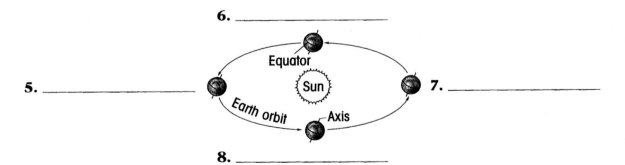

CRITICAL THINKING

How would the lengths of day and night change where you live if the Earth were not tilted on its axis? Write your answer on a separate sheet of paper.

21.3 Dividing Up the Earth:
Lines of Latitude and Longitude

Exercise 89

Study the maps below. Then answer the questions.

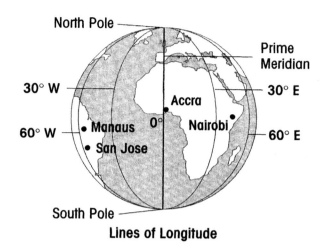

Lines of Longitude

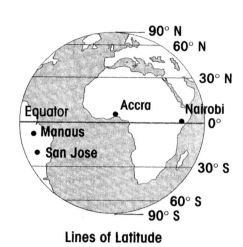

Lines of Latitude

1. Which lines are continuously the same distance apart, lines of latitude or lines of longitude? _____

2. What city in the map is closest to the equator? _____

3. At what degree of latitude is the North Pole? _____

4. Which two cities on the map lie on the same line of longitude?

   _____

5. Which city on the map is closest to the prime meridian? _____

6. Which line of longitude passes through the smallest amount of land?

   _____

7. At what two points do all the lines of longitude meet? _____

CRITICAL THINKING

If you travel eastward along a line of latitude, you can circle the Earth completely and always be traveling eastward. However, if you travel northward along a line of longitude, you will begin to travel southward as soon as you cross the North Pole. Why do you think this is so? Write your answer on a separate sheet of paper.

21.3 Dividing Up the Earth:
Time Zones Around the World

A. You live in Los Angeles and work as a telephone sales person. You sell your products to offices all over the United States. Use the time zone map to answer the questions below.

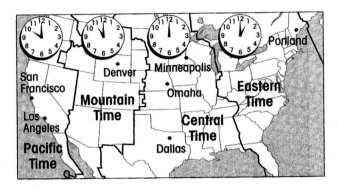

1. During what hours in *your* time zone should you not call the East Coast because offices will be on their noon lunch hour?

   _____

2. The switchboard of your customer in Omaha closes at 5:30 P.M. What is the latest time in *your* time zone that you can get a call through?

   _____

B. Your company transfers you to Dallas. You are still selling your products to offices all over the United States. Use the map to answer these questions.

3. You are supposed to return a call to Minneapolis at exactly 3:00 P.M. Minneapolis time. At what time in *your* time zone should you call?

   _____

4. You want a fax to arrive in Portland, Maine, at 1:00 P.M. What time in *your* time zone should you send it?

   _____

CRITICAL THINKING

Time zones have only been in use since the late 1800s. Why are time zones more important now than they would have been many years ago?

▶22.1 Plate Tectonics: Exercise 91
Breaks in the Earth's Crust

A. Complete each sentence with a term from the box.

geologists	magma	volcanoes
lava	earthquake	

1. Magma that has reached the Earth's surface is _____.

2. Melted rock formed in the Earth's mantle is _____.

3. Scientists who study rocks to learn about the history and structure of the Earth are _____.

4. Openings in the Earth's surface that release magma from the mantle are _____.

5. A sudden violent shaking of the Earth is called an _____.

B. Rewrite each sentence to make it true. Replace the underlined term with the correct term.

6. The Earth's crust is made up of several <u>mantles</u>.

   _____

7. Plates drift because they float on the hot, soft rock of the <u>crust</u>.

   _____

8. Most geologists think that all of the Earth's <u>seas</u> were once part of Pangaea.

   _____

CRITICAL THINKING

Will a physical map of the world look the same 5 million years from now as it does today? Why or why not? Write your answer on a separate sheet of paper.

▶ 22.1 Plate Tectonics: Shifting Plates   Exercise 92

A. Several things can happen as the Earth's plates move.
Read the descriptions below. Decide what will happen
and write it on the line. Choose from the statements in
the box.

A trench will form.	An earthquake will occur.
A volcano may erupt.	A mountain range will form.

1. Two plates move toward each other and begin to pile up.

_____

2. Two plates move toward each other, and one gets pushed down
under the other.

_____

3. Two plates suddenly slip as they rub past each other.

_____

4. Two plates move, and an opening is formed in the crust.

_____

B. A newspaper reporter is on the scene of either a volcanic
eruption or an earthquake. Write a brief news report
describing what the reporter sees and hears. Use a separate
sheet of paper if you need more space.

_____

_____

_____

_____

CRITICAL THINKING

Why do volcanic eruptions and earthquakes often occur in the same
areas? Write your answer on a separate sheet of paper.

22.1 Plate Tectonics: Earthquakes and Volcanoes

Exercise 93

A. Read the list of events below. Write *volcano* or *earthquake* next to each one, whichever describes the event best.

1. Plates slide past each other. _____

2. Shock waves travel through the Earth's crust. _____

3. Magma rises in a vent. _____

4. A fault forms. _____

5. Lava flows out and becomes rock. _____

B. Label the parts of the volcano, using the terms in the box.

| lava | magma | vent | gas and ash |

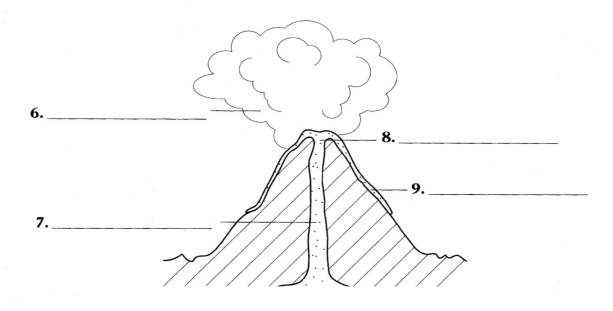

6. _____

8. _____

9. _____

7. _____

CRITICAL THINKING

Geologists are trying to find a way to predict earthquakes. What might be some signs that they would look for? Write your answer on a separate sheet of paper.

Name _____   Date _____

22.2 Rocks and Minerals: Kinds of Rock   Exercise 94

A. Match each term with its definition. Write the correct letter on the line.

_____ 1. igneous rock

_____ 2. sedimentary rock

_____ 3. metamorphic rock

_____ 4. weathering

_____ 5. soil

_____ 6. erosion

_____ 7. glacier

a. a type of rock formed by the pressing together of smaller particles of rock or the remains of living things

b. a large, slow-moving field of ice

c. a type of rock formed when igneous or sedimentary rock changes under very high temperatures or pressure

d. a type of rock formed from magma

e. the wearing away of rock or soil

f. a process that breaks down rocks and minerals

g. rocks on Earth's surface broken down by weathering into very tiny pieces that mix with the nutrients from living and once-living things

B. Look at the three rocks below. Use the pictures and the labels under them to decide whether each one is *igneous*, *sedimentary*, or *metamorphic*. Write the correct rock type under each picture.

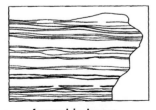

formed in layers

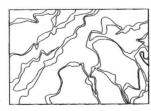

was once another type of rock called limestone

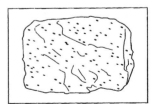

formed from lava

8. _____   9. _____   10. _____

CRITICAL THINKING

How can an igneous rock become a sedimentary rock? Write your answer on a separate sheet of paper.

22.2 Rocks and Minerals: Weathering and Erosion

Exercise 95

A. Put a check next to each statement below that describes a cause of either weathering or erosion.

_____ **1.** ice freezing in the cracks of rocks

_____ **2.** people sitting on a sandy beach

_____ **3.** a glacier moving down a mountainside

_____ **4.** a river flowing over boulders

_____ **5.** energy from the sun heating the ground and making air rise

_____ **6.** magma rising in volcanic vents

B. Write *true* or *false* on the line after each sentence. If the sentence is false, rewrite it to make it true.

7. Running water, rain, ice, and chemicals can weather rocks and minerals. _____

_____

8. When water freezes, it contracts and acts like a wedge to break rock. _____

_____

9. Weathering breaks rocks down into tiny pieces of soil. _____

_____

10. Glaciers create mountains as they flow downhill. _____

_____

CRITICAL THINKING

A geologist has two rocks. One has sharp edges, and the other has rounded edges. Which one has been weathered by flowing water? Explain your answer on a separate sheet of paper.

Name _____ Date _____

Study the following pictures. To the right of each picture, draw
a second picture showing what the scene might look like in
1,000 years.

1.

2.

3.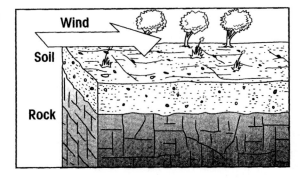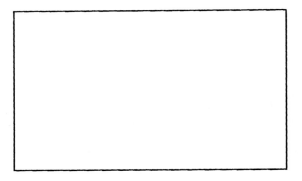

CRITICAL THINKING

Because of weathering and erosion, landforms change over time.
List three other things in nature that change in appearance over
time. Explain why each changes. Write your answers on a separate
sheet of paper.

23.1 Air All Around Us

A. Use the terms in the box to label the layers of the atmosphere on the drawing below. Write the correct terms on lines 1 to 6.

ionosphere	mesosphere	stratosphere
thermosphere	troposphere	ozone

1. _____
2. _____
3. _____
4. _____
5. _____
6. _____

The Earth

B. Match each description below with its correct layer in the atmosphere. Write the correct letters on lines 6 to 10.

_____ **7.** reflects radio signals   **a.** troposphere

_____ **8.** has thin air   **b.** stratosphere

_____ **9.** is the third layer   **c.** mesosphere

_____ **10.** has clouds   **d.** ionosphere

_____ **11.** has the ozone layer   **e.** thermosphere

CRITICAL THINKING

Mount McKinley is the highest mountain in North America. The top of it is more than 20,000 feet (6,000 meters) above sea level. What advice would you give people who want to climb this mountain? Write your answer on a separate sheet of paper.

Name _____ Date _____

Rewrite each sentence to make it true. Use the correct term from the box to replace the underlined term.

warmer	pressure	uneven	radiation
Earth	gases	faster and spread out	

1. Air pressure is the weight of <u>clouds</u> pressing down on the Earth.

   _____

2. A barometer is an instrument that measures air <u>temperature</u>.

   _____

3. Energy from the sun reaches the Earth as <u>gravity</u>.

   _____

4. The <u>even</u> heating of the atmosphere causes convection currents to form.

   _____

5. Heat causes molecules in matter to move <u>slower and come together</u>.

   _____

6. At night, clouds act as a blanket and make the land <u>cooler</u>.

   _____

7. Heat energy radiating from the <u>sun</u> warms the atmosphere.

   _____

CRITICAL THINKING

Where would you expect to find a greater difference between daytime and nighttime temperatures, at the seashore or in the desert? Explain your answer on a separate sheet of paper.

Name_____ Date_____

A sailor is planning a trip around the world. Help him plan his trip. Use the map and your knowledge of wind to answer the questions below.

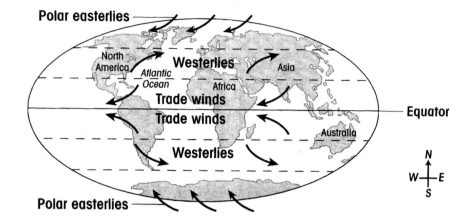

1. After the sailor crosses the Atlantic Ocean, he sails down the coast of Africa. There, near the equator, it is very warm. Heat makes air molecules rise. Do you think this will make the equator a windy place or a calm place? Explain your answer.

   _____

   _____

2. After passing between Australia and Asia, the sailor is headed across the Pacific Ocean. He is just north of the equator. What winds is he fighting against?

   _____

3. As the sailor heads north, aimed at the West Coast of the United States, he finally gets into a wind system that helps him. What is it?

   _____

CRITICAL THINKING

The Midwestern states, such as Iowa, Nebraska, and South Dakota, are known for their very hot summers and very cold winters. Washington is farther north, but its west coast has milder weather all year round. It does not get as cold, but it does not get as hot, either. Why is this so? Write your answer on a separate sheet of paper.

▶ 23.3 Water and Air: Precipitation   Exercise 100

A. The terms in the box refer to different forms of water in the atmosphere. Match each term with its definition. Write the term on the line.

water vapor	fog	rain	snow	hail	sleet

_____   **1.** low-lying clouds

_____   **2.** water in the form of a gas

_____   **3.** rain that freezes as it falls through a layer of cold air near the ground

_____   **4.** lumps of ice that form as water freezes around ice crystals that are moving up through rain clouds

_____   **5.** water droplets that fall to the Earth

_____   **6.** water vapor that crystallizes because the temperature in a cloud is below freezing

B. The following statements describe how rain occurs. Place the statements in the order in which they occur. Write the correct numbers (1 to 6) on the lines.

_____ **7.** Droplets collect to form clouds.

_____ **8.** Water vapor in the air forms tiny droplets of liquid water.

_____ **9.** Water enters the air by evaporation.

_____ **10.** Droplets become larger and heavier.

_____ **11.** Droplets fall to the ground as rain.

_____ **12.** Air is cooled below the dew point.

CRITICAL THINKING

It is morning. You want to plan a picnic for the afternoon, but no weather forecast is available. All you know is that right now it is sunny, the humidity is high, and the temperature is dropping. Do you think that today would be a good day for a picnic? Why or why not? Write your answers on a separate sheet of paper.

23.3 Water and Air: Clouds   Exercise 101

A. Match each term with its definition. Write the correct letter on the line.

_____ **1.** cirrus cloud	**a.** a low-lying gray cloud that covers a wide area
_____ **2.** cumulus cloud	**b.** the amount of water in the air at any given time
_____ **3.** dew point	**c.** a high-altitude cloud made of ice crystals
_____ **4.** humidity	**d.** a low-lying layer of cloud
_____ **5.** fog	**e.** the temperature at which water vapor turns into liquid water
_____ **6.** stratus cloud	**f.** a big, puffy, low-altitude cloud that usually signals good weather

B. Use the descriptions in the box below to fill in the cloud chart. You may use some descriptions twice.

made of ice crystals	made of water droplets	thin and feathery
broad, flat layers	unbroken cloud cover	big, puffy
low in sky	often sign of stormy weather	gray colored
usually bright white	sign of fair weather	seen in mountains

cirrus clouds	stratus clouds	cumulus clouds

CRITICAL THINKING

On a cold day outside, you can "see your breath." How is this like a cloud? Write your answer on a separate sheet of paper.

Name _____   Date _____

▶ 24.1 Air on the Move   Exercise 102

A. Complete each sentence with one of these terms: *front,*
climate, weather, air mass, occluded front.

1. A huge body of air that moves from place to place is an _____.

2. The place where two air masses of different temperatures meet
   is a _____.

3. The average weather in a region over many years is _____.

4. The condition of the atmosphere at a certain time and place
   is _____.

5. An _____ forms when a cold front overtakes a warm front.

B. Look at the weather map below. Use the information on it
to answer the questions.

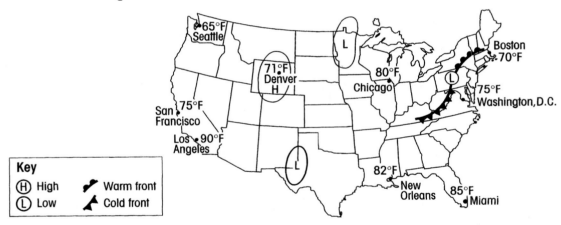

6. Is the temperature higher in Los Angeles or Chicago? _____

7. What will the weather be like during
   the next day or so in Washington, D.C.? _____

CRITICAL THINKING

You are sitting outside in shorts and a short-sleeved shirt. Suddenly
the wind picks up. There is a brief but heavy shower that forces you
to go inside. When the rain ends, you have to put on a heavy
sweater to sit outside. What type of weather system has passed? On a
separate sheet of paper, explain how you can tell.

Name_____ Date_____

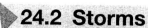 **24.2 Storms**

A. Complete each sentence with a term from the box.

wind	tornado	thunderhead	hurricane

1. A tall, thick cloud that produces lightning and thunder is

   a _____.

2. Air moving from high to low pressure areas is _____.

3. A stormy cyclone with high winds is a _____.

4. A swirling column of air that extends down from a cumulonimbus

   cloud is a _____.

B. Complete each sentence with a term from the box.

funnel-shaped	low air
cumulus clouds	lightning

The Earth's surface heats moist air. The air rises and cools,

which causes **(5)** _____ to form. An updraft

blows up through the clouds. Then cumulonimbus clouds form.

A thunderstorm begins. Electric charges build up and then are

discharged. Heat from **(6)** _____ expands the

air and we hear thunder.

A cyclone is a storm with circling winds in an area of

(7) _____ pressure. A cyclone extends down

from a cumulonimbus cloud and forms a **(8)** _____

cloud. The formed cloud begins to spin rapidly. It can cause a great

deal of damage.

CRITICAL THINKING

The TV weather forecaster says that a high pressure system will arrive
tomorrow. Should you plan on taking your umbrella to school?
Explain your answer on a separate sheet of paper.

Name _____   Date _____

A. Use the climate zone map below to answer the questions.

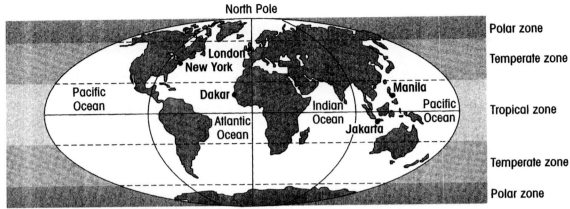

1. Is Manila or London more likely to have no real winter season? _____

2. Which city, New York or Jakarta, has warm summers and

   cold winters? _____

3. What type of clothing would you wear to spend Thanksgiving

   in Dakar? _____

B. Answer the questions below.

4. What is one good thing and one bad thing about living in a
   tropical climate?

   _____

5. What is one good thing and one bad thing about living in a
   temperate climate?

   _____

6. What is one good thing and one bad thing about living in a
   polar climate?

   _____

CRITICAL THINKING

Choose a climate zone other than the one in which you live. How
would your life be different if you lived in that climate zone? Write
your answer on a separate sheet of paper.

▶25.1 The Story in the Rocks

A. Use the diagram of rock layers below to answer the questions.

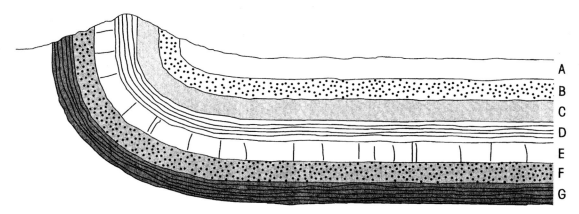

1. Which layer is the oldest? _____

2. Which layer is the youngest? _____

3. Why are the layers on the left side of the diagram curving up rather than lying flat?

   _____

   _____

B. What methods or processes do geologists use to learn about the Earth's history? Name two and describe them.

   _____

   _____

   _____

   _____

   _____

CRITICAL THINKING

Fossils tell only part of the story of what life was like millions of years ago. How else can we learn about the history of the Earth? Write your answer on a separate sheet of paper.

Name _____   Date _____

▶ 25.2 Geological Time: Eras   Exercise 106

A. Finding the age of fossils is not always easy. Sometimes scientists start by ruling out certain time periods. For each fossil described below, cross out the eras the fossil could *not* be from. If you think you know the era the fossil came from, circle your guess.

1. Large dinosaur leg bone

   Precambrian   Paleozoic   Mesozoic   Cenozoic

2. A human skull

   Precambrian   Paleozoic   Mesozoic   Cenozoic

3. A mud tunnel made by worms

   Precambrian   Paleozoic   Mesozoic   Cenozoic

4. A large deposit of coal

   Precambrian   Paleozoic   Mesozoic   Cenozoic

B. Geologists find three rock layers on top of one another. In the bottom layer, there are small skeletons of sea animals. In the middle layer, there are skeletons of land animals. In the top layer, there are skeletons of sea animals. Explain the geological events that occurred in the area.

_____

_____

_____

_____

_____

_____

CRITICAL THINKING

The Cenozoic era is the present geological era. However, it may not be the last era. Why? Write your answer on a separate sheet of paper.

25.2 Geological Time: Past Life   Exercise 107

A. List the organisms in the two groups from simplest (lowest number) to most complex (highest number) below. Then, next to each organism's name, write the name of the era in which it first appeared.

humans, bacteria, birds, dinosaurs

1. _____   2. _____

3. _____   4. _____

algae, flowering plants, ferns

5. _____   6. _____

7. _____

B. Answer the questions below.

8. What group of animals listed above became extinct?

_____

9. Which kingdom, plant or animal, developed more new species between the Mesozoic and Cenozoic eras? Explain.

_____

_____

10. Of all the organisms listed above, which are ancient and which are new in the Cenozoic era?

_____

_____

CRITICAL THINKING

Do you think fossils provide a record of every kind of organism that lived in the past? Explain your answer on a separate sheet of paper.

25.2 Geological Time: Ordering Eras   **Exercise 108**

Label each picture below with an era from the box.

| Mesozoic era | Precambrian era | Cenozoic era | Paleozoic era |

a. _____

b. _____

c. _____

d. _____

CRITICAL THINKING

Name five different kinds of animals. Put them in the order in which their group first appeared on Earth. Explain why you chose that order. Write your answer on a separate sheet of paper.

26.1 Features of the Oceans: Water — Exercise 109

A. Write *true* or *false* on the lines below each sentence. If the sentence is false, rewrite it to make it true.

1. The oceans cover 70 percent of the Earth's surface.

   _____

   _____

2. The study of the ocean is called paleontology.

   _____

   _____

3. The ocean's salinity is the measure of how much water is in it.

   _____

   _____

4. An ocean current is a mass of water that flows like a river through an ocean.

   _____

   _____

B. Match each current below with its description. Write the correct letter on the line.

_____ **5.** Gulf Stream system

_____ **6.** density current

_____ **7.** North Atlantic current

a. any current caused by cold, salty water sinking below warmer water

b. a river of water that flows through the Atlantic Ocean

c. the current that moves from Newfoundland toward Europe

CRITICAL THINKING

How would life on Earth be different if all of the world's water were as salty as the ocean? Write your answer on a separate sheet of paper.

Name _____ Date _____

A. Label the parts of the ocean floor, using the terms in the box.

mid-ocean ridge	ocean trench	continental shelf
ocean basin	continental slope	

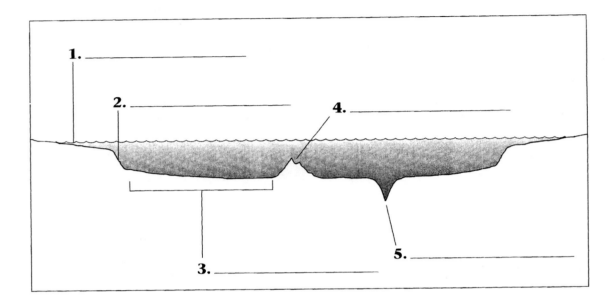

1. _____

2. _____

4. _____

3. _____

5. _____

B. Use the diagram above to answer the questions.

6. You walk into the ocean from the beach. Which part of the ocean floor are you standing on?

_____

7. Which part of the ocean floor looks like a cliff?

_____

8. What is the largest part of the ocean floor?

_____

CRITICAL THINKING

Much of the deep ocean is still unexplored. Why is the study of the deepest parts of the ocean so difficult? Write your answer on a separate sheet of paper.

26.1 Features of the Oceans: Comparing the Ocean Floor to the Land

A. Answer these questions.

1. Name four formations that occur on both the ocean floor and on land.

   _____   _____

   _____   _____

2. Which one of these ocean floor features do you think oceanographers know the least about? Explain your answer.

   _____

   _____

3. Which part of the ocean floor do you think oceanographers know the most about? Explain your answer.

   _____

   _____

4. Where do most underwater earthquakes occur?

   _____

   _____

B. Match each ocean feature with the landform that is most similar. Write the correct letter on the line.

_____ **5.** mid-ocean ridge   **a.** valley

_____ **6.** trench   **b.** plain

_____ **7.** continental slope   **c.** mountain range

_____ **8.** basin   **d.** cliff

CRITICAL THINKING

Some mountains under the ocean are bigger than those on land. Why might this be the case? Write your answer on a separate sheet of paper.

Name _____   Date _____

26.2 Waves and Tides: Understanding Waves   Exercise 112

A. Match each word with its definition. Write the correct letter on the line.

_____ **1.** undertow

_____ **2.** seismic sea wave

_____ **3.** tide

a. a giant wave caused by an earthquake on the ocean floor

b. the rise and fall of the oceans, caused by the sun's and moon's pull of gravity

c. the backward movement of ocean water near the shore

B. Use the diagram to answer the questions.

4. Draw an arrow on the diagram that shows the direction in which the energy of the waves is moving.

5. Draw another arrow under one of the waves in the diagram to show the direction in which the water is moving.

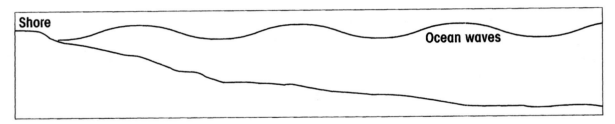

Shore

Ocean waves

C. Rewrite each sentence to make it true. Replace the underlined term with one of the following terms: *winds, breakers*.

6. Local <u>tides</u> cause most ocean waves.

_____

7. <u>Rivers</u> form as the tops and bottoms of waves move at different speeds near shore.

_____

_____

CRITICAL THINKING

What do you think would happen if the water in ocean waves moved forward toward shore instead of the way it really moves? Write your answer on a separate sheet of paper.

26.2 Waves and Tides: Looking at Tides   Exercise 113

A. Use the following terms to complete the sentences below:
low tide, moon, neap, coast, gravity, spring.

1. A tide is the up and down movement of water on the _____.

2. The pull of the _____ and the sun causes tides.

3. Tides that vary greatly in height are _____ tides.

4. During _____, the tide pulls away from the shore.

5. Tides that are neither very high nor very low are _____ tides.

6. Wind causes most waves, but _____ causes tides.

B. Look at the diagrams below. One shows the positions of the Earth, sun, and moon during a neap tide. The other shows their positions during a spring tide. Label the diagrams *neap tide* or *spring tide*.

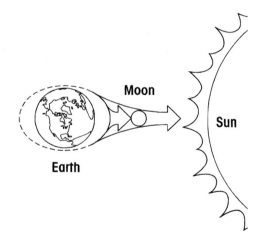   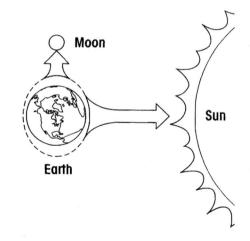

7. _____   8. _____

CRITICAL THINKING

Would it be better to explore the coast at high tide or at low tide?
Explain your answer on a separate sheet of paper.

26.3 Ocean Resources: Ocean Life Exercise 114

Read the following paragraphs about whales. Then answer the questions below.

Many whales migrate between polar and tropical regions. They spend the summer months in Arctic and Antarctic waters. The cold water has a large supply of plankton, which whales eat. The whales build up thick layers of fat in these feeding areas. The whales then migrate south in the fall before the polar waters freeze.

The water is much warmer in the tropical oceans near the equator. The whales give birth to their young there. The babies would not survive if they were born in the cold polar oceans. But food is scarce in the tropical oceans. So adults live off their fat in the warm waters. Babies live off their mother's milk. In late spring the whales migrate north again.

1. Where do whales feed in summer?

   _____

2. Where do whales give birth?

   _____

3. According to the paragraphs, what would happen to a whale that stayed north all winter?

   _____

   _____

4. According to the paragraphs, what would happen to a whale that stayed south all summer?

   _____

   _____

CRITICAL THINKING

Do you think whales are an ocean resource? Why or why not? Write your answer on a separate sheet of paper.

▶26.3 Ocean Resources: How We Use Them   Exercise 115

A. Put a check next to each resource that people get from the ocean.

_____ fish   _____ coral

_____ oil   _____ vegetables

_____ fruit   _____ salt

_____ oxygen from algae   _____ wood

_____ tides (as an energy source)   _____ natural gas

_____ coal   _____ metals

B. Use the ocean resources you chose above to fill in the lines below.

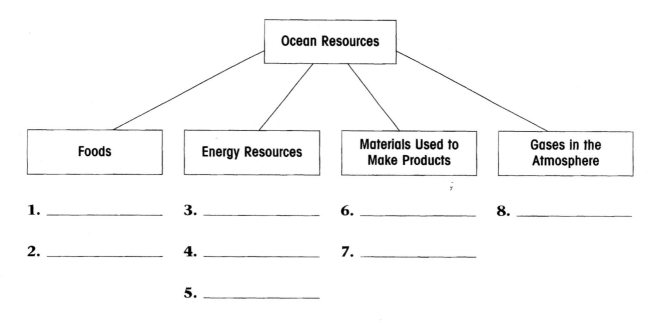

1. _____   3. _____   6. _____   8. _____

2. _____   4. _____   7. _____

                        5. _____

CRITICAL THINKING

Which ocean resource above do you think is the most important to people? Why? Write your answer on a separate sheet of paper.

Name _____ Date _____

A. Complete the sentences below with these terms: *astronomy, universe, galaxy, stars.*

1. The _____ is all the matter, energy, and space that exists.

2. The Milky Way is a _____ that contains the Earth and the rest of the solar system.

3. The study of the stars, planets, and all of space is _____.

4. The Milky Way contains billions of _____.

B. There are four types of galaxies below. Each one has a different shape. Circle the galaxy that has the same shape as the Milky Way.

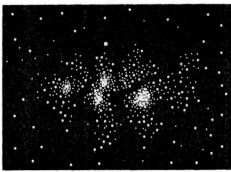 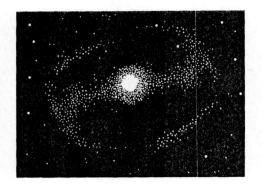

CRITICAL THINKING

Astronomers group galaxies by their shape. What is another property of galaxies that astronomers might use to group them? Write your answer on a separate sheet of paper.

▶ 27.2 The Solar System: The Inner Planets   **Exercise 117**

The inner planets are Earth, Mars, Mercury, and Venus. On the
diagram, label them. Then, on the lines below that, write their
names in order from closest to the sun to farthest from the sun.
Write two facts about each planet.

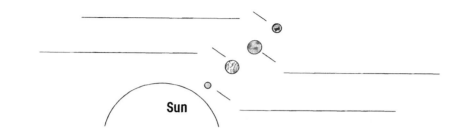

Sun

1. Planet _____

Facts _____

_____

2. Planet _____

Facts _____

_____

3. Planet _____

Facts _____

_____

4. Planet _____

Facts _____

_____

CRITICAL THINKING

The fuel that powers the sun is hydrogen and helium. What is the
process the sun uses to produce its light and heat? Name and explain
that process on a separate sheet of paper. (Hint: Look at Chapter 15
in your textbook if you need help.)

27.2 The Solar System: The Outer Planets   Exercise 118

The outer planets are Jupiter, Neptune, Pluto, Saturn, and
Uranus. On the diagram, label them. On the lines below, write
their names in order from closest to the sun to farthest from the
sun. Then write one fact about each planet.

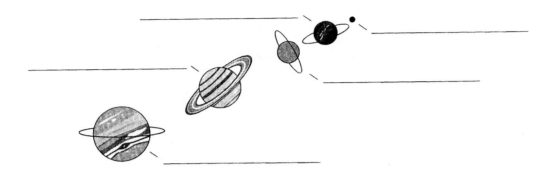

1. Planet _____

Fact _____

2. Planet _____

Fact _____

3. Planet _____

Fact _____

4. Planet _____

Fact _____

5. Planet _____

Fact _____

CRITICAL THINKING

The large outer planets all have many moons and rings. Do you
think the moons and rings are related to each other? Explain your
answer on a separate sheet of paper.

27.2 The Solar System:
Asteroids, Comets, and Meteors

A. Match each word with its definition. Write the correct letter on the line.

_____ **1.** satellite   **a.** a ball of ice and dust that orbits the sun

_____ **2.** asteroid   **b.** an object that orbits a planet

_____ **3.** comet   **c.** a meteoroid that falls to the Earth

_____ **4.** meteor   **d.** a small, rocky object that orbits the sun

_____ **5.** meteorite   **e.** a bright streak of light caused by a meteoroid
                                      burning up in the Earth's atmosphere

B. Label the drawings below with these terms: *asteroid, satellite, comet, meteor.*

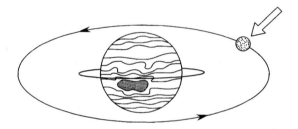

6. _____   **7.** _____

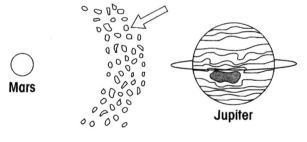

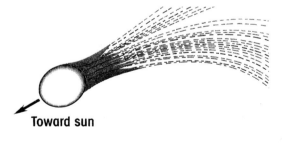

8. _____   **9.** _____

CRITICAL THINKING

Objects from space enter the Earth's atmosphere constantly. Why don't we see pieces of rock falling to the ground around us all the time? Write your answer on a separate sheet of paper.

27.3 Space Exploration   Exercise 120

A. Match each event with the year it happened. Write the correct letter on the line.

_____ **1.** *Viking* sends photos from Mars.   **a.** 1983

_____ **2.** *Explorer 1*, the first U.S. satellite, is launched.   **b.** 1957

_____ **3.** First American woman goes into space.   **c.** 1958

_____ **4.** Space exploration begins.   **d.** 1976

B. Think about what it would be like to take part in a space shuttle mission. Then answer the questions below.

5. Choose something that you would like to do experiments on in space. Draw a line under one of the choices below. Or think of something different, and write it on the lines.

How does appetite change in space?

What effects does space travel have on the growth of plants?

Does space travel have an effect on the behavior of insects?

Does friction change when there is less gravity?

_____

_____

6. Now think of an experiment that would help you answer the question. Describe how you would set up and carry out your experiment.

_____

_____

_____

_____

CRITICAL THINKING

In the future, astronauts may travel to other planets in the solar system. What planet do you think would be best for space exploration? Why? Write your answer on a separate sheet of paper.